Inside the Presidential Debates

Inside the Presidential Debates

THEIR IMPROBABLE PAST
AND PROMISING FUTURE

Newton N. Minow and Craig L. LaMay

The University of Chicago Press   Chicago and London

The University of Chicago Press, Chicago 60637
The University of Chicago Press, Ltd., London
© 2008 by Newton N. Minow and Craig L. LaMay
All rights reserved. Published 2008.
Paperback edition 2016
Printed in the United States of America

25 24 23 22 21 20 19 18 17 16   3 4 5 6 7

ISBN-13: 978-0-226-53041-3   (cloth)
ISBN-13: 978-0-226-43432-2   (paper)
ISBN-13: 978-0-226-53039-0   (e-book)
DOI: 10.7208/chicago/9780226530390.001.0001

Library of Congress Cataloging-in-Publication Data

Minow, Newton N., 1926–
    Inside the presidential debates : their improbable past and promising future /
Newton N. Minow and Craig L. LaMay.
        p. cm.
    Includes bibliographical references and index.
    ISBN-13: 978-0-226-53041-3 (cloth : alk paper)
    ISBN-10: 0-226-53041-8 (cloth : alk paper)
    1. Presidents—United States—Election. 2. Campaign debates—United States.
3. Television in politics—United States. 4. United States—Politics and
government—1945–1989. 5. United States—Politics and government—1989–
I. LaMay, Craig L. II. Title.
JK524.M563 2008
324.7—dc22
                                                            2007026792

♾ This paper meets the requirements of ANSI/NISO z39.48-1992 (Permanence of
Paper).

To the memory of Dr. Frank Stanton, 1908–2006,
visionary broadcaster, advocate of presidential debates,
and champion of the First Amendment.

Contents

Foreword

In 1986 the Twentieth Century Fund needed someone to lead a study and a national conference on presidential debates. A program officer at the Fund wrote to the acclaimed presidential historian and journalist Theodore White seeking advice about Newton Minow, who had been suggested for the job. Was Minow "knowledgeable about and influential in this area?" the program officer asked. "Does he have a good grasp of the policy issues involved, and can he render those issues intelligible to a general audience?"

White wrote back, "That's equivalent to asking whether Pavarotti can sing, Horowitz can play the piano or Isaac Stern the violin. Of all those interested in the central role of the presidential debates in our election campaigns, I know of no one more influential than Newton Minow."

Newton Minow's place as a preeminent leader in U.S. communications history and policy is impossible to overstate. He is perhaps best known as the young Federal Communications Commission (FCC) chairman who, in 1961, challenged the nation's broadcasters to rescue the promise of television from the "vast wasteland" many felt it had become—a phrase both poetic and biting enough to have permanently entered the public lexicon. Mr. Minow's tenure as chairman of the FCC under the administration of President John F. Kennedy was notable, however, for much more than his trenchant commentary. It was marked by successful legislative efforts to promote several landmark undertakings including the 1961 All Channels Act, which mandated UHF reception for all television sets and hence greatly increased the number of television channels available to Americans. Minow was also the driving force behind what eventually became the International Telecommunications Satellite

Consortium (Intelsat), the organization that launched the modern era of satellite communications. Mr. Minow championed the development of public television and public radio and contributed to the growth of cable television as well.

After leaving government service, Minow, a distinguished lawyer, stayed active in communications industry practice and policy. He helped the National League of Women Voters resume the televised presidential debates in 1976, and today he is vice chairman of the current debate sponsor, the Commission on Presidential Debates. He has been chairman of the Public Broadcasting Service (PBS) as well as chairman of Chicago's outstanding public television station, WTTW; a director of a national commercial network (CBS); a director of independent commercial broadcasting stations (the Tribune Company); and a director of a leading advertising and communications company (Foote, Cone & Belding). Among many other positions he's held, he has been the chairman of the RAND Corporation, a trustee of the Mayo Clinic and an early advocate of using communications technology to provide health care, and Walter Annenberg Professor of Communications Law and Policy at Northwestern University. As a scholar, Mr. Minow has written dozens of important articles and books on issues ranging from journalists and criminal justice to telemedicine. He has advised Democratic and Republican administrations on communications policy issues ranging from diplomacy and international broadcasting to data mining and citizen privacy.

But at the center of Minow's important body of work is a rich investigation and commentary on political broadcasting. His first major contribution to the field was the 1964 book *Equal Time: The Private Broadcaster and the Public Interest,* in which he developed many of the themes and issues he revisits in this volume, with a weather eye on the digital age. His next book, *Presidential Television,* published in 1973, warned of how television had seriously tipped constitutional checks and balances in favor of the executive branch. In 1987 he cowrote *For Great Debates: A New Plan for Future Presidential TV Debates,* an examination of how television has affected presidential debates.

In 2001 Mr. Minow turned his attention to the technological revolution and the opportunities it offers to increase public access to knowledge and learning. In *A Digital Gift to the Nation,* supported by the Century Foundation and coauthored by Lawrence K. Grossman, former president of both NBC News and the Public Broadcasting System, Minow made an innovative proposal. He called for the establishment of a Digital Opportunity Investment Trust aimed at stimulating creative, experimental ideas and techniques to enhance learning; broaden knowledge; encourage an informed citizenry and self-government; make available to all Americans the best of the nation's arts, humanities, and culture; and teach the skills and disciplines needed in an information-based economy. The trust would be financed with revenue from auctions of licenses to the publicly owned electromagnetic spectrum (the frequencies that transmit radio and television signals, as well as a new array of digital information) and would be governed by a board of distinguished and diverse citizens from many fields.

Carnegie Corporation of New York was pleased to have supported the efforts leading to *A Digital Gift to the Nation*. It was with equal enthusiasm and an appreciation of the urgency and importance of Mr. Minow's most recent project—a return to research and analysis in the field of presidential debates—that the Corporation funded this new book, *Inside the Presidential Debates*. It is the second volume that Mr. Minow has collaborated on with Craig LaMay, a journalism professor and expert on international mass communications. In 1995 Mr. Minow and Mr. LaMay had coauthored *Abandoned in the Wasteland: Children, Television, and the First Amendment*, which profoundly influenced the Clinton administration's policies aimed at encouraging broadcasters to provide high-quality, nonviolent television programming for children. One of the authors' recommendations, that the V-chip be made a required component in all TV sets so parents can block reception of unwanted shows, is now mandated by law.

When Mr. Minow first proposed undertaking a new examination of the current presidential debate system, he had not written at length on the presidential debates for almost a decade. In the interim much had changed on the political scene: in particular, the advent of third-party candidates was having an increasing effect on almost every aspect of presidential campaigns. In 1992, billionaire businessman Ross Perot, running on an independent platform that included support for such issues as trade protectionism and balancing the federal budget, became a force to be reckoned with. He joined the two major-party candidates—Bill Clinton and George H. W. Bush—on the debate stage and eventually pulled in over 18 percent of the popular vote. In 2000 and again in 2004, another third-party candidate, Ralph Nader, sought to participate in the debates. In the 2000 election, according to some, Nader played an important role in determining the electoral outcome. Many political scientists and journalists believe that independent and third-party political movements will continue to gain momentum in the next decade.

What would be the consequences of such a development? Is the third-party phenomenon a blip on our national radar screen? An evolutionary development in our political system? Or an indication of a new fracture in the American polity? One could make arguments for each of these. After all, we are a different nation from the one we were in 1976, when televised presidential debates (between Gerald R. Ford and Jimmy Carter) resumed after a sixteen-year hiatus. Since then, there has been a major demographic change: the U.S. population has risen from around 218 million to more than 300 million and is projected to surpass 400 million by midcentury. We are also a more diverse nation: today immigrants account for 11.5 percent of our population. By the end of this decade, the percentage of immigrants among the total population will surpass the previous 1890 high of 14.8 percent. At the same time, the United States, not unlike many other nations, is being transformed by unprecedented technological, scientific, environmental, educational, and security challenges, as well as by the seemingly unstoppable forces of globalization. How we choose our leaders in this complex world beset by many challenges is a critical matter for all Americans, and as citizens of the one predominant world power, we make choices that have a direct impact around the globe. Since television is such a dominant force in our society, the televised presidential debates may be the seminal events in the presidential election process.

In 1960 television and radio first gave almost everyone the chance to be part of the national audience for the debates between Vice President Richard Nixon and Senator Jack Kennedy. Today America's presidential elections continue to be among the great levers of our democracy, but they also serve as one of the shared national experiences that are indispensable to our unity and to our identity as citizens. Presidential debates have become a hallmark of that experience. Fifty years on, political communication in the twenty-first century is digital, viral, and ubiquitous, but often as not, its purpose and effect are to divide us rather than to unite us.

Our ever-evolving nation faces many dangers and many opportunities. As citizens, we continue to confront the task of strengthening and supporting our nation and its institutions so that not only our generation but also those that follow after us may continue to live lives enriched by freedom and enlightened by free and open inquiry about the issues, social forces, and ideas that affect our destiny. How can televised presidential debates help to fortify our ideals and continue to uplift our democracy? How can the debates better serve American voters in the digital age? How can they help to build the bonds between us that both enrich our individual lives and contribute to the common good? There is no one more qualified to address these questions than Newton Minow. Along with his colleague Craig LaMay, he here provides us with the framework for a new national dialogue about these issues. Let the discussion begin.

Vartan Gregorian

Acknowledgments

This book is a memoir of a life spent thinking about, developing, and working to improve the televised presidential debates. I was involved from the beginning, serving first as assistant counsel and later as law partner to Illinois governor Adlai E. Stevenson, the man who first proposed the idea in 1960 and whose vision led to the Kennedy-Nixon debates. In the 1970s and early 1980s, the National League of Women Voters asked me to help organize its presidential debates. Later, while a fellow at Harvard's Kennedy School, I worked with others to create the Commission on Presidential Debates, which I serve today as a vice chairman.

In telling the story of that journey, I have had a lot of help. First, I thank my coauthor, partner, and colleague, Craig Llewellyn LaMay. Craig and I have worked together for more than fifteen years, teaching, writing, collaborating, and thinking about how communications can better serve our country. When the idea for this book hit me in the fall of 2000, Craig and I were teaching law and graduate journalism students at Northwestern University. We first discussed the idea during a class break; though he was enthusiastic about the idea, Craig was busy with his own book at the time. Less than two months later, we spent the last class session with all of the students in my Chicago apartment on a Monday afternoon, watching on CNN as the Florida Supreme Court made its ruling in *Gore v. Katherine Harris*. Craig and I agreed to join forces and undertake this history and analysis of the presidential debates, and we began it in earnest in 2004.

When we began writing, we wrote in the third person. Craig pointed out, however, that my intimate involvement in the debates required regular use of the first-person singular if the narrative was to make sense. Our superb editor at the University of Chicago Press, Robert Devens, and several outside readers agreed with this assessment. We accepted that advice, but I want to emphasize that the book is a joint effort, reflecting not only my personal experience but also research, interviews, and materials that Craig and I both assembled. This book is Craig's as much as mine. He is a full partner, an exceptionally gifted scholar and writer, and a cherished friend.

We were supported in the research for this book by the Carnegie Corporation of New York. In 1992, Carnegie had supported another research and writing project of ours through a grant to the American Academy of Arts and Sciences. This time the Corporation made a grant to Northwestern University, where Craig is a professor in the Medill School of Journalism and where I have been a trustee and member of the faculty for many years. We are grateful to Vartan Gregorian, the Carnegie Corporation's president, and Gerry Mannion, director of the Corporation's U.S. Democracy Program, for their confidence in our work.

We thank Robert Devens, whose skill as a historian and whose editorial counsel contributed immensely to the book. To Kathy Schultz, my assistant for the last thirty-two years, much appreciation for keeping us organized and focused. We thank Janet Brown, the executive director of the Commission on Presidential Debates, and Lewis Loss, exceptionally able legal counsel to the Commission, for their thoughtful and constructive assistance. For their time and their insights into the televised presidential debates, we offer special thanks to former FCC chairman Richard Wiley, whose leadership at the Commission helped make the debates possible in 1976; journalist and frequent debate moderator Jim Lehrer; and Dorothy Ridings, whose service to the debates began in 1976, when she was an officer of the National League of Women Voters, and who continues today as a board member of the Commission on Presidential Debates. We thank Mitch Webber, who as a Harvard law student did a splendid job researching the legal issues, and Scott Gordon, a skilled young journalist who helped us gather and review the legislative and regulatory history of the televised debates.

Friends and colleagues read early drafts of the book and gave us enormously helpful comments in response to our questions, as well as several good quotes and anecdotes. We take a deep bow to broadcaster and author Lawrence Grossman; historians Tim Gilfoyle and Jonathan Fanton; my law partners Howard Trienens and Eden Martin; communications lawyer and scholar Henry Geller; my son-in-law and Harvard law professor Joseph Singer; and Craig's father, Edward H. LaMay. All of them improved the manuscript. Craig also thanks his friend Clare for her love and patience while he worked on this book.

My deepest debts are personal. My daughters Nell, Martha, and Mary (all lawyers) are my toughest critics. They each went over the manuscript and caught many errors and proposed valuable changes. Jo, my wife of fifty-eight years, is always the most creative member of the family. Once again Jo came up with the best ideas.

Of course, Craig and I take full responsibility for the historical interpretations and arguments that follow. As a former trustee and chairman of the Carnegie Corporation, I hope the book may in a small way fulfill the 1911 dream of Andrew Carnegie when he created the Corporation "to promote the advancement and diffusion of knowledge and understanding among the people of the United States."

Introduction

President John F. Kennedy told me more than once that without the televised debates he would not have been elected president in 1960. The debates were the first ever face-to-face encounters between major-party presidential candidates.[1] Going into the campaign, Kennedy was not nearly as well known as Richard M. Nixon, who had been vice president for eight years.

And yet today almost no one remembers the issues the two men discussed. The candidates spent much of their time arguing over China's intentions toward two tiny Pacific islands, Quemoy and Matsu, claimed by Nationalist Taiwan, a matter quickly forgotten after the election.[2] The matter of "south Indochina" came up so briefly that no one noticed it. Besides, the vice president assured the audience, "the civil war there was ended . . . and the Communists have moved out."[3]

But for better *and* worse, the Kennedy-Nixon debates changed presidential elections forever, propelling them into the age of television. In 1960 it had been only four years that a majority of American homes had a television set,[4] and the "great debates," as they were called, brought the candidates into the living rooms of millions of voters, allowing them to see, hear, and judge them in a way never before possible. At the same time, the experience stoked the public appetite for and the modern campaign's emphasis on the image and the sound bite—those who saw the debates on television gave them to Kennedy, while those who heard them on the radio thought Nixon the winner.

Don Hewitt, who produced the first debate in Chicago for CBS, later said, "It was not important who won or lost that debate. That first debate launched Jack Kennedy onto the national scene." Vice President Nixon had arrived at the television studio first, Hewitt said, and "banged his knee getting out of the car. He looked sort of green and sallow and unhappy. Then in walks this handsome Harvard kid who looks like a matinee idol. I said to both of them, 'Do you want some makeup?' Kennedy, who didn't need any, said no. Nixon heard him say no and decided, 'I can't have makeup because it will look like I got made up and he didn't.' He went off in another room and got made up with something called Lazy Shave, and looked like death warmed over.

"Four years later," Hewitt said, "I'm sitting in a makeup room in San Francisco. Richard Nixon is being made up to go out on the rostrum to introduce the [Republican] nominee, Barry Goldwater. And I said, 'You know, Mr. Nixon, if you'd let Franny here make you up four years ago, Barry Goldwater would be going out there now to introduce you.' He looked in the mirror. And then he turned very slowly to me and he said, 'You know, you're probably right.'"[5]

*　　*　　*

Three short years after those first televised encounters between Nixon and Kennedy, the president would be assassinated, and with him went the nascent "tradition" of televised presidential debates. Politics and the law stood in the way: In 1960, Congress suspended Section 315 (the "equal time" law) of the Federal Communications Act so as to make possible the nation's first presidential debate. Without such a change, the law would have required every candidate for the office to be afforded equal time on television—and there were at least a dozen more candidates. President Kennedy had already signaled his intention to ask for another waiver, having promised his friend Barry Goldwater that if Goldwater won the Republican nomination in 1964 the two men would travel the country together and debate.[6] But in 1964, incumbent president Lyndon Johnson sent clear word to the Senate that he did not want a similar suspension of the law, because he did not want to debate Republican nominee Goldwater.[7]

In 1968 there was no incumbent, and though Vice President Hubert Humphrey wanted desperately to debate, Nixon—perhaps because of his experience in 1960—did not. The equal time law was not suspended. In 1972, President Nixon again told Congress that he would not debate his challenger, South Dakota senator George McGovern. So again the law was not changed. Of course, Democrats controlled the Congress then and could have pushed the issue, but they were horribly divided. Their 1968 convention in Chicago had been a disaster, and they were poorly prepared in 1972.

Not until 1975, after Nixon left office, was the law changed, this time without any congressional action. Instead, the Federal Communications Commission (FCC) revised its interpretation of the equal time law to make debates possible. With the change in the law, as in 1960, the opportunity for debates in 1976 was fortuitous. As a result of Watergate and his pardon of former president Nixon, President Gerald Ford entered the 1976 campaign trailing far behind his challenger, Georgia Governor Jimmy Carter, in the polls. Ford felt he *had* to debate to win back public support. Seizing the moment, a handful of skilled and determined public officials from both major parties worked with citizens and civic groups to make the presidential debates happen. The tradition begun by President Ford and Governor Carter has survived, but it has not been easy.

*   *   *

You may be already asking yourself why you should care about televised presidential debates. The answer is simple: in modern democracies, including our own, television is the essential medium for political communication. In any country in the world—democratic or otherwise—you can watch television for a day or two and get a good idea of what that country's social and political values are. How does it regard its leaders? its schools, cultural and religious institutions? How does its programming serve special or vulnerable audiences, like children or ethnic minorities? And how does its programming present and explain to citizens the important choices they are expected to make at the ballot box? In many of the world's developing regions, in Africa, Southeast Asia, and Latin America, broadcast television and radio are essential to democratization because they reach the remote rural corners of countries where there are no newspapers or magazines and where many people cannot read. Without broadcasting, democracy would be impossible in many of these countries, because "citizenship" would have no meaning.

Americans sometimes forget that the same is true in the United States. In 1962, I was chairman of the Federal Communications Commission when I received a phone call from Eleanor Roosevelt, whom I had met earlier when my senior law partner Adlai Stevenson introduced us, and who had visited me at the agency not long after I arrived in 1961. "Why aren't you doing anything to help Reverend Smith?" she asked me.

"I'm sorry, Mrs. Roosevelt," I answered, "I don't know anything about this. Who is Reverend Smith?"

Mrs. Roosevelt then told me about television station WLBT in Jackson, Mississippi (the state capital), which had refused to sell campaign airtime to the Reverend Robert L. T. Smith, a successful grocery owner and black pastor. He was running for a seat in the U.S. House of Representatives, the first black man to do so since Reconstruction. When Reverend Smith's campaign manager, local pharmacist and state NAACP president Aaron Henry, approached television station WLBT with a request to buy advertising time, the station manager had said to him, "Nigger are you crazy? Get out of here. We're not going to sell you any time."[8] Reverend Smith later recalled that when he made the same request, he was told that if he appeared on WLBT "they would find my body floating upside down in the river."[9]

Reverend Smith and Aaron Henry had then taken their case to the FCC, though I was not aware of it. Their letters had disappeared into the bowels of the bureaucracy and gone unanswered. "The reason I'm calling you," Mrs. Roosevelt said in our phone conversation, "is that the election is next week." I promised her I would look into the matter immediately.

After checking around, I found Reverend Smith's letters sitting on somebody's desk. I called my staff together and asked what was going on. One of our lawyers explained that under the law WLBT had to treat candidates equally. If the station sold time to one, it had to sell time to another. If it gave time to one, it had to give time to another.

"I know that," I said. "What's the point?"

"Well," the staffer told me, "we checked with Congressman John Bell Williams [the incumbent opponent], and he's not buying any time. So WLBT is treating them equally."

"That's ridiculous," I said. "Are you telling me that if one candidate doesn't want to buy time, that means the other can't be on the air?"

"That's our interpretation of the law," I was told.

Disgusted, I dictated a telegram to WLBT: "Explain why you think it's in the public interest not to have any discussion of this congressional race on your station during the campaign period. And explain it today." After all, Jackson was more than 50 percent African American, and the station's decision not to sell campaign time effectively denied all of the city's citizens an opportunity to learn anything about one of the candidates.

Late that afternoon, a lawyer representing WLBT showed up at my office. "We're putting him on the air," he said.

"Soon," I replied.

Reverend Smith bought thirty minutes of airtime on WLBT the day before the primary election. He lost the election to segregationist Williams, but Reverend Smith's appearance was a victory for the black community. Myrlie Evers, whose husband Medgar Evers would be shot to death outside their home in Jackson a year later, later said that seeing the Reverend Smith on television "was like the lifting of a giant curtain. He was saying things that had never before been said by a Negro to whites in Mississippi."[10]

Months later I appeared in a hearing before the House Commerce Committee, which supervises the FCC. John Bell Williams was on that committee, and he questioned me sharply: "Why is the government telling a station what to put on the air?"

I said to myself, "I'm not a career person and I'm not going to be around here forever," and so I decided to reveal the background of this controversy. "I think we ought to show for the record what this is all about," I said, and proceeded to explain to the full committee what Congressman Williams's question had to do with his own election contest. Williams got up and walked out of the hearing.

I left the Commission in 1963, but in 1964 WLBT was sued by the United Church of Christ for failing to serve Jackson's black citizens. The case wound its way through the FCC and the federal courts for almost a decade, until finally the U.S. Court of Appeals for the District of Columbia revoked WLBT's license. This has been the only time in American history that a television station has lost its license through such judicial action for failing to serve the public interest.[11]

Many years later, in 1996, the Democratic National Convention came to my hometown of Chicago, and I was invited by a friend—John Bryan, chairman of the Sara Lee Corporation, who grew up in Mississippi—to a breakfast for the Mississippi delegation. At the breakfast I was introduced to an elderly black gentleman who asked me, "Are you the Minow who was chairman of the FCC?"

Yes, I said.

"Don't you know who I am?" the man asked.

"No, I'm sorry, sir, I don't," I replied.

He said, "I'm Aaron Henry. I was the campaign manager for Reverend Smith in 1962. I'm the one who was sending you and Mrs. Roosevelt all those letters."

I was stunned. "What do you do now?" I asked.

It was his turn to be stunned. "You don't know what I do now? You don't know my job today? I'm chairman of WLBT."

It was an "only-in-America" moment. The next year, 1997, Aaron Henry died after a lifetime of civil rights activism. He had led voter registration drives, boycotts, and sit-ins. He was threatened, beaten, and arrested more than thirty times, on one arrest chained to a garbage truck. His home was firebombed twice and his pharmacy once. But he had transformed his community, his state, and his country for the better, and he had established in practice what we proclaim as theory—that television, when used wisely, is a powerful tool for democracy and freedom.

*   *   *

The televised presidential debates occupy a different chapter in that story, and an important one, a fascinating survey of our past and an essential building block of our future. Beginning in 1976 and through the election of 1984, the presidential debates were organized by the nonpartisan League of Women Voters, an organization that had long experience organizing debates in local and state elections around the country.[12] In 1988, the sponsorship of the debates entered a new chapter: The League was replaced by the Commission on Presidential Debates, a not-for-profit organization created in 1986 that was originally backed by the two major political parties. The Commission has organized all the debates since. Between these two sponsors, the United States has now had eight consecutive presidential contests that have featured multiple televised presidential debates as well as vice-presidential debates in every election but one (1980).

The first of the 2004 debates between President Bush and Senator John Kerry, at the University of Miami, attracted 62.5 million viewers, the largest audience for any debate since 1992.[13] The second debate had 47.7 million viewers, exceeding viewership for any of the presidential debates in 1996 or 2000.[14] The third and final 2004 presidential debate, at Arizona State University, attracted 51.2 million viewers despite competing against nationally televised baseball playoff games between the Red Sox and the Yankees and, in another part of the country, the Astros and the Cardinals.[15] The one 2004 vice-presidential debate between Vice President Dick Cheney and Senator John Edwards had 43.6 million viewers.[16]

How did this extraordinary accomplishment happen? Many other democracies do not broadcast debates between major party candidates or, if they do, began the practice only recently. Rather, as in Britain's case, they provide public-service broadcast time without charge to the candidates and the parties so these can make their case directly to the voters. Sometimes citizens themselves get the opportunity to grill the candidates individually, and often unmercifully, in televised public forums. There is much to admire in this: everywhere in the democratic world—including the United States—the airwaves by law belong to the public, not to the broadcasters. "Free time" is therefore a misnomer—incorrect as a matter of law and economics—for candidate time. If the public owns the air-waves to begin with, it makes no sense to talk of "free" or "donated" time. It is more accurate to call it public-service time or voters' time, and for al-most fifty years I have advocated the British approach of providing public service time to candidates.[17]

On the matter of televised presidential debates, however, the United States is a model for other countries. American-style debates, where the candidates face off against each other, have until recently been a rarity else-where. Many of the world's emerging democracies—from Latin America, Africa, and Eastern Europe—have experimented with electoral debates, and they frequently come to the United States to learn from us. Specifi-cally, they seek advice from the Commission on Presidential Debates.

In every democracy, the desire to hold televised political debates im-mediately confronts a problem of fairness discussed throughout this book. The basic policy dilemma is how to permit and encourage radio and tele-vision coverage of candidate debates while not being unfair to minority-party candidates who want to participate in them. Democracy points in the direction of both. But there is a practical problem. If a debate has to include all minority candidates, it will be reduced to a meaningless cha-rade. In the United States, for example, more than two hundred people declare themselves presidential candidates every four years. Where do policy makers strike the balance between encouraging debates and treat-ing legitimate minority party candidates fairly?

*   *   *

I have been lucky enough to participate in the American experience with televised presidential debates from the beginning. I served as assistant counsel and later as law partner to Illinois governor Adlai E. Stevenson, the man who first proposed the idea in 1960. As FCC chairman in 1962, I made a decision in a case that resulted in delaying subsequent debates until 1976—a huge mistake, I realized later, as I discuss in chapters 2 and 3 of this book. That year and again in 1980, I served as cochair of the pres-idential debates for the League of Women Voters. And in 1986, while a fel-low at Harvard's Kennedy School, I worked with others to create the Com-mission on Presidential Debates, which I serve today as a vice chairman.

Over the past half-century, I have seen and participated in the enormous effort that goes into organizing the debates under a variety of sponsors and approaches and among a wider variety of candidates and campaigns, with behind-the-scenes arguments about everything from the format to the questioners to the length of the response time, the placement of cameras, the height of podiums, and the location of water glasses. I have observed—and made—a number of mistakes along the way. I know the enormous effort that goes into organizing the debates. I have participated in the struggle to reconcile the competing interests of the public, the candidates, debate sponsors, and broadcast networks. Press indifference and press hostility are familiar to me. Well-publicized charges of bias from critics across the political spectrum and legal challenges from excluded candidates are par for the course. Despite it all, I know that televised presidential debates are a gift to the American people, a valuable and now essential part of our democratic process. The irony of this success is that today we take the debates for granted, not realizing that but for the foresight and determination of a few people, legal obstacles would have prevented them from ever happening.

Unlike other books on this subject, this one does not seek to critique the debates as television programming or political theater. Neither does it deal with primary debates, nor with voter attitudes and behavior. Rather my and my colleague Craig LaMay's goal is to examine the combination of historical accident and creative policy making that produced this remarkable political and social institution and to propose realistic ways to improve the debates in an increasingly fragmented political and media environment. Now in my eighties, I speak freely and candidly for the record, to tell the story of how the debates evolved.

The debates are not perfect, but they give voters a chance to see the candidates on a stage armed with nothing but their character and intellect, confronted not with softball questions from those who want them to look good but challenges on fundamental issues from opponents who have spent as much time on the issues, thought as hard about them, and want to win as much as they do. Debates provide what lawyers call "demeanor evidence"—a chance for voters to see how the candidates respond to challenges, on the spot and under stress, to hear the timbre of their voices, to see whether they blink or seem nervous or flustered.

The presidential debates are not academic debates—"real debates," as critics sometimes say—nor should they be. Academic debates are about the arguments for and against a policy or proposition—for example, a law. Candidates for state legislatures, not surprisingly, often do engage in academic-style debate, because we need to know what they think about particular policies. The presidency is something else entirely. The president is chief executive of the government and commander in chief of the armed forces. The president can propose laws and veto them, and he leads his party members in the legislature. But his role is much larger than crafting and winning support for laws; the president is required to lead and organize the country. Presidents have to sit down with the chief executives of other countries, allies and enemies. The debates give us a chance to see how presidential candidates handle pressure, how well they think on their feet. We do not want to know who is the best debater or the better policy wonk. In presidential debates we want the candidates to demonstrate something of their general education, leadership ability, character, and personality. There will always be scripted lines and canned speeches, but always, always there are moments of authenticity that we would otherwise miss, moments that inevitably seem to capture the essence of the candidate and the campaign. To paraphrase Winston Churchill's famous commentary on democracy, presidential debates are the best of many alternatives.

It is not my argument in this book that the debates are perfect or even ideal. I have great admiration, for example, for the British approach to broadcasting and elections, and I have long advocated emulating some of its best features here. But the truth is that the American system of free expression, and the American system of broadcasting, is unique. We do not have the British approach, and it is unlikely we could achieve it. My argument is that the U.S. presidential debates do an excellent job of giving the electorate insights about the candidates; they attract huge audiences and are now well established; and presidential candidates, even popular incumbents, can no longer avoid them. The important issue, then, is how to improve them.

Broadcast political debates in the United States began with the earliest days of radio. Before the 1928 presidential election, the then-new League of Women Voters sponsored a ten-month series of nationally broadcast debates. The candidates did not participate; instead, journalists, scholars, and other politicians argued on their behalf. The same year, the Mutual Broadcasting System launched *American Forum of the Air*, a regular public affairs and debate program moderated by lawyer Theodore Granik, who grilled candidates for lesser national and state offices and interrupted any candidate who tried to avoid his questions.

In March 1935, NBC Red, one of two NBC radio networks at the time, went national with *The University of Chicago Round Table*, a public affairs debate program. At the same time, NBC Blue began a more formal debate program, *America's Town Meeting of the Air*, in which two candidates were each given twenty uninterrupted minutes to make their case to the listening audience at home and a live audience in the studio.[18] The balance of the hour-long program consisted of questions from members of the studio audience on matters of national interest, and a prize was awarded to the audience member who asked the best question. At the height of its popularity the program had five million listeners weekly. The program's moderator, George V. Denny Jr., believed that radio was a medium much better suited to political discussion than newspapers because, he claimed, the latter were always editing candidates' remarks to make favored candidates and parties look better. "If we persist," said Denny, "in the practice of Republicans reading only Republican newspapers, listening only to Republican speeches on the radio, attending only Republican political rallies, and mixing socially only with those of congenial views, and if Democrats . . . follow suit, we are sowing the seeds of the destruction of our democracy."[19] President Franklin Roosevelt strongly shared this opinion of newspaper reporting, which he thought was too often ideologically driven, and for that reason he took to radio with his "fireside chats" so he could communicate directly with the public.

A generation later, the new broadcast technology of television changed American politics even more profoundly. When Vice President Richard M. Nixon and Massachusetts Senator John F. Kennedy met in Chicago in September 1960 for the first of their four televised debates, it was the first time in U.S. history that the nominees of the major parties had joined in such a face-to-face encounter.[20] Some 77 million Americans — 60 percent of the adult population — watched that first Kennedy-Nixon debate, more than five thousand times the average audience for what had been until then the most famous political debates in American politics — the 1858 meetings between Abraham Lincoln and Stephen Douglas, who were running against each other for an Illinois Senate seat. Lincoln understood very well the importance of debates: he kept notes as to what was said in his encounters with Douglas, including verbatim reports from newspapers, and then published a book on the debates — the only book our sixteenth president ever published.

Today the Lincoln-Douglas debates are the benchmark for critics who decry the televised presidential debates as high-stakes political theater with little or no real substance. Minority parties and their supporters scorn the debates as a sham—except when their nominees are included in them.[21] Before and after the debates, the candidates' campaign staff and party spokespersons spin them for political advantage. Political pundits and journalists scour the candidates' performances looking for the "winner." Media watchdog organizations and political advocacy groups question the debates' legitimacy, even their legality.[22] The candidates themselves pose and posture before acceding to the debates, like prize-fighters trying to intimidate each other. But citizens watch the debates in total numbers that rival or even exceed the Super Bowl for viewership. The debates are their one opportunity in the campaign to see and hear the candidates speak directly to each other in a face-to-face encounter.

It was this way from the beginning. Anticipating the first of the four 1960 debates between Vice President Richard Nixon and Senator John Kennedy, the print media were deeply skeptical of their broadcast competitors. A *Wall Street Journal* editorial warned that the televised encounter would be "rigged more for entertainment than for enlightenment."[23] The *New York Times* wrote dismissively that the debate would appeal most to voters "who are influenced not so much by logic and reason as by emotional, illogical factors—the candidate's personality, whether he talks too much or too little, a desire to be with the winner or sympathy for the underdog, and many other far less rational factors."[24] The paper predicted that "Mr. Nixon and Mr. Kennedy will each be trying to bring the audience to his point of view, . . . but the danger is that they will be attempting to do this not so much by explanation and logic but by personality projection, charges and counter-charges, empty promises, and plain gimmicks of one sort or another. The fear is that they will not discuss the issues as much as put on a show."[25] Jack Gould, the eminent television critic for the *New York Times*, panned the decision to rely on a panel of journalists to ask the questions: "What is very definitely wanted rather than mere questions and answers is a discussion between the two men. . . . For the candidates to agree that serious issues discussed in 'the great conference' can be handled in one and a half or two and a half minutes is not an encouraging augury of the campaign to come."[26] On the morning of the first Nixon-Kennedy encounter, September 26, a *Times* writer compared the coming evening's program with the Lincoln-Douglas debates of 1858 and intimated that the 1960 debates would be found wanting by comparison.[27]

If the press was not fully satisfied, neither were the candidates. The press secretaries for both candidates—Pierre Salinger for Senator Kennedy and Herbert Klein for Vice President Nixon—complained prior to the first debate that the panel of journalists included no one from the nation's major print media but only representatives from the three networks.[28] Also prior to the first debate, an "independent" candidate who had unsuccessfully sought the Democratic nomination, Andrew J. Easter, sued in federal district court to be included in the program. Easter claimed that the congressional action that made the debates possible was an unconstitutional abridgment of his right to participate, for it was allowing the networks to engage in "discriminatory and unfair practices in silent unison."[29] Among many others, Easter named as defendants in his suit both houses of Congress, FCC Chairman Frederick Ford, NBC President Robert Kintner, Vice President Nixon, and Senator Kennedy.[30]

Neither was the broadcast industry uniformly happy with the debates. Though the programs represented a professional milestone for the television networks, which had long wanted to prove themselves important contributors to the national political discussion, many of their affiliates were angered by the debates because of program preemptions and lost advertising revenue. In testimony before Congress, CBS president Frank Stanton promised that his network would not accept commercial sponsorship for the debates. Speaking afterward, NBC chairman Robert W. Sarnoff was equivocal on the issue, noting at one point that NBC had received "expressions of sponsor interest" in the debates and that he "felt it desirable in the public interest to encourage sponsorship of informational programs in the field of public affairs."[31] The sponsorship issue was a critical one: in the agreement hammered out between the networks and Congress, the networks each had promised to provide a minimum of eight hours of public-service time without charge to the major-party candidates in 1960.[32] Eventually the 1960 debates ran without interruption even for local station breaks. Trade magazine *Broadcasting* estimated that each of the four debates that year cost each of the networks approximately a half million dollars in forgone advertising revenue and program preemptions—about $6 million overall—and their affiliates many millions more.[33]

Moreover, the 1960 debates were not entirely free from instant polls and political spin. For the first debate, on September 26, the Gallup Poll assembled sixty avowed "independent" voters in a movie house in Hopewell, New Jersey, to watch the program and, with an electronic box, to register their "approval" or "disapproval" of the candidates' remarks.[34] The point of the exercise, said the *Wall Street Journal*, was "to uncover new clues as to what issues concern American voters this year and how they will vote November 8."[35] By the end of the week, the *New York Times* would report, based on a handful of random interviews throughout the country, that the debate had done little to change voters' minds.[36] The same day, however, ten southern governors who had previously been at best luke-warm to Kennedy's candidacy strongly endorsed him, citing his "superb handling of Mr. Nixon and the issues facing our country."[37] A scientific survey of the nation's voters done for CBS by pollster Elmo Roper found that 44 percent believed the debates had influenced their vote; 5 percent said their presidential choice was based solely on the debates.[38]

The morning after the first debate, newspaper reviews of the program were mixed, but a common theme to most was that television was too superficial a medium for such a serious business as national politics. The *New York News* called the program a "powderpuff performance" and charged that the "TV tycoons" had prevented the candidates from fully engaging each other by their use of a panel of journalists to ask questions.[39] The *Wall Street Journal*, confirming its own predebate prediction, complained that "those ghostly figures with their backs to the cameras were nothing but distractions. Even good questions would have derailed the conversation. . . . If instead the two candidates had been left alone to speak, to question and reply to each other, they would have inevitably pushed themselves to the hard questions about labor policy, taxes, civil rights, government spending or about the role of government in welfare legislation."[40] The *New York Mirror* criticized even more harshly the decision to have journalists ask the questions, saying the debate was "bad television, and whoever arranged the show either was overawed by the occasion and the personalities or he just did not know his business. . . . The questions asked by the commentators got the argument just about nowhere. In the future these fellows can be dispensed with."[41] Other newspapers were more charitable, if not entirely enthusiastic. The *Baltimore Sun*, for example, wrote that "the 'great debate' wasn't exactly great and it wasn't exactly a debate, but it was the best political program of the year."[42] The *St. Louis Post-Dispatch* called the program "a stiff and formalized occasion" but allowed that a "real discussion of the issues did take place."[43] The *Seattle Times* concluded that "both candidates handled tough questions with professional skill but seemed somewhat confined by the program's rigid format. There was too much emphasis on seeing to it that each candidate had the same number of seconds in which to speak."[44]

Journalists were not alone in their criticism. The eminent historian Henry Steele Commager wrote in the *New York Times Magazine* that "televised press conferences in future campaigns could be a disaster" and offered his view that neither George Washington nor Abraham Lincoln would have fared well in "such televised press interviews."[45] The journalist-scholar Norman Cousins was harsher, writing in the *Saturday Review* that the debates ran "counter to the educational process. They require that a man keep his mouth moving whether he has something to say or not. . . . Thoughtful silence is made to appear a confession of ignorance."[46] Only the British seemed to think the debates an unalloyed success. The British Broadcasting Corporation (BBC) showed the first debate in its entirety, and London's *Daily Mirror* called the program "a brilliant lesson from America on how to make an election come vividly alive."[47] The London *News Chronicle* suggested Britain copy the idea: "Set rival leaders together on the same screen and the most partisan of viewers is forced to hear both sides of the question."[48]

Problems notwithstanding, history records the 1960 debates as a great success with voters: according to data compiled by the ratings firm Arbitron, 73.5 million Americans saw that first debate, and two-thirds of the nation's 45 million households with television sets tuned in to watch.[49] If the political experts and pundits had their doubts, the public did not. One Detroit woman told the *Wall Street Journal,* "I learned more about what each man stands for in an hour than I have in two months of reading the papers." A young Anchorage sales clerk who would be voting for the first time told the paper, "Before, I was concerned only with things like Kennedy's grin and his religion, but now I feel the campaign is seriously grounded on issues. It was something I know I wouldn't have taken the time to read in the papers." Though most newspaper editorials called the debate a draw, anecdotal reports from viewers suggested that Kennedy had significantly increased his standing among undecided voters. A Jacksonville, Florida, real estate broker told the *Journal,* "I always thought Kennedy was a kiddie, but he really came out last night. I'd been leaning toward Nixon, but now I think Kennedy's the boy. He has more brains— an amazing memory and he's a better speaker." Nixon supporters, by contrast, were concerned. Said one Dallas man, "Nixon looked sick. He looked as though he's really lost weight, and I kept noticing beads of sweat on his forehead. Kennedy looked better." Reporters traveling with Nixon said the vice president was disappointed in his performance.[50]

The fourth and final debate of the 1960 campaign was broadcast from ABC News studios in New York. Like the previous three, the fourth drew an audience of more than 60 million viewers; an average of 71 million viewers watched each of the four debates, and a total of more than 115 million Americans watched at least some part of the four debates on television or listened to them on the radio.[51] On television, all four debates attracted audiences averaging 20 percent larger than the entertainment programs they replaced.[52] At the conclusion of the final program, moderator Quincy Howe of ABC News said: "Vice President Nixon and Senator Kennedy have used a new means of communication to pioneer a new type of political debate. . . . Surely they have set a new precedent. Perhaps they have established a new tradition."[53]

But it would not be that easy.

1 *How Adlai Stevenson Put John F. Kennedy in the White House*

> What I am proposing now is . . . the establishment of what I hope will become a national institution, a great debate for the Presidency. ADLAI E. STEVENSON, March 1960

Let's begin by addressing the questions posed by Admiral James Stockdale, the distinguished and straightforward U.S. Navy veteran who appeared in the 1992 vice presidential debate representing Ross Perot's Reform Party: "Who am I? And why am I here?"

My involvement with presidential debates began with heart attacks that in 1955 struck two of the most powerful men in the country, President Dwight D. Eisenhower and Senate Majority Leader Lyndon Baines Johnson. At the time I was a young law partner of former Illinois governor Adlai E. Stevenson, and in the fall of that year I was with Stevenson when he gave a speech at the University of Texas. The governor and I were invited to spend that night at Johnson's Stonewall, Texas, ranch, where LBJ was recovering from his illness. After Adlai's speech in Austin, we drove to the ranch with Texas congressman Sam Rayburn, the powerful speaker of the House. We arrived in Stonewall late at night, but LBJ was waiting up for us (much to the dismay of his wife Lady Bird, as his doctors had told him to get more rest). Johnson announced that it would be unseemly to have the top three Democrats in the country appear to be conspiring to take over the government while President Eisenhower was recovering from his own heart attack, so we would be out all the next day, meeting in the open where the press could see us.

Afterward Adlai and I flew back to Chicago, and in the course of the plane ride Adlai said, "Lyndon and Sam say that if I want the nomination next year, I will have to fight for it in the primaries. What do you think?"

I said, "They're right. If President Eisenhower does not run for reelection, the Democratic nomination will be very appealing. There will be a lot of candidates who want it. On the other hand, if President Eisenhower does run again, he's going to be reelected and you should forget about it. But if you want the nomination, you're going to have to campaign for it."

Adlai said, "I'm not going to do that. I'm not going to run around to shopping centers shaking hands like I'm running for sheriff."

Eventually, of course, President Eisenhower did decide to run again in 1956, and Adlai did enter the primaries, did run around shaking hands at shopping centers, and won his party's nomination. The two electoral contests between Eisenhower and Stevenson were a turning point in presidential campaigns. Both traveled the country meeting voters, but the Republicans made extensive use of television, too. The last true whistle-stop campaign in American presidential politics had occurred in 1948, with President Truman's train swing across the nation. That year there were only twenty-nine television stations operating in the United States, broadcasting to only about 1 million television sets, less than 9 percent of the nation's homes. Two years later there were 108 stations on the air around the country broadcasting to 10 million sets. By 1952 television penetration had jumped to nearly 40 percent of American homes, and that year both the Republican and Democratic presidential nominating conventions were broadcast to national audiences for the first time. Both parties made use of television advertisements, each with different objectives. General Eisenhower was already widely popular, so his campaign needed only to shore up support in key areas of the country. It hired six different advertising firms to produce more than a dozen twenty- and sixty-second commercials featuring the general answering recorded questions read by nonprofessional performers. The Democrats' advertising strategy was to make Adlai into more of a national figure, and it bought five-minute segments at the end of popular entertainment programs to give their candidate exposure. The Republicans eventually did the same.[1]

As the presidential campaign of that year wore on, it seemed to me that the combination of countrywide barnstorming and spot television advertising was physically exhausting for the candidates and made very little sense as a way to explain their views on important issues to the voters. I wrote a memo to Adlai proposing an alternative. Modern technology would enable voters to have a much better understanding of the candidates through radio and television, I argued, and because President Eisenhower's health was still not fully restored, Adlai should propose a series of televised nationwide joint discussions instead of traveling across the country shaking hands at rallies. Stevenson's advisers debated the idea, and though some of them agreed with me, they eventually rejected it. A few thought the idea would be perceived as a gimmick. Others thought Adlai would not do well in such a face-to-face debate. My guess is Eisenhower would have rejected the idea, too.

Then, very near the end of the campaign, a major international crisis erupted. On October 31, war broke out between Egypt and an alliance of Israel, France, and Britain over control of the Suez Canal, which Egyptian president Gamal Nassar had moved to nationalize. The Soviets threatened to intervene on the side of Egypt, thus raising the specter of a wider war that would involve the United States. The United States resolved the crisis by compelling the British and French to withdraw, thus for the first time asserting its power in the Middle East. But in what was clearly a moment of international danger, President Eisenhower asked for and received from the television and radio networks fifteen minutes of prime time to talk to the country about the war.

Jim Finnegan, an old-time professional politician from Pennsylvania whom I was assisting on the Stevenson campaign, said to me, "Our candidate should have an opportunity to answer President Eisenhower's views on Suez, and you're now in charge of getting us time on radio and television to do that."

This was my first specific exposure to issues involving political campaigns and broadcast regulation. Citing Section 315 of the Federal Communications Act, we asked the networks for equal time. In those days, the law made no distinction between news programs and other kinds of televised appearances, so we thought we had a good case. But the networks turned us down on the ground that President Eisenhower was speaking not as a candidate but in his capacity as the president. Therefore, the networks said, they were under no legal obligation to offer Stevenson equal time in which to respond. Naturally, we did not see how the two functions of president and candidate could be separated, so with the help of the Democratic National Committee we went to the Federal Communications Commission (FCC) and asked the agency to order the networks to provide the time. The FCC, as it turned out, was badly split on the issue and could not make up its mind how to resolve it.[2] When it did, it ruled against us by limiting its decision to the particular controversy before it: "We do not believe that when Congress enacted Section 315 it intended to grant equal time to all presidential candidates when the President uses air time in reporting to the nation on an international crisis."[3]

Meanwhile the clock was ticking. The election was only a day or two away. Finally, the Mutual Broadcasting System decided to give Stevenson time, which we promptly accepted. When that happened, all the networks gave him time, and Stevenson went on the air and gave his views about the Suez crisis.

Though the Republicans won the election, they were very upset by the networks' decision to grant us time. Remarkably, they then asked the FCC to order the networks to give the president time to answer Stevenson, even *after* the election. Nothing came of it.

In 1959 Adlai asked me to help him with an article about television and politics for *This Week* magazine, a Sunday supplement that appeared in newspapers throughout the country. The first drafts were done by the respected political writer John Bartlow Martin, and subsequently both Adlai and I worked on the piece. In the article, Adlai called for a series of half-hour blocks of broadcast time, on television and radio, to be made available without charge to the major party candidates and to the candidate of any other party that had won 20 percent or more of the popular vote in the previous election or "could demonstrate substantial national support."[4] The proposal was that during the final eight weeks of the campaign the candidates should give their views on the issues in a national forum, and that would become the centerpiece of the campaign.

That article changed history. It attracted the attention of leaders in the Senate, among them Senator Michael Monroney (Oklahoma) of the Commerce Committee, a onetime newspaper reporter and political columnist who had long been concerned about the rising costs of purchasing television time for political campaigns. In 1960, when Congress first explored how the still-new technology of television might be used to enhance the electoral process, its focus was not on debates but on a different idea entirely. That idea, from Stevenson's article, was to provide broadcast airtime to the candidates to present themselves and their ideas to the public in their own way.

Stevenson began the article by noting what were, even then, the prohibitive costs of "political television."[5] As a remedy for this problem, he wrote, "I would like to propose that we transform our circus-atmosphere presidential campaign into a great debate conducted in full view of all the people. . . . Imagine a debate now, or at least a discussion on the great issues of our time with the whole country watching. How we decide [those issues] may fix our children's future, and mankind's. And we can decide them not after canned rhetoric and TV spectaculars but only after intelligent discussion, which the candidates and the networks can provide."[6]

Despite the title ("Adlai Stevenson's Plan for a Great Debate"), and Stevenson's description of a "great debate," the governor did not in fact propose debates, events with which he was both personally familiar and famously skilled. Only a few years before, in the 1956 Florida Democratic primary, Stevenson had debated Tennessee senator Estes Kefauver in a nationally televised ABC broadcast moderated by Quincy Howe of ABC News; in 1952, Republican and Democratic aspirants for their respective parties' presidential nominations—or in some cases their appointed representatives—had answered two questions each at the national convention of the League of Women Voters. To the extent that that forum constituted a debate, it was the first nationally televised political debate in the nation's history, and two months later Michigan senator Blair Moody proposed that the eventual nominees of the two parties meet in a nationally televised debate in the weeks before the November election. Both NBC and CBS agreed to broadcast such a meeting, but neither of the nominees—Stevenson and Eisenhower—accepted the networks' offer.[7]

The idea of a *broadcast* debate was not new: the first nationally broadcast political debate was on radio on May 17, 1948, between Republicans Harold Stassen of Minnesota and Thomas Dewey of New York. The sponsor of the Stassen-Dewey debate was a small ABC station in Portland, Oregon, whose program director seized on the idea of a debate before the state's primary election. In a foretelling of what would later become one of the biggest obstacles to broadcast debates, the two candidates negotiated the terms of their encounter almost to the last day before going on the air. Governor Stassen insisted on audience participation and expected that "there will be applause, . . . maybe some heckling" because "that's the American way."[8] Governor Dewey refused to allow any audience participation. Stassen wanted a wide-ranging discussion; Dewey insisted the one-hour program be limited to a single question: "Shall the Communist Party in the United States be outlawed?"[9] Stassen finally agreed to Dewey's terms, and the broadcast was carried by nearly nine hundred radio stations across the country.[10] Each candidate gave a twenty-minute opening argument; each then gave an eight-and-a-half-minute rebuttal in which he lambasted his opponent. During the debate, AT&T operators reported that long-distance calls dropped by 25 percent.[11]

When Stevenson wrote his article in 1960, he came at the issue from personal experience and knowledge. And he did not propose debates. Rather he proposed that the candidates appear on television consecutively, not simultaneously, to present their ideas to the American people in the final weeks before the election. They should not have to purchase the time, Stevenson said; it would be provided to them as a public service by the nation's broadcasters: "Suppose that every Monday evening, at peak viewing time, for an hour and a half, from Labor Day to election eve, the two candidates aired their views. They might on each evening take up a single issue. Each in turn might discuss it for half an hour, followed by 15-minute rebuttals of one another for the third half hour."[12]

Stevenson acknowledged that this airtime could be used in other ways, "including face-to-face debate," but the critical matter was that "in some manner the candidates for president appear together at the same prime time each week for a serious presentation of views on public questions." Of similar importance, he said, was that "the time should cost them and their parties nothing." Stevenson acknowledged that many more parties than just the Republican and the Democrat would ask for time under his proposal. At least ten other parties put forward presidential candidates in 1956, but giving time to all of them, he said, would be "manifestly absurd." He proposed as a solution that public-service time be provided only to parties that polled at least 20 percent of the vote in the previous election and "to new parties which can demonstrate substantial national support."[13]

Stevenson's article caught the attention not only of Senator Monroney but also of Rhode Island senator John Pastore, chairman of the Subcommittee on Communications of the Senate Commerce Committee. A little more than two months later, Pastore's subcommittee held hearings on a Senate bill modeled after the governor's proposal.[14] Specifically, the bill required "each TV broadcast station and each TV network to make available without charge the use of its facilities to qualified candidates for the office of President of the United States. . . . Each candidate is entitled to 1 hour of time a week for the 8-week period beginning September 1 preceding the election. . . . This time is required to be made available in prime viewing hours and to be scheduled in programs of 1 hour each, equally divided between the two candidates."[15] By its terms the bill did not apply to radio broadcasters, only television, and it required that the candidates themselves appear on their own behalf.[16] The bill differed from Stevenson's original proposal in one key respect: where Stevenson had proposed a threshold of 20 percent public support to qualify for airtime, the Senate bill provided time to any party whose "candidate for president in the preceding election was supported by not fewer than 4 percent of the total popular vote cast."[17] In hearings on the bill in May 1960, Pastore noted that even under this 4 percent rule only the Republican and Democratic candidates would qualify for time in that fall's presidential contest; he claimed (incorrectly) that no third party had won more than 1 percent of the popular vote going back to 1944.[18] (Henry Wallace's Progressive Party won 2.4 percent of the vote in 1948.)

Governor Stevenson was the first to testify in favor of the bill. After noting that "the technology of our civilization is equal to its problems," Stevenson bemoaned the cost of modern campaigning, especially television advertising. The networks' inflexible prime-time scheduling, compounded by prohibitively expensive commercial time, forced serious candidates to resort to the sort of advertising agencies that traffic in "the jingle, the spot announcement, and the animated cartoon."[19] Stevenson suggested that the antidote to the two major difficulties in modern campaigning—physical exhaustion and the chronic use of ghostwriters—was a more extensive and more efficient use of television.

Senator Pastore pressed the governor on the objections that many broadcasters had already made to the proposal. Did "free time" encroach on broadcasters' First Amendment rights? Did it amount to a seizure of broadcasters' property without compensation? Stevenson was adamant in his response to both questions:

> I find no criticism of this measure more unjustified than the charge that it is Government interference with free speech. Rather it represents a guarantee of free speech. The freedom of speech which our Nation's founders fought to preserve was more than the right of a peddler on Boston Commons to hawk his oysters without restraint. It was the right of public discussion of political issues. Their devotion to it was not to an abstract right, but born of conviction that full discussion of alternatives was prerequisite to an intelligent choice between them. The same conviction motivates the sponsors of this bill. . . . To require 8 hours every 4 years for a particular type of public service programming would involve preemption of three one-hundredths of 1 percent of each station's total broadcast time during that period, or one one-hundredth of 1 percent of each station's prime time. . . . [This] is not a very large amount that we are talking about. The television stations are licensees of the public, they enjoy monopolies, granted by the public, of great value; they already have an obligation to provide public service programs, to operate in the public interest.[20]

Near the end of Stevenson's testimony, Texas senator Ralph Yarborough asked what the governor would think if "for this year 1960, that we try this out on a voluntary basis, and if doesn't work in 1960, postpone the enactment of this law and then pass this law for the 1964 campaign." Stevenson was intrigued by the idea, provided the voluntary system conformed to his original proposal of "an hour a week to be divided between the two parties." If it did not, he said, "I would prefer to see legislation."

When Stevenson complimented Yarborough on the suggestion, the senator replied, "Well, the voluntary system was not suggested by me, Governor Stevenson. It has been suggested and I merely brought that up to get your opinion."[21] Yarborough, it would turn out, thought that only legislation would do, that the broadcasters could not be trusted to act voluntarily.

Pastore's committee took testimony and statements from a number of people and organizations. Former president Herbert Hoover, who as commerce secretary to President Calvin Coolidge had been the early architect of the nation's communications laws, opposed the Presidential Campaign Broadcasting Act, saying that "if we are to avoid government censorship of free speech, we had better continue the practice of the supporters of candidates providing their own television and radio programs."[22] Norman Thomas and the Socialist Party also objected to the bill, saying that while they favored the idea of using television more productively in campaigns, the Senate proposal "would provide the powerful and relatively affluent major parties with free time while the small and impoverished parties would have to purchase their airtime. If anything, the procedure should actually be reversed."[23] The American Civil Liberties Union also wished to amend the proposal—with a requirement that *all* legally qualified presidential candidates get free time, irrespective of any showing in the previous election.[24] Both Vice President Richard Nixon and former New York governor (and presidential candidate) Thomas Dewey objected to the bill on the grounds that free time represented an "expropriation" of broadcaster property. Dewey argued that the purpose of the bill could be accomplished more easily "by amending the law so that broadcasting stations and networks be permitted to give such free and equal time to the candidates of the two major parties as they, in the exercise of their editorial discretion, consider wise and proper. I have always understood that they were eager to do this but that the anachronistic restriction in the law has prevented them from doing so."[25]

The broadcast industry strongly and loudly opposed both the Senate and House bills. *Broadcasting* magazine characterized the Senate bill as a property "seizure" in violation of the Fifth Amendment.[26] In testimony before Pastore's subcommittee, NBC executive vice president David C. Adams said the legislation raised "grave constitutional questions" both because it interfered with the broadcasters' free expression rights by compelling speech and, he said, because it deprived broadcasters of their property for public use without providing just compensation. As counsel to the National Association of Broadcasters, Whitney North Seymour made a different constitutional argument: that the government cannot, however benign its intent, regulate political speech. The First Amendment, he said, "would seem to forbid favoritism by the federal government in providing free platforms as between candidates of major and minor parties."[27]

But Congress was clearly determined to do something. The networks counter-offered with various proposals of their own for providing time for the candidates. CBS was the first to make an offer of voluntary public-service time; represented by CBS president Frank Stanton, the network proposed eight one-hour prime-time telecasts to be used for debates and discussions. Importantly, Stanton also asked that these debate programs be exclusive—in other words, that only CBS would be able to air them. NBC said it would air, on a nonexclusive basis, eight one-hour *Meet the Press* broadcasts in prime Sunday-night time, with six of them to include appearances by the Republican and Democratic presidential nominees. ABC suggested that the three networks provide, on a rotating basis, their three best time slots with the largest audiences for nine weeks prior to the election; again, the two major-party candidates would be able to use the time as they chose.[28] Of these proposals, only NBC's did not require a change in the law, since the 1959 amendments to the Communications Act exempted "bona fide news interviews" from the equal opportunity requirement. Both the ABC and CBS proposals required congressional action.

The day after Governor Stevenson's appearance before Senator Pastore's subcommittee, Stanton followed, giving a more measured industry view of the proposed legislation. Since the early 1950s Stanton had wanted to have televised presidential debates, and in 1955 he had published an essay in the *New York Herald Tribune* urging Congress to amend or revoke Section 315 to make such debates possible.[29] In his congressional testimony, Stanton was careful not to attack the proposed legislation as an offense to broadcasters' free speech or property rights; instead he argued that if Congress was serious about putting the candidates before the American public in the weeks leading up to the election, there were much better ways to do it, and moreover that the networks' news divisions were eager to do it. The Senate bill, Stanton said, "does nothing but give time to the nominees to do with as they like—the 16 hours would be forthcoming without regard to their interest, their news significance or even to their relevancy." And there was a bigger problem:

> You see the headline in the paper this morning says "Stevenson urges TV great debate." Well I don't think the testimony up to this point, the bill itself, isn't talking about a debate. The bill itself is talking about free time to be used as the candidate chooses to use it, so I don't see how you can talk about this

bill as a great debate. . . . I think [political television] should be done on the basis of issues that are decided upon in advance and you select a group of journalists who are qualified to ask those questions, and then television can go wherever the candidates are and put the questions to each candidate. This is the kind of face-to-face discussion I am talking about.[30]

Stanton also objected, on news judgment and First Amendment grounds, to the idea that only a candidate or party that had received 4 percent of the popular vote in the previous election could qualify for inclusion in the bill's free time proposal. Trying to establish a free time requirement around a percentage figure, he argued, was arbitrary. It would have excluded the Republican candidate for president in 1856 because his party had not received 4 percent of the vote in 1852, though by 1860 the Republicans would begin twenty-four uninterrupted years in the White House. The Bull Moose Party would have been excluded in 1912 even though its candidate, Theodore Roosevelt, was an illustrious former president who would go on to win more votes that year than the Republican incumbent. Senator Robert LaFollette would have been excluded in 1924 even though he drew more than half the votes of his Democratic opponent. Strom Thurmond would have been excluded in 1948 despite the powerful support he had in the South and his eventual strong showing in the electoral vote. The decision of who was newsworthy, Stanton emphasized, was for journalists to make, not Congress: "I would approach it in terms of giving the broadcaster the freedom to make the decision rather than try to put him in a straitjacket and anticipate now what the conditions are going to be 4, 8, 12, and 16 years hence. . . . The whole fault I have to find with S. 3171 is that it invades, from my point of view, the journalistic function of television and a free press."[31]

Finally, Stanton objected, the Senate bill was "too narrow and inflexible." If televised presidential debates were important, he said, just as important were campaigns for a multitude of other local, state, and federal offices around the country. Under the Senate proposal, he told the committee, the Lincoln-Douglas debates of 1858 would not have been televised, because the two were running not for the presidency but for the Senate.[32]

At one point in his testimony, Wyoming senator Gale McGee asked Stanton why, if he found the bill so troublesome, he and CBS did not provide more time to political candidates on their own initiative. He was surprised when Stanton told him that the law prevented him from doing so, and Senator Pastore quickly confirmed Stanton's view of the matter: "If the stations or networks were to offer an opportunity of debate to two candidates, they subject themselves to granting equal time to all other candidates for the same office, and as a result this has discouraged broadcasters from offering time in the first place."[33]

The window of opportunity now open, Stanton pressed it throughout his testimony. At the suggestion of his lawyer, CBS counsel Leon Brooks, he pledged that if Congress would suspend the equal opportunities requirement for the 1960 presidential and vice-presidential races, the networks would undertake to present several debates between the candidates. In his written statement to the subcommittee, Stanton had called for the relevant section of the law to be amended to allow freer news coverage of candidates, but in the absence of such an amendment he proposed an experiment:

> What I would like to do as far as CBS television network is concerned is to offer the candidates for President an hour each night in prime evening time for debates or face-to-face discussions during the campaign. . . . I think if you have an industry that wants to do it, and I think the record of the industry is pretty good, then I think the industry ought to be given an opportunity to do it. If we don't do it, then I think you ought to bring us up short. I think we are subject to public censure and criticism if we don't do it, but I think we ought to be given the opportunity to see what we can do if we are allowed to do it voluntarily.[34]

So that was what Congress did: it suspended that portion of the equal opportunities law that made it impossible for broadcasters to air candidate debates, *but only for 1960* and only for candidates for the offices of president and vice president.[35] Because the incumbent, President Eisenhower, could not run again, there was no obstacle of incumbency to work against the experiment. That fall, Vice President Richard Nixon and Massachusetts senator John Kennedy would have four televised debates, each lasting sixty minutes, each sponsored by the host network.[36] The dominant theme of the meetings was the threat of global communism, particularly threats from China and Cuba. There was no vice-presidential debate.[37]

The first of the presidential debates aired on September 26 from WBBM-TV in Chicago, a CBS-owned-and-operated station. Newsman Howard K. Smith served as moderator and three journalists asked questions. All three networks simultaneously carried the program, which aired at 9:30 p.m. on the East Coast. Adlai Stevenson's visionary belief that "the technology of our civilization is equal to its problems" enabled nearly 70 million Americans to watch as the candidates for the presidency faced each other on television for the first time in history. Many people remember only the first debate, in which the vice president, recovering from the flu, looked pale and sluggish while Kennedy appeared poised and fit. "Kennedy was bronzed beautifully, wearing a navy suit and a blue shirt," Stanton recalled later. "Nixon looked like death because he had been in the hospital. And you could run your hand inside his collar without touching anything—it was that loose. His color was terrible; his beard was not good and he didn't want any makeup. I felt sorry for him."[38]

After the broadcast was over, Stanton said, he could not find Nixon to thank him; he had left the studio immediately, leaving behind his coat and his briefcase. Stanton then went to thank Kennedy, whom he found on the phone, his shirt soaked through with perspiration, but agreeing with his caller that "we sure took this one." When Kennedy hung up, he introduced Stanton to Chicago mayor Richard J. Daley, who offered the CBS president a ride downtown. As they walked out of the CBS studio, Stanton reports, Daley said to him, "You know, I'm going to change my mind and tell my men to go all out for Kennedy."[39] Before that first debate, Daley had been lukewarm to the Massachusetts junior senator; now his support made all the difference. The state of Illinois played a major role in determining the outcome of the election two months later.

Daley was not the only one to conclude that Kennedy had won. After the debate, the *New York Times* declared that "on sound points of argument, Nixon probably took most of the honors," but the impression of those who watched on television was that the more telegenic Kennedy had carried the contest.[40]

In his classic work *The Making of the President 1960,* Theodore H. White described the debates as a "revolution . . . born of the ceaseless American genius in technology; its sole agent and organizer had been the common American television set," which permitted "the simultaneous gathering of all the tribes of America to ponder their choice between two chieftains in the largest political convocation in the history of man."[41] Walter Lippmann called the debates "a bold innovation which is bound to be carried forward into future campaigns and could not now be abandoned."[42] Both men's optimism was premature. At midnight of Election Day—November 7, 1960—the federal law that made the revolution possible expired by its own terms. There would not be another presidential election with televised debates for sixteen years.

2 *Presidential Debates and "Equal Opportunity"*

> There is hardly a political question in the United States
> which does not sooner or later turn into a judicial one.
> ALEXIS DE TOCQUEVILLE, 1840

From the vantage point of the twenty-first century, it is easy to overlook the fact that much of the long controversy surrounding the debates had nothing to do with the debates themselves but with legal controversies involving the *broadcast* of the debates.[1] While Congress in 1960 changed the law temporarily to make the Kennedy-Nixon debates possible, it left on the books the legislation that had the practical effect of making further such debates *impossible* until well after 1960. When the law finally did change, it was not Congress that changed it but the FCC and the federal courts. As a result, the story of presidential debates is in significant measure a story of legislatures, regulatory agencies, candidates, broadcasters, and reformers struggling to adhere to, amend, and reinterpret rules so that the public might benefit from a more robust, elevated campaign dialogue. The obstacles to regular broadcast debates have included laws and federal regulations whose practical effect was to make all but impossible the broadcast of debates—and certainly debates between the major-party presidential candidates. In theory, of course, broadcasters have always been able to present debates, but had they done so the Communications Act would have required them to give equal time to potentially dozens of minor-party candidates, some serious and some silly. The law, in short, created a powerful if unintended practical incentive to avoid debates between candidates for public office.

The irony of this is that the modern presidential campaign is a television event. Most Americans see, hear and come to know the candidates *only* through television. Especially in uncontested states, where one candidate has an insurmountable lead over the other, or in states with few electoral votes, the television campaign *is* the campaign, and the televised debates between the candidates mark the high point of the contest. Few understand the key regulatory and constitutional issues that surround the televised presidential debates—indeed, *any* broadcast debate between and among *any* candidates for *any* political office in the United States. This history is poorly understood by the debates' many critics, most of whom tell it incompletely or selectively, or ignore it entirely.[2]

The central problem began in 1927, with the drafting of the Federal Radio Act, the first piece of comprehensive legislation regulating what was then a new technology and a rapidly growing industry, radio broadcasting. That law and the one that replaced it, the Communications Act of 1934, created what is known as the "equal time" rule in Section 315. The law requires broadcast stations that provide airtime to a candidate for public office also to provide "equal opportunity" to other qualified candidates for the same office. But which candidates? All or some? And how much time? When? And what distinguishes a legitimate news story about a candidate from a donation of airtime? Assuming one knew the difference, was a broadcast debate a news event, a donation of time, or something else?[3] The Communications Act, like the Radio Act before it, was all but silent on these matters, and the congressional record on both statutes offered little guidance to broadcasters or to the federal agency responsible for making the rules, the Federal Communications Commission.[4] Just what the law meant would eventually be decided by the courts.

*   *   *

As Alexis de Tocqueville observed, American political questions usually turn into judicial issues. So it was with the Communications Act, which requires broadcasters to serve "the public interest, convenience and necessity."[5] The reason for this requirement is that the electromagnetic spectrum broadcasters use belongs not to them but to the public. An important judicial opinion written by then U.S. circuit judge Warren Burger in 1966—stemming from Reverend Smith's effort to buy time on WLBT in Jackson, Mississippi—stated that a broadcaster's use of that spectrum is therefore based on a legal quid pro quo: "A broadcaster seeks and is granted the free and exclusive use of a limited and valuable part of the public domain; when he accepts that franchise it is burdened by enforceable public obligations. A newspaper can be operated at the whim or caprice of its owners; a broadcasting station cannot. . . . [A] broadcast licensee is a public trust subject to termination for breach of duty."[6]

Perhaps the foremost of broadcasters' public interest obligations, and certainly the most explicit one, requires broadcasters to carry political broadcasts.[7] Two sections of the Communications Act speak to that obligation: Section 315 of the 1934 law (today incorporated into the Telecommunications Act of 1996)[8] and Section 312(a)(7) (the legislative history of which is discussed in appendix C). These two sections require broadcasters to sell "reasonable" amounts of time to qualified candidates for federal office at the lowest possible charge for the time sought—in other words, as inexpensively as possible.[9]

My focus in this chapter is Section 315 and the "equal opportunities" or "equal time" rule, which essentially says that if a broadcaster gives or sells airtime to one candidate for public office, it must provide the same opportunity to all other candidates for the same office. The policy justification for the rule, according to Nicholas Zapple, long-time legal counsel to Senator Pastore, was in "assuring a legally qualified candidate that he would not be subjected to unfair disadvantage from an opponent through favoritism in selling or donating time or in scheduling political broadcasts."[10] Congress first wrote the equal opportunities rule into law as Section 18 of the 1927 Radio Act, the nation's first attempt at a comprehensive law regulating the developing technologies of radio and telephony. Legislators were concerned that without such a requirement broadcasters would use the airwaves to manipulate elections by favoring some candidates and ignoring others. Said one congressman at the time, "American politics will be largely at the mercy of those who operate these stations."[11] An opposing view of the proposal was, as one Texas senator put it, that "bolshevism or communism" might be entitled to airtime under the new regulatory scheme.[12] The sponsor of the bill, Senator Clarence Dill of Washington, assured his colleagues that by restricting the use of radio to "legally qualified candidates" for public office, the Communist Party, among other radical groups whose activities were criminalized, would not qualify for time.[13] In the House, at least one representative bluntly objected that the equal opportunity provision violated the right of free speech, but Commerce Secretary Herbert Hoover, speaking before a House committee, touted the bill as a protection against censorship.[14] Senator Dill, trying to postpone controversy over these issues, urged that a bipartisan commission (what became the Federal Radio Commission) have jurisdiction over interpretation and enforcement of the equal time provision.[15] Without such a commission, he said, radio stations might censor themselves for fear of offending the administration and by extent Hoover and his Interstate Commerce Commission, which under existing law at the time was required to renew broadcasting licenses every ninety days.[16]

Less than a decade later, Congress included the equal time rule as Section 315 of the 1934 Communications Act, providing that "if any licensee shall permit any person who is a legally qualified candidate for any public office to use a broadcasting station, he shall afford equal opportunities to all other such candidates for that office in the use of such broadcasting station. . . . Provided, That such licensee shall have no power of censorship over the material broadcast under the provisions of this paragraph. No obligation is hereby imposed upon any licensee to allow the use of its station by any such candidate."[17]

The government agency whose job it is to interpret and enforce this law is the Federal Communications Commission (the FCC), a creation of the 1934 law. The FCC made relatively few rulings about the meaning of Section 315 over the first two decades of its existence. Tellingly, almost all of those rulings came after 1956, the same year that television sets first could be found in the majority of American households.[18] American politics has not been the same since.

Prior to 1956, the FCC had made few rulings on Section 315. In 1951, for example, the Commission determined that the law did not apply unless a candidate personally appeared in a program; friends and supporters could appear on his or her behalf without triggering the equal time requirement.[19] But perhaps the more important ruling came in 1940, when the agency defined a "legally qualified candidate" under the law as one who "has publicly announced his or her intention to run for nomination or office; is qualified under the applicable local, state or federal law to hold the office for which he or she is a candidate."[20] The FCC said that a candidate must qualify for a place on the ballot or have made a public commitment to seeking election through a write-in candidacy and also must be able to show that he or she is a "bona fide" candidate for that office. Such a showing, the agency said, can be done in several ways, including "making campaign speeches, distributing campaign literature, issuing press releases, maintaining a campaign committee, and establishing campaign headquarters (even though the headquarters in some instances might be the residence of the candidate or his campaign manager.)"[21]

Section 315 caused no serious problems until the advent of television, and then it quickly became clear that access to this new medium was essential for any politician seeking to gain or maintain public office. It also became apparent that the law was frustratingly silent on a central question: what constitutes a candidate's "use" of a broadcast facility? In the 1956 presidential campaign, the FCC addressed this question twice, both times in response to Democratic challenges to President Dwight Eisenhower. The first ruling followed a three-and-a-half-minute televised appeal by the president on behalf of a charity, United Community Funds, which at the time was engaged in its annual fund drive. When Democrats sought equal time, the FCC granted it. After all, the law had no exception for "public service" appearances, nor did it require that a politician's appearance had to be "political."[22] In other words, the FCC decided, virtually any appearance by a candidate triggered the equal opportunities rule.

A second test of this proposition was the 1956 Suez Crisis, discussed in the last chapter, when as a member of Governor Stevenson's presidential campaign staff I was given the task of obtaining equal time for Stevenson to respond to President Eisenhower's televised speech on the crisis. The FCC hedged at first, then denied our request.[23] To the extent that one can separate the roles of president and candidate, Eisenhower's appearance on television was clearly in the former role. But again, the FCC had no guidance on the term *use* and was not disposed to take up the matter of definition on its own.

Congress finally intervened to change the law in 1959, the result of a challenge to the FCC by a third-party candidate, Lar Daly, who was running for mayor of Chicago under the banner of the America First Party. Daly was a colorful and perennial candidate for public office who often campaigned while dressed as Uncle Sam. He died in 1979, after he had run unsuccessfully to be Chicago's mayor, Illinois governor, a U.S. senator, a U.S. congressman, and, in 1960, president of the United States as the candidate of the Tax Cut Party. In 1959 he had run in the Chicago Republican Party primary for mayor but lost. He then chose to run as an independent. In the midst of the mayoral campaign, Daly petitioned the FCC for equal time as the result of television appearances by his opponents, Democrat Richard J. Daley (the incumbent) and his Republican challenger. Among the broadcast segments Daly used to make his claim for time was a forty-six-second clip that showed the major party candidates filing their papers with the city elections office. Other clips included a twenty-nine-second broadcast of Mayor Daley in an appeal for the March of Dimes and a twenty-one-second broadcast of the mayor greeting President Arturo Frondizi of Argentina at Chicago's O'Hare Airport.[24] Lar Daly demanded broadcast time of his own in order to counter Mayor Daley's appearances in these film clips, and the FCC gave it to him. In a long opinion, the Commission ruled that all three clips triggered the equal time provision, and it dismissed as irrelevant the objection that none of the clips constituted a formal campaign appearance. "Of no less importance," the Commission wrote, "is the candidate's appearance as a public servant, as an incumbent office holder, or as a private citizen in a non-political role." Such "appearances and uses of a nonpolitical nature may confer substantial benefits on a candidate who is favored."[25] In short, the FCC agreed that simply because *Mayor* Daley had appeared on television, *candidate* Daly was entitled to the same airtime.[26] More generally, the apparent conclusion of the FCC was that the word *use* in Section 315 applied to all regularly scheduled newscasts.[27]

If that were true, of course, television and radio stations would have a strong incentive not to cover politics at all, never mind electoral campaigns, for fear of triggering an unsustainable onslaught of demands for airtime—an unacceptable policy outcome that Congress clearly had never intended. The networks were furious at the FCC ruling, though the agency chairman at the time, John Doerfer, told CBS newsman Howard K. Smith that the Commission had ruled in such a narrow and mechanical fashion with the thought that it could compel Congress to repeal Section 315 altogether.[28] If strictly enforced, a Senate report concluded, the *Lar Daly* decision would "tend to dry up meaningful radio and television coverage of political campaigns," and the real losers would be the listening and viewing public: "The inevitable consequence is that a broadcaster will be reluctant to show one political candidate in any news-type program lest he assumes the burden of presenting a parade of aspirants."[29] The FCC knew its decision would bring a storm of protest because it undermined newscasts, including broadcasters' journalistic judgment about what is newsworthy. But a new FCC chairman, Frederick Ford (who succeeded Doerfer after the latter was compelled to resign because of a scandal), also believed that it was Congress's job, not the agency's, to fix the law.[30]

Congress quickly did. In 1959 it amended Section 315 to allow for four exceptions to the equal opportunity rule. According to those amendments, legally qualified candidates may appear in (1) bona fide newscasts, (2) bona fide news interviews, (3) bona fide news documentaries, or (4) "on-the-spot coverage of bona fide news events" without triggering the equal opportunity requirement.[31]

Those who supported these changes in the law referred constantly in floor discussion about them to their concern about the FCC's *Lar Daly* decision, mentioning in nearly every session that Mayor Richard Daley made "use" of Chicago's TV stations only briefly, and then more as a dignitary than as a candidate. The supporters admitted that making changes to Section 315 was a gamble but concluded that their best bet was to pass a reasonable bill and see what the FCC would do with it. Senator John

Pastore, the bill's sponsor in the Senate, said that if the decision turned out badly Congress could always correct it: "I cannot look at a crystal ball and say that everything we hope to avoid will be avoided. . . . If we do not do something this session about the situation, we shall have a very chaotic situation come next election."[32]

The most difficult issue, though, was determining what kinds of programs were exempt from the equal time provision. Early on, debate in the House revealed that language exempting "bona fide" news programs was too vague on its own, as a station's politics could easily influence its news judgment. One legislator noted that the changes could give broadcasters too much discretion in their coverage of political conventions. Many legislators argued that "news documentaries" and "panel discussions" (neither of which was ever clearly defined in the course of the congressional debate) functioned more as political soapboxes than as news programs. One representative wanted to define "bona fide newscast[s]" narrowly as broadcasts that run only as "bona fide news *develops*" (our italics), which would seem to rule out any kind of news analysis or "week-in-review" programs.[33]

Senator Pastore thought a "news documentary" could be any program that fleshed out the context and background of the news and therefore was not inherently political or even beneficial to a featured candidate. A conference report extended to documentaries the requirement that a candidate's appearance be "incidental" to the presentation of news. A documentary that "deals predominantly with a candidate," on the other hand, was not exempt. Legislators were skeptical of the idea that "panel discussions"—which presumably meant programs like *Meet the Press* and *Face the Nation*—were "incidental" to the presentation of news. One pointed out that such programs "more frequently than not have to do with what the candidates did or did not do some years before, rather than with any newsworthy item as of the moment."[34] In other words, those programs were apparently more susceptible to "use" by candidates and their content was harder for broadcasters to control. Another legislator argued that there is news value in "the opportunity of Americans to hear face-to-face debate by opponents."[35] Senator Spessard Holland of Florida met with no opposition when he pointed out that exempted panel discussions could unfairly affect primaries, especially in states that are dominated by one party. He noted that in Florida it was then common for "anywhere from 5 to 15 candidates" to run for governor. Pastore replied that exempting panel discussions was not particularly important to him "because it is a little broader than the news category or on-the-spot news coverage."[36]

Legislators generally agreed that panel discussions had less claim to news value and were more open to political unfairness than other kinds of news programs.

Overall, legislators seemed more concerned with the effects that the equal time provisions could have on nightly newscasts than on panel programs like *Face the Nation* or *Meet the Press*. Representative Oren Harris's version of an exemption bill was the most restrictive. It allowed panel discussions to be exempt only as part of "regular bona fide" newscasts. Including them (or documentaries) or anything beyond "bona fide news programs or on-the-spot coverage of news events," Harris said, could expand the bill to cover "all kinds of programs not intended to be covered."[37] In the end, legislators concurred that documentaries were easier to fold into the category of "bona fide" coverage—and, implicitly, that the public and FCC would find it easier to spot political abuses in the news-documentary format. But language exempting "panel discussions" seemed to allow too much room for abuse.

There were other issues, too: It was unclear whether "equal time" meant that candidates should or could use their time for comparable broadcast formats. As one congressman put it, "The first candidate who appears has no choice in the means and methods whereby the station carries his utterances, whereas his opponents have a complete choice and control over their means and methods of appearance."[38] Further, there was some concern that the proposed amendments to Section 315 would have the effect of knocking important minor-party candidates off the air and out of the public eye. Without the right to demand equal news coverage, one representative argued, these parties would not have a fair shot at getting their message heard on television.[39] Other critics of the amendments said they effectively diminished equal opportunities for challengers because they enabled "the party in power to manipulate and saturate the news," especially in presidential contests.[40]

Not surprisingly, all legislators in the debate were concerned with how the changes might affect incumbents. One Washington senator brought up a very tricky gray area between newsworthy public duties and television campaigning: "In my section of the county . . . there was a very close race for district attorney. A week before the election there were two murders in the city of Seattle, and the two guilty persons were captured. The incumbent district attorney used every television station every night after the two criminals confessed to the murders. The citizens forgot about the other man who was running. We encounter difficult situations like that, but that was news."[41]

The anecdote reveals a broader subtext in the congressional debate over the amendments: those who supported them were willing to give broadcasters room for some discretion rather than make it more difficult for them to cover the news, and they willingly let the FCC work out the problem of enforcement. The prevailing view was that the public benefits of the amendments "are so great that they outweight [sic] the risk that may result from the favoritism that may be shown by some partisan broadcasters."[42] Asked if a station could cover "all the news involving one candidate, and no news regarding the other," Pastore responded, "Absolutely. The only thing Section 315 prohibits is exposure of the candidate himself."[43] The distinction may sound paper thin, but in light of the *Lar Daly* decision it made perfect sense at the time. Congress wanted to balance its guarantee of equal treatment for candidates for public office with two other, equally important policies—encouraging maximum coverage of politics and public affairs and preserving independent journalistic judgment in broadcasting.[44] Those who supported the amendments felt it was essential to give the FCC something a little more reasonable and less mechanical with which to work in resolving the tension between these goals. And they were willing to leave the details to the FCC. Pastore summed up the approach this way: "What is a newscast? We are saying to the Commission, 'Tell us what it is, and make rules and regulations, so that all may know.' What is a news documentary? We say to the Commission, 'Define it by rules and regulations.'"[45]

Implicit in this approach was the understanding that enforcing the law would depend somewhat on complaints from the public—not just from candidates—and therefore on public perceptions of fairness. Oklahoma senator Fred Harris expressed faith that any program that "tries to go beyond the spirit and the letter of the law and begins to abuse it . . . is going to be detected immediately."[46] The final bill was careful to include the provision that the "format and production" of exempt broadcasts would be determined by the broadcaster, language that Harris saw as a compromise that protected the equal time provision from broadcasters clamoring for its outright repeal.[47] Still, when it was all done, lawmakers seemed to think that the category of "panel discussions," adaptable to so many purposes, was harder for the public, and perhaps the FCC, to understand and regulate in time for the 1960 election. The final version of the bill thus allowed "news interviews" and "news documentaries" to qualify for exemption but left out "panel discussions" and, even more significantly, "debates." If Congress had included those words, this would be a much different book.

As Frank Stanton promised, the networks in 1960 provided political programming far beyond the televised debates. Often overlooked is all the *other* political programming made possible by the temporary suspension of Section 315; the networks afforded a total of thirty-nine hours and twenty-two minutes of airtime to the presidential and vice-presidential candidates during the campaign.[48] NBC proceeded with its plans for special presentations of *Meet the Press,* while ABC scheduled eight *Presidential Roundup* programs in which candidates Nixon and Kennedy, as well as vice-presidential candidates Henry Cabot Lodge and Lyndon Johnson, were invited to appear individually for interviews. CBS aired nine half-hour campaign reports called *Presidential Countdown,* with Walter Cronkite. The Mutual Broadcasting radio network devoted nine of its Friday night *World Tonight* programs to documentaries on the week's campaign developments.[49] The networks provided so much candidate airtime in 1960 that the campaigns could not use it all and even sold back to the networks some time for which they had paid.[50] Much of that programming was unique, the likes of which have never been seen again. "For the first time," wrote CBS News president Richard Salant, "the political diet in television was not the set speeches by the candidates, the carefully staged rallies, the screened and rehearsed 'telethons,' but rather the more meaningful beginnings of a national dialogue and a systematic portrait of the nature of the candidates."[51] At the end of the campaign, the FCC reported to Congress that the suspension had been a brilliant success and that no broadcasters abused it, as some members of Senator Pastore's subcommittee had feared.

For broadcasters, in fact, their success in Congress meant an opportunity to prove themselves the journalistic equal of the print press, and thus, they hoped, to persuade Congress to repeal the equal opportunities rule entirely.[52] With the industry still reeling from the quiz show scandals of a little more than a year before, *Broadcasting* magazine editorialized:

> By political accident broadcasters have been given a chance, and a good one, to cover the 1960 election campaigns with the same freedom accorded to the press. . . . This is an opportunity that cannot be ignored by any broadcaster who aspires to a status superior to that of jukebox operator or popcorn concessionaire. It is an opportunity that has come when it was most needed—by broadcasters and the public. Great national policies will be formed during the 1960 campaigns. If broadcasting covers the campaigns with wisdom, ingenuity and thoroughness, the electorate that goes into the polls next November will be the best informed in history, and the image of broadcasting, now defaced by the investigations of recent months, will have been fully repaired.[53]

But if there was an opportunity to change the law, *Broadcasting* warned, there was also significant risk in the deal the networks struck with Congress. In an editorial written two weeks after Stanton's proposal for the voluntary provision of candidate time, the magazine observed,

> There's a good chance the U.S. Congress will give broadcasters enough rope to enable them to climb to freedom in political broadcasting. The same rope is long enough for broadcasters to hang themselves with. . . . The new freedom imposes new responsibilities. Operating as they have under rigid rules applying to political broadcasting, broadcasters have little experience in deciding for themselves how and at what length to cover candidates and issues. . . . The main thing to hope for is that a majority of broadcasters will do an honest and thorough job. If they do that, they can appeal for total repeal of Section 315 on a record of true contribution to journalism.[54]

The National Association of Broadcasters had twice before urged Congress to repeal the equal opportunities rule, in 1952 and 1956, but had gotten nowhere.[55] The industry hope that followed the 1960 suspension, it turned out, was short-lived. Congress did not amend the law further to make the suspension a recurring feature for subsequent elections, nor did it repeal Section 315.

President Kennedy appointed me chairman of the Federal Communications Commission in 1961.[56] It was the only job in government that appealed to me, because of the deep interest in television I had developed while working on Adlai Stevenson's 1956 presidential campaign. Though I was, of course, in contact with the FCC on Adlai's behalf during the Suez Crisis, the key moment for me had nothing to do with the Stevenson campaign but came on a walk with Robert Kennedy. Bob was often my roommate when we traveled for the campaign, and on a trip to Springfield, Illinois, he suggested we skip the speeches (we'd heard them before) and go visit Abraham Lincoln's house instead. On the way, Bob said something I've never forgotten: he said that when he grew up, the three great influences on the family were home, church, and school, but in observing his own family he believed there was now a fourth major influence, television.

That resonated with me. Like Kennedy, I had young children at the time, and so both of us were focused on television and its impact on children. Years before, as a U.S. Army sergeant in a battalion working to build a telephone line from India to China, I had come to believe that telecommunications could transform a society for the better. I believe that television's potential to improve the lives of our children and the life of our country ranks among the most vital public issues in democratic governance. When Pierre Salinger, President Kennedy's press secretary, called me in late December 1960 to report that the president would announce my appointment as FCC chairman, I was ready.

About a year into my tenure at the Commission, in 1962, a case came to the agency involving the radio broadcast of a political debate. A Socialist Labor Party candidate complained that a Michigan radio station had broadcast a dinner debate between the Democratic and Republican gubernatorial candidates and that he was entitled to equal time. The debate host, the Economic Club of Detroit, had held gubernatorial debates between "the two principal candidates (Republican and Democratic) for the past several years. On October 8, 1962, Station WJR broadcast a debate sponsored by the Economic Club between Democratic Governor John B. Swainson and Republican candidate George Romney, complete with a question-and-answer period." WJR's role in the event was entirely passive; it had played no part in scheduling the debate, inviting the candidates, or determining the format or the questions. It had simply covered the debate as a news event. Nonetheless, the Socialist Labor Party candidate sued WJR and its owner, Goodwill Station, demanding equal time, and the FCC decided that the station had a legal obligation to comply.[57] According to the Commission, WJR had violated the equal time law by broadcasting a debate in which the sponsors had not invited a third, legally qualified candidate.[58] In the previous Michigan gubernatorial election, Socialist Labor had "received only 1,479 votes out of a state-wide total of 3,255,991."[59] Nevertheless, the FCC decided that absent the explicit mention of *debates* in the 1959 amendments, Congress had intended not to exempt them:

> As you may know, at the time of the enactment of the 1959 amendments to the Act, both Houses of Congress had considered bills which would have exempted *debate*, panel discussion and similar type programs. However, neither the bills passed by the respective Houses nor the conference substitute bill, which was enacted into law, provided an exemption for appearances by candidates on a *debate* program. The conclusion that appearances on *debate* programs were not exempt was strengthened when Congress apparently reached the same conclusion and enacted S.J. Res. 207 (Public Law 86-677), exempting the Great Debates. Thus, it seems clear from the above that neither the language of the amendment, the legislative history, nor subsequent Congressional action contemplated an exemption from the "equal opportunities" provision of Section 315 of the broadcast of a *debate* between legally qualified candidates.[60]

When the *Goodwill Station* case came before the Commission, I voted against the station at the urging of my colleagues and staff. So as chairman of the Commission, I helped undo all the work we had done to promote debates in 1960. I should have urged my fellow commissioners to rule otherwise and decide that a debate set up by someone other than a television or radio station is a bona fide news event. Senator Pastore had all but invited us to reach that conclusion in his own remarks on the 1959 amendments.

In retrospect, there is no decision I made in public life that I regret more. I regret it because I now believe it to have been an incorrect legal interpretation of Section 315. I also regret it because it led to bad policy effects in 1964, 1968, and 1972. In 1975 the FCC would change its interpretation of the law, a subject I discuss more in the next chapter. In 1962, however, we assumed that a rational, conscientious Congress would do the obvious thing and make the 1960 suspension permanent, at least for the presidential and vice-presidential general elections, which are so much in the limelight that no network would act in an unfair, partisan fashion. We were wrong in that assumption. We also believed that leaving the problem to Congress, an elected body, was the democratic thing to do. If we had known Congress would fail to act, we should have construed the law much more broadly and hoped that the courts agreed with us. As it was, our decision in the case had an effect we never intended, depriving the public of the robust debate the law was supposed to promote.

If the *Goodwill Station* case was a setback, the apparent deathblow to broadcast debates came the same year in a case involving NBC. There, a Prohibition Party candidate filed a complaint against the network for its coverage of a California gubernatorial campaign debate between Governor Pat Brown and challenger Richard Nixon. United Press International had sponsored and set the ground rules for the debate. NBC broadcast the event, along with "all the major newspapers in California," which had covered the debate, assessing it as "singularly newsworthy." Still, we at the FCC stood by our advisory letter in the *Goodwill Station* case, holding that NBC was required to provide equal opportunity to the Prohibition candidate in order to compensate for NBC's debate broadcast.[61]

The "Great Debates" of 1960 had appeared to usher in a new age of political communication. But in 1962, hopes for future televised debates were all but extinguished. And I had participated in this setback, while Congress remained silent.

3 "If You're Thirty-two Points Behind, What Else Are You Going to Do?"

You may be wondering at this point if you have read correctly: surely the law did not prohibit the broadcast of political debates for the nation's highest office. But *in effect* it did. The 1960 temporary exemption to the Equal Time law provided by Congress was thus all the more remarkable. The exemption marked the formal beginning of televised presidential debates in the United States. That they happened at all, however, owed largely to the fact that no incumbent president was a candidate in the 1960 election. Three presidential elections would pass before another fortuitous set of political circumstances made it possible for the televised debates to happen again.

The 1976 election presented an ideal climate for change. While there was a Republican incumbent, President Ford, he faced great initial difficulties in the campaign because of the Watergate scandal and his unpopular pardon of Richard Nixon. He needed to debate to close the gap. His Democratic challenger, Georgia governor Jimmy Carter, was also eager to debate—many Americans knew little about him. However, the demands for equal time from the many minor-party candidates remained a problem. There seemed no legal way to make the debates happen.

That there were debates in 1976 owes to the work of a handful of far-sighted people who put aside partisan politics and worked together to change the law. In 1975 the Brookings Institution held a conference in Washington to discuss the equal opportunities rule and other issues. I was not there, but three important shapers of the nation's communications policy were: first, there was Democrat Nicholas Zapple, who as former counsel to Senator Pastore knew the congressional nuances on the subject of debates better than anyone; second, there was Larry Secrest, legal counsel to FCC chairman Richard Wiley; and third, there was Henry Geller, who had been my right arm and chief adviser when I was FCC chairman and was an expert on Section 315. During discussion at the Brookings conference, Zapple stated with great certainty that there would be no legislative action to suspend or reform Section 315 for 1976; if there were to be broadcast debates, they would have to come from some FCC administrative action. When the conference ended, Geller approached Secrest with an idea: acting on behalf of the Aspen Institute, where he was a Communications Fellow, Geller would file a petition with the FCC seeking a new interpretation of Section 315's exemption for on-the-spot coverage of a "bona fide news event" that would permit the debate to go forward.[1] Secrest assured Geller that Wiley, a strong, activist, can-do FCC chairman, would give such a petition serious consideration.

Geller prepared the petition, which the Aspen Institute, under the leadership of Douglass Cater, a former White House assistant to President Johnson, filed with the Commission. Geller argued that a debate between Ford and Carter, under the auspices of, say, the League of Women Voters, would clearly be a "bona fide news event" covered by almost all news outlets. While it was true that the law did not specifically mention debates, he wrote, that simply left the matter ambiguous and for the FCC to determine. A ruling in favor of exempting debates, he went on, would further the obvious public interest in robust political discussion and an informed electorate. As evidence for his assertion, Geller pointed to the huge success of the 1960 debates.

The FCC under Chairman Wiley agreed. It reviewed the legislative history behind both the 1959 amendments and the 1960 exemption and concluded that Congress *had* meant to exempt debates from the equal opportunity doctrine. The 1962 decision in the Goodwill Station case, the agency said, had been based on an "incorrect reading" of this broader legislative history. The fact that Congress provided a one-time-only exemption in 1960 did not mean that Congress thought debates were not exempt under the 1959 amendments to Section 315, the Commission said, but instead reflected Congress's belief that by 1960 the FCC had not had enough time to fully figure out how the amendments applied to different kinds of programs. Now, with more than a decade of experience to guide it, the FCC concluded that the "automatic and mathematical" application of the equal time rules in political campaigns was no longer warranted and was not good public policy.[2] Congress clearly had included an exemption to 315 for news programs, the agency reasoned, which means it had distinguished between "campaigning" and "news." Although that distinction is vague and hard to understand, the FCC had no power to ignore it. The question, then, was whether debates were news, and, *if structured properly,* the FCC decided, they could be.

This means that Congress' refusal to include an explicit exemption for debates did not necessarily indicate a clear intent to apply the equal time provision to all debates. It merely shifted onto the courts—and the FCC in the first instance—the job of figuring out when a debate amounted to a "news" program. In other words, the statute was ambiguous, and given that ambiguity, the FCC was acting within its authority to reinterpret the law. In what is now known as the *Aspen* decision, the FCC ruled: "Debates between qualified political candidates initiated by nonbroadcast entities . . . will be exempt from the equal time requirements of Section 315, provided they are covered live, based upon the good faith determination of licensees that they are 'bona fide news events' worthy of presentation, and provided further that there is no evidence of broadcaster favoritism."[3] To give its decision added emphasis, the FCC even invoked the famous 1964 U.S. Supreme Court case of *New York Times v. Sullivan,* announcing, "We believe that the public's interest in 'uninhibited, robust, wide-open' debate on public uses far outweighs the imagined advantages or disadvantages to a particular candidate."[4]

Not all the FCC commissioners supported the change.[5] Two of them argued that the *Aspen* decision had no support in the legislative history of the 1959 amendments (discussed in chapter 2) and that the new rule was susceptible to broadcaster abuse. Commissioner Benjamin Hooks, a Democrat, disputed the Commission's characterization of debates as bona fide news events:

> [Debates] are a species of quasi-news used as potent devices for the promulgation of the claims of a political candidate in the course of an election; they are staged, structured and premeditated campaign tools imparting very little of news value. . . . Political debates are hard to imagine as fast-developing news exigencies, since they are ordinarily scheduled long in advance, with partisan hype and hoopla, and the issues in a debate are framed and restricted by the disposition of the participants.[6]

Commissioner Robert E. Lee, a Republican, worried about unchecked broadcaster discretion: "Pursuant to the legal interpretation adopted today, a broadcaster may determine that only major candidates are newsworthy and, while covering their debates and press conferences, may ignore similar appearances of other candidates."[7]

After the FCC's decision, Representative Shirley Chisholm, the National Organization for Women, and the Democratic National Committee all sued the FCC, in each case arguing that the new FCC rule would provide President Gerald Ford—who had announced his intention to run for reelection a full fifteen months before the November election—with unchecked access to the public.[8]

The U.S. Court of Appeals for the District of Columbia did its own review of the legislative history behind the 1959 amendments, found it inconclusive (as Geller had argued), and so decided it was "obligated to defer to the Commission's interpretation" of the law. "The inherent newsworthiness of speeches and debates seems no greater or less than that of 'political conventions and activities incidental thereto,' events expressly within the scope of the exemption," the court wrote. An extended dissent, written by Judge J. Skelly Wright, pointed out that Congress had specifically considered including debates in the 1959 exclusion amendments but declined to do so. Further, Wright argued, by refusing to overrule the FCC's 1962 *Goodwill Station* opinion with additional amendments, Congress had, in effect, ratified the FCC's original interpretation.[9]

Following the FCC's *Aspen* ruling and the D.C. Circuit Court's opinion in *Chisholm v. FCC,* broadcasters found themselves working with equal opportunity rules that were different and much more lenient than they had ever been.[10] But if the *Aspen* decision was an advance, it came with a significant hitch: it did not allow stations themselves to organize candidate debates. Instead the Commission ruled that a debate was a "bona fide news event" only when sponsored by organizations other than broadcasters themselves, and if the debate was broadcast live and in its entirety.[11]

The *Aspen* proposal was made with a willing sponsor in mind: the League of Women Voters of the United States.[12] After the FCC ruled favorably on the proposal, the League got immediately to work. With a fifty-thousand-dollar grant from the Benton Foundation, the League hired Jim Karayn, a public broadcaster and a strong and energetic promoter, to put the debates together for 1976. The League also began a nationwide petition drive with a goal of getting 4 million signatures in support of debates. That effort led to news coverage about the possibility of debates, most of it skeptical but encouraging. As the *Cincinnati Post* put it, "Generally the favored candidate shuns debates out of fear of making his underdog opponent better known. . . . If the candidates try to duck the debates, the women plan to bring enough pressure to change their minds. The League is on the right track, and we wish it luck."[13] League president Ruth Clusen publicly announced the League's debate plans on May 5 at its annual convention in New York City: "The country is ready for face-to-face discussions of the issues, the public has said it wants this kind of dialogue, and candidates themselves have claimed there is a desperate need for full airing of the issues."[14]

At the time I read about this in the newspapers but otherwise was not involved in it. Then in 1976 I was an elected delegate to the Democratic National Convention in New York. When I came home, there was a phone message from Mrs. Clusen. When I returned her call, she said, "We are trying to organize presidential debates this year. We would like you to be our chairman and help us get it done."

I asked, "Mrs. Clusen, how did you happen to come to me?"

She replied, "We went to Frank Stanton first, but because of his involvement with CBS he can't do it. He recommended you." Shortly afterward, Mrs. Clusen and Jim Karayn came to see me in Chicago and tell me what they had in mind.

At one point in our discussions I said, "Mrs. Clusen, with all respect, this is not the way to go. If you want to get this accomplished it will have to be nonpartisan. I'm a Democrat. There will have to be a Republican cochair. The most important thing we have to establish here is trust. The candidates have to trust you. They are staking everything on these debates, and that is why you need to have a Republican and a Democrat. They are not going to do anything they perceive as unfair."

She agreed: "Fine, whom do you recommend?" I recommended Dean Burch, who had also been an FCC chairman (under President Nixon), had managed the 1964 presidential campaign of Barry Goldwater, and was a past chairman of the Republican National Committee.

I did not know it at the time, but Dean was then working in the White House. When I called him there, he told me he had left his law practice and was working for President Ford's campaign. When I told him what I wanted, he of course said he could not do it. Not one to walk away empty-handed, I asked, "Well, would you find out if President Ford is willing to debate?"

"Let me get back to you," he replied. Not long afterward Dean called back: "Yes, President Ford wants a debate."

I said, "Do you mind telling me why?"

He said, "Newt, if you're thirty-two points behind, what else are you going to do?" But, Dean added, "he will have some things he wants."

The president wanted at least three ninety-minute presidential debates and probably a vice-presidential debate. He wanted one on foreign policy, one on domestic policy, and one general debate. He wanted a panel of journalists to ask questions, and he did not want televised reaction shots of the candidates.

I called Mrs. Clusen and said, "Believe it or not, I think the president is willing to do this. Let me see about the Democrats." I knew Robert Lipshultz, Jimmy Carter's counsel in Atlanta, who later became counsel to the president when Carter was elected. I called Bob and asked him about the debates, and he said, "Let me get back to you." After a few days he called me back: "Jimmy wants a debate."

I said, "Do you mind telling me why?"

He answered, "Well, we know we are thirty-two points ahead in the polls, but Jimmy doesn't think the country knows him. And there are some things he wants. Jimmy is a confident debater. He debated when he ran for governor. He will want to be sure that there are at least three presidential debates and maybe one for vice president. He wants the debates to be ninety minutes each. He wants to be sure there is one on domestic policy and one on foreign policy and one general debate. He wants to be sure that there is a panel of journalists asking questions, and he does not want reaction shots of the candidates."

I could not believe it. It was as if the Republican and Democratic candidates had been talking to each other. They had not, but their respective advisers had given the candidates the same advice. So I called Mrs. Clusen and said, "I think this may happen, but we still need to get a Republican cochair."

She said, "Well we would like to get a woman." I agreed, and we went over a list of possibilities. She mentioned Rita Hauser, whom I knew. Rita was very active in Republican politics and is a very accomplished international lawyer. I called her, but she was in Asia somewhere and out of telephone contact. It would not work.

I called Mrs. Clusen back: "How about a friend of mine named Charls Walker?" Charls was a former Republican deputy secretary of the U.S. Treasury, a respected citizen, and a part-time lecturer at the University of Texas.

Mrs. Clusen gave the okay, so I called Charls and he agreed to do it. Then Rita's secretary called back: "We have reached Mrs. Hauser, and she wants to do it." Suddenly I had two Republicans as cochairs. I told Mrs. Clusen that was fine—that one Democrat can always handle two Republicans.

On August 18, 1976, Ruth Clusen held a press conference at a hotel near the Republican National Convention in Kansas City to announce that the League had that morning telegrammed President Ford and Jimmy Carter, inviting the two men to participate in a series of debates. The telegram had been carefully written and rewritten by several people, including me, and urged each candidate to "designate a representative to meet with [the League] as soon as possible to consult on the project in more detail." A total of eleven reporters showed up at the League's press conference. It seemed no one took the project too seriously.

The next day, August 19, in accepting his party's nomination for president, Gerald Ford challenged Jimmy Carter to a series of nationwide debates. "I'm ready," he said, "to go before the American People and debate the real issues face to face."[15] The announcement was right at the top of the president's remarks, and the convention hall went wild.

Just like that the debates went from a notion to a promise.

In late August, the representatives for the two campaigns and the League began negotiating ground rules for the debates. The Ford campaign sent three lawyers, Dean Burch, William Ruckelshaus, and Mike Duval. The Carter campaign also sent three people—all of them media people, including press secretary Jody Powell—but no lawyers. One of the early sticking points was whether the debates would have a live audience. Neither campaign had wanted one because both were concerned about audience reaction, visual and vocal, but the League insisted that without an audience the debates might not qualify as bona fide news events. Eventually all sides agreed that there would be an audience composed equally of journalists and League representatives and their guests, but that there would be no television shots of the audience during the debates.[16]

Before negotiations began, the League had said publicly that it wanted the candidates to question each other for the last third of each debate. Douglass Cater, who had been a panelist in the third of the 1960 debates and was now the director of the Aspen Institute and a member of the League's campaign steering committee, expressed his hope that the 1976 debates would improve on what he said had been the "lackluster" format of the Nixon-Kennedy meetings: "I hope the League will demand at least one old-fashioned debate where contestants face each other frontally and are allowed abundant time for explanation and rebuttal."[17] But it was not to be. The League repeatedly pressed the candidates to question each other for at least part of each debate, but the campaigns' representatives rejected the idea every time it came up. There had to be panelists asking the questions.

President Ford's lawyers were trying to figure out who the panelists should be, and one suggested a process analogous to a labor arbitration: each side would submit a list of names independently, and the names that appeared on both lists would constitute the panel. We tried it and did not have any difficulty agreeing to a list of names.

Between 1976 and 1984, there was never an assumption on the networks' part that they would have their own representative on the panel. Because I knew many journalists, many called me asking to be on the panel. If they were not already on the list for consideration—and they almost always were—I would add them to the list, but that was all I was willing to do or could do. Nor did it matter what I did. The League had its own ideas about panelists. Its leaders always wanted to be sure we had at least one woman on the panel, and we also felt we should try to make it geographically, racially, and ethnically diverse. But otherwise it did not matter to us whether the panelists were from the print or broadcast media or what the media balance was. Of course, what the candidates cared about was not getting people they thought would be unfair.

On September 18, Charls, Rita, and I organized a meeting in Washington to which we invited the heads of the news divisions of ABC, NBC, and CBS and the head of PBS and told them what we wanted to do. They listened but did not say very much. They were still upset that they could not organize the debates themselves, and they did not like the idea that somebody else was doing it.[18] When I told the network news representatives what the ground rules would be, my friend Dick Salant, the head of CBS News, was furious. All the television people thought the agreement between the League and the candidates infringed on their journalistic judgment, particularly the prohibition on camera shots of the audience once a debate was under way. Salant called it censorship. He said, "You're going to tell us how to cover the event? You're going to tell us that there will be no reaction shots in the debate?"

I said, "Dick, it's not that we, the League, are telling you anything. The candidates have agreed on these rules, and we are going to honor their agreement. We are inviting you to cover an event—not your event, the League's event. If you don't want to cover it that's fine with us, because I'm sure NBC and ABC and the radio industry will be very happy that you are gone."

At one point Charls got so frustrated that Salant was repeatedly interrupting him with objections that Charls barked at him to "shut up." Salant became so upset that he got up and left. (He left his briefcase behind. About fifteen minutes later his assistant sheepishly came back to retrieve it.)

The others stayed. They did not like the situation either, but they did not walk out. We agreed to take their objections back to the campaigns to see if we could get them to change their minds. And we did, twice, on September 15 and September 18, with less than two weeks to the first debate in St. Louis—but the campaigns would not budge.[19]

*　　*　　*

In 1976 we had three presidential debates and one vice-presidential debate (between Senators Walter Mondale and Bob Dole). Under federal election law at the time, the League could not accept corporate or union donations for the debates, so it had to rely on individual donations. The total cost of the four debates was $322,000, and through newspaper and magazine advertisements the League raised most of that money—a little more than $250,000—from the public.[20] Perhaps a hundred donations were in the $1,000 to $10,000 range, but most were for $15 to $25.[21]

At the second debate between President Ford and Governor Carter in San Francisco, Max Frankel of the *New York Times* asked a question about Poland, to which President Ford responded that Poland was no longer under communist domination. The audience gasped, and of course the remark became the big news of the debate, if not the big news of the entire 1976 debate series.[22] It became one of those defining moments in which a candidate makes a gaffe or turns a rhetorical flourish, and that single moment—rather than the broader and more complex features of the debate or the discussion of the issues—becomes the whole story.

Other such moments live on in public memory even among those who never saw them: Richard Nixon's wiping perspiration from his brow in 1960; vice-presidential candidate Lloyd Bentsen's reply to opponent Dan Quayle—"You're no Jack Kennedy"—when in 1988 the junior senator from Indiana compared himself to the former president; President George H. W. Bush looking at his watch during a town hall debate with challenger Bill Clinton in 1992, impatient for the evening to end; Al Gore's audible sighs in his 2000 presidential debate with George W. Bush; and Bush's inexplicably quizzical facial expressions in his first 2004 meeting with Senator John Kerry. And who can forget Ronald Reagan's angry retort to a moderator, "I am paying for this microphone!" in a 1980 Republican primary debate in New Hampshire?[23] The incident helped solidify Reagan's public image as firm and decisive and marked the beginning of his rise in the national polls.[24]

More broadly, only one presidential election has gone by since 1976 without a series of parallel debates on NBC's *Saturday Night Live*. In the program's first season, 1975, comedian Chevy Chase appeared as President Ford in the fourth episode, turning Ford into the first pop-culture president and beginning a comic tradition that continues today. Chase never made the slightest effort to mimic President Ford's speech or appearance but lampooned the supposedly accident-prone president in skits that always ended with spectacular pratfalls. Later in that first season, President Ford actually introduced the program to a national television audience with the famous words, "Live, from New York, it's *Saturday Night!*" and then turned the program over to that week's guest host—Ron Nessen, his press secretary. In 1976, Chase and fellow cast member Dan Aykroyd, playing Jimmy Carter, did their own series of three presidential debates, one of them a beauty pageant. (Aykroyd's Jimmy Carter was a cardigan-wearing micromanager who personally answered calls from despondent Americans and urged them to relax by listening to the Allman Brothers.)

In 1980, when the League of Women Voters managed to have only one debate between Carter and Reagan, *Saturday Night Live* fared even worse: because of an actors' strike, the season did not start until after the election in November, and there were no "debates." Other memorable "presidential" debate performances on *Saturday Night Live* include Dana Carvey's George H. W. Bush and Ross Perot, Darrell Hammond's Bill Clinton and Al Gore, and Will Ferrell's perpetually confused George W. Bush. Seven different actors portrayed Ronald Reagan, among them Robin Williams. So popular were some of these hyperbolic parodies that in 2000, to prepare Gore for his second debate with Bush, his campaign staff made the vice president sit and watch Hammond's portrayal of his exasperated sighing in the first debate.

President Ford reportedly loved the Chevy Chase skits, and after Ford's death in December 2006, the comedian gave the former president credit for boosting his career. Years after Ford left office, Chase recalled, the former president and his wife Betty joined Chase and his wife for lunch at the Betty Ford Clinic, where Chase was being treated for addiction to painkillers. At the president's suggestion, a television and VCR were brought to the dining room with several audition tapes of actors seeking to play the president in a film biography of his wife. When the VCR began to malfunction, Chase recalls, he started to get up to adjust it but felt a hand on his arm, restraining him. It was President Ford. "'No, no, Chevy. Don't even think about it," he said. "I'll probably get electrocuted, and you'll be picked up and arrested for murder."[25]

*   *   *

Whether it is journalists focusing relentlessly on a sound bite or a gaffe, or a *Saturday Night Live* parody, these are precisely the kind of things the print press worried about in advance of the 1960 debates. Then as now the amplification of such incidents was the result of press coverage. Today, however, that amplification is further distorted by the spin provided by the campaigns themselves, by the need of twenty-four-hour cable news channels to report news where there is none, by the rise of partisan "news" sources on cable and the Internet, and of course by the entertainment media, from Jon Stewart's *Daily Show* to YouTube. Arguably, many of the "defining" moments captured by these media reflect or exemplify rather than establish areas of concern voters already have.

News coverage of the debates can, of course, be both highly critical and substantive, but sometimes the news media (with the helpful assistance of spin doctors in the campaigns) simply make mischief with relatively minor mistakes or even innocuous statements.[26] In either case, candidates have always known that they could do so, and it puts them under tremendous pressure. From the beginning the campaigns have tried to control the debates' formats and presentation, but no matter how hard they try they cannot control everything. During the Philadelphia debate in 1976, for example, the sound went out completely in the middle of the debate while Carter and Ford were standing on their platforms on the stage. The two of them stood frozen at their lecterns for seventeen minutes. After about ten minutes, my cochairs and I raced down there to figure out what to do. Neither of the candidates walked over to shake hands with, or talk to, the other. They simply stood there like statues. Finally the sound came back on, and the debate continued. After it was over, reporters were interviewing Senator Eugene McCarthy—who had sued the League for not including him in the debate as an independent candidate—about his reaction to the debate. One of them asked, "Senator McCarthy, what did you think of the 17-minute gap when the sound went out?" He responded, with his delicious sense of humor, "I never noticed."

The third debate in 1976 was at Williamsburg, Virginia, where the League organizers took our pictures with the candidates. President Ford had met me before, and he had been in Congress when I was at the FCC, but he really did not know me. As we gathered for our picture, I said, "Mr. President, we thank you for participating. This is the first debate since 1960 and the first debate in which an incumbent president has agreed to participate. You have set a very important example for the future."

He put his arm around me and he said, "Well, I hope so." And then he said, "It's nice to see you, Mint." Somehow he had put "Newt" and "Minow" together in his mind to get "Mint."

I never forgot that, and neither have I forgotten the president's example. The fact that we have presidential debates today, that they are virtually required of anyone wishing to hold that office, can be attributed in significant measure to Gerald Ford. And his understanding of the value of the debates was correct: notwithstanding his gaffe in the first debate, he came from thirty-two points behind to almost win the election. The Carter people had thought they would win the election by a much bigger margin than they did.

Years later, I was invited to participate in a panel discussion at the Ford Presidential Library in Grand Rapids, Michigan. My wife Jo and I had a most congenial lunch with President Ford and his wife, Betty, during which we talked about the 1976 debates. I told President Ford he had established a major American tradition by participating in the 1976 debates and that history would honor his decision to debate. President Ford replied that he believed the debates had helped him.

But the most important thing about 1976, our bicentennial year, is that the debates happened at all. They broke the ice after a sixteen-year hiatus. They proved that a nonbroadcast sponsor could do the job. They established the practice of holding three debates of ninety minutes each, with one general debate, one on foreign policy, and the third on domestic policy. They established the practice of having one vice-presidential debate. The 1976 debates also continued the practice, begun in 1960, of journalists' asking questions.

In 1960, of course, the networks themselves had organized the debates and naturally wanted their own reporters to participate in them. But why did journalists participate as panelists in 1976? Why not have the candidates question each other directly? I personally do not believe that the presence of an intermediary, whether a panel of journalists or a single journalist (as we have had for the last several sets of debates, with Jim Lehrer of PBS's *NewsHour* as moderator)[27], somehow discredits the exchange between candidates. But in 1976 the advisers to the campaigns each told their candidate that by having a panel of journalists asking the questions he could avoid having to question his opponent himself and thus risk appearing mean or overly aggressive. Each side wanted its candidate to come across as a nice guy, and that could not happen if the candidates questioned each other very intensively. The candidates and campaigns still think this way. In 2000, President Clinton told Jim Lehrer in a PBS documentary, "It's a little harder in these debates to go after your opponent unless people serve you up the right question. Otherwise the picture is of a debater being disrespectful to the citizens."[28]

Many scholars, including presidential historian Michael Beschloss, argue that journalists do not ask the questions the public wants answered, or if they do they ask them in a manner intended to elicit a yes or no answer when in fact a nuanced reply may be more appropriate.[29] My own feeling is that over the years a number of journalists on the panels saw the debates as their opportunity to audition before the country, to show how smart they are or to ask questions that, they hoped, would elicit a gaffe or provoke a candidate to respond emotionally. The famous question Bernard Shaw of CNN asked Michael Dukakis in 1988 about how he would react if his wife were brutally raped appeared to be just such a question—not informative but somehow a defining moment for the candidate because he did not react with a display of anger at the hypothetical. (The question was related to one of the campaign's most tawdry commercials, the celebrated "Willie Horton" revolving-door spot about Massachusetts's letting violent criminals out of jail when Dukakis was governor. Shaw later said the experience convinced him that there should be no panel of journalists, just a moderator.)[30] In 1976 our message to the journalists was, "You're on your own. Ask whatever questions you want. The only thing we would hope is that you talk to each other ahead of time so you don't ask the same question. But that's up to you." So we gave them no instructions, and we never asked nor considered asking to see their questions beforehand.

In 1980 the League again asked me to cochair the debates, this time with Carla Hills, a former assistant U.S. attorney general and cabinet secretary under President Ford. The president of the League then was Ruth Hinerfeld, and we had a Public Advisory Committee made up of Democrats, Republicans, and independents. The committee was mixed racially and by gender. Both the Republican nominee, Ronald Reagan, and President Jimmy Carter had earlier made firm and enthusiastic public assurances they would participate in the debates, but John Anderson's strong independent candidacy soon tested those commitments. Having failed to get the Republican Party nomination, Anderson was running as an independent with a substantial following.

At the time, the presence of a strong third-party candidate wanting to be included in the debates was, as the League put it, "uncharted territory."[31] Dozens of candidates wanted to participate in addition to Anderson, but the League feared that admitting them would lead the major-party candidates to withdraw. It decided to add to its existing requirements for debate eligibility a new one, "demonstrated significant voter interest and support."[32] The League established two ways of meeting the new requirement: nomination by a major party or "a level of voter support in the polls of 15 percent or a level of support at least equal to that of a major-party candidate."[33] The League announced its new selection criteria at a press conference in New York City on August 10 and found, as the Commission on Presidential Debates would later, that the 15 percent requirement caused both confusion and controversy. Critics said the figure was simply arbitrary, with no historical precedent. Neither of those claims was quite true; after the 1976 debates Congress at one point considered a bill that used the records of third-party candidates from the 1912 (Theodore Roosevelt), 1924 (Robert LaFolette), 1948 (Henry Wallace and Strom Thurmond), and 1968 (George Wallace) presidential elections to set a standard for debate inclusion.[34]

On August 19, a week after the Democratic Convention made Carter the party's nominee, the League formally invited both Carter and Reagan to meet in a series of three debates. Starting on August 26, the League found itself negotiating with the campaigns' representatives on the entire debate program, including the number of debates and their formats, where they would be held and when. Carter wanted earlier debates and Reagan later ones; Carter wanted more debates, Reagan fewer. But both sides were holding out to see what would happen with Anderson, and on September 9 the League announced that based on poll results Anderson would be invited to the first debate in Baltimore on September 21.[35] Anderson and Reagan both accepted the invitations immediately, but Carter refused, saying he would participate in a three-way debate only after a two-way debate with Reagan. There was speculation in the press, completely unfounded, that for the first debate we might put an empty chair on the stage with Jimmy Carter's name on it, and the story got enough play that the White House was extremely upset about it. No one at the League ever seriously considered putting out an empty chair; rather a *Washington Post* reporter had suggested it in an interview with a League official and then reported the negative response, making it seem as though the League was considering the idea. The League held out hope for Carter's participation to the last, going so far as to keep a third podium available should he show up at the last moment, but he did not. The Reagan-Anderson debate took place as scheduled, with a moderator and a panel of journalists asking questions, but without the president of the United States in attendance.[36]

The negotiators for the Republicans and the Democrats that year were Robert Strauss and Jim Baker, both old political hands, both from Texas. At one meeting in Washington we were at an impasse on one issue with the League, and Baker looked at me and said, "Excuse me, I have to go the men's room." A couple of minutes later Strauss looked at me and said, "Excuse me, I have to go to the men's room."

They were gone about ten minutes. They came back with a little piece of paper. They had solved the problem, worked out some kind of compromise, and said, "Here is the way it's going to be." They had reached an agreement without the League, but the League accepted it.

Against this kind of maneuvering, that first debate between Reagan and Anderson was both a great success and a disappointing failure for the League of Women Voters. The League had held firm to its selection criteria, establishing a precedent that is now largely forgotten but that set the standard for future presidential debates. But in holding fast to its principles the League also paid a price, failing to give voters an opportunity to see and hear all of the serious presidential contenders at the same time. And matters only got worse. Carter refused to change his terms, and with Anderson holding steady in the polls it appeared as though there would be no further debates in 1980 though the public clamored for them. Trying to rescue something from the situation, the League made a new pitch to the candidates, offering a two-way debate between Carter and Reagan if all three would agree to a three-way debate afterward. This time Carter and Anderson accepted, but Reagan did not, and the League withdrew its offer.

At the same time, the League invited the three vice-presidential candidates—Democrat Walter Mondale, Vice President George H. W. Bush, and Independent Patrick Lucey—to debate in Louisville, Kentucky. Mondale and Lucy accepted. Bush did not, leading Mondale to withdraw, with the result that the entire event was canceled.[37] Finally, in mid-October, a debate between Carter and Reagan was arranged after four of the five national polls taken between September 27 and October 16 showed Anderson's level of support had fallen below 15 percent.[38]

On October 17 the League invited Carter and Reagan to debate in Cleveland on October 28, and both accepted what became, by default, a winner-take-all meeting between the two major-party candidates. Realizing the significance of the Cleveland meeting, the League of course wanted to maximize its benefits to voters, and so it urged the use of a single moderator rather than a panel of journalists. The League had used a single moderator (ABC's Howard K. Smith) in a February 1980 "presidential nominees forum" in Chicago with the seven candidates seeking the Republican nomination, with great success.[39] The single-moderator format, the League believed, put the burden of presentation on the candidates and thus encouraged a more robust discussion between them. The Chicago forum had also included questions from the audience.

For all of these reasons, press commentators also urged the single-moderator format, but both Carter and Reagan refused, insisting on a moderator and a panel of journalists to ask the questions—a virtual press conference—and threatening to walk away if they did not get it. Moreover, the candidates insisted on their right to veto any journalists the League chose for the panel, from an original roster of one hundred reporters and editors. We told them how we had done it in 1976, and they said, "That's fine, but we want to be able to strike people from the list who we don't think are fair or would be objective." The campaigns originally agreed to use their veto power sparingly, but instead each of them employed it in a show of gamesmanship intended to unnerve the other side, with the League and me in the middle.

As a result of the parties' behavior, some journalists and news organizations refused to participate in the debates. Gerald Boyd and Hedrick Smith, both of the *New York Times,* refused invitations when asked, and the newspaper's Washington editor, Bill Kovach, eventually announced that the *Times* would not allow any of its people to participate in the 1980 debates: "We cannot encourage a process that has a political saliva test administered by the candidates. We all know where that leads—to asking the White House who we can assign to cover it."[40] CBS News president Ed Joyce also refused to allow his reporters to participate in the debates.

I remember spending one entire Sunday at home on the phone from 7 in the morning until 10:30 at night, alternately with the Republicans, the Democrats, and the League, trying to find panelists whom everyone would find acceptable. The last sticking point was that the League wanted to be sure we had a woman in the group. Finally, at about 10:30 at night, Strauss and Baker agreed on Barbara Walters, a great choice I thought. When I called to report the decision to the League, their negotiators said, "Barbara Walters? We were hoping we would not have a celebrity but a woman who is not so well known."

I said, "Well, if that is what you want you can negotiate this by yourself, because I've had it. Besides, Barbara Walters would do a great job."

The candidates' campaign representatives complained about everything, large and small, and never should have been allowed in the process, but at the time there was no way to avoid dealing with them. In 1980 the League had no real institutional leverage or historical experience that it could use to force the candidates to debate. The choice was to let the candidates call the shots or nothing—no debates. As a result, the three-way debate that the American public said it wanted and that the League had originally planned never happened. There was only one presidential debate between the major-party candidates, rather than three, and no vice-presidential debate.

Again, the experience was both disappointing and exhilarating. The Cleveland debate between Carter and Reagan was watched by the largest audience ever to watch a presidential debate, 80.6 million Americans in nearly 46 million households, at the time the most-watched television program in U.S. history.[41] After that debate, Reagan jumped ahead in a Gallup poll, and by Election Day he had won over almost all of those voters who, before the debate, had identified themselves as undecided. The Voice of America broadcast the debates in English to a global audience, and in Spanish to all of Latin America.

The debate in Cleveland was the only one between the major-party candidates, and it proved very influential. I attended it, and I remember when President Carter made the mistake of saying he had consulted with his daughter Amy about nuclear weapons policies. That debate, many people felt, decided the election for Reagan when he asked, "Are you better off now than you were four years ago?"

The experience of 1980 was also a turning point for me. It taught me that letting the candidates have anything to say about who was on the panel was simply wrong and unacceptable. I vowed we should never do it again. The obvious solution was that in the future the sponsor should permit no participation by the candidates or parties in the selection of the journalists who participated in the debates.

Given the success of 1976, in which President Carter had played a part, I was disappointed that he did not agree to participate with both Reagan and Anderson in 1980. Anderson was a serious candidate. But the Carter campaign staff believed Anderson drew from the president's base even though he came from the Republican Party perspective, and they were adamant about not including him. Today, with the 15 percent rule used by the Commission on Presidential Debates, and having had the experience of including Ross Perot in 1992, we would not even *allow* a debate unless a qualified third-party candidate was included. That is, if a third-party candidate qualifies under the rules, the major parties cannot exclude him or her. If they tried to do so, the Commission should say fine, there will be no debate.

In 1984 the League of Women Voters asked me to remain on its advisory committee but not to continue as cochair. I sensed at the time that the relationship between the League and the parties was not as good as it had been in 1976, or even in 1980, when I first began to see it deteriorate.

Subsequently I heard that the negotiations between the parties and the League went from tense to hostile, though I did not participate in them. The campaigns were upset with the League, and the League was upset with the campaigns. The candidates would insist on conditions for their participation, then hide behind the League when critics came calling. There was a basic problem of truth in advertising, of public accountability.

4 *The Commission on Presidential Debates and Its Critics*

As I participated in the frustrating inside negotiations for the 1980 debates, I began to think that sponsorship of the debates needed to be strengthened if they were to continue. Institutionalizing presidential debates had been the goal of the League of Women Voters, but by 1984 it was clear to me that despite its valiant efforts the League simply did not have the clout to succeed. Under its sponsorship, the debates were ad hoc affairs, often put together at the last minute. The painful negotiations that produced the 1984 debates showed that they were susceptible to behind-the-scenes manipulation by the campaigns, which would establish the terms for the debate and complain about or veto the moderators, then pretend that it was all the League's doing. In 1976, 1980, and 1984, the debates occurred only after a long period of sporadic negotiations followed by a late flurry of eleventh-hour negotiations between the leading candidates and, in an ever-diminishing role, the League.

I was very conscious of the experience of 1960, when the debates were such a huge success and everyone assumed that they would be a permanent feature of American politics, only to see the long drought that followed. 1976 was an anomaly: not only was President Ford far behind in the polls, but he had never been elected president. In 1980 the whole enterprise almost fell apart. In 1984 the League and the campaigns went through a list of 103 journalists before finding four whom all three could agree on as panelists.[1]

The League had served admirably and thanklessly as a debate sponsor but could not ensure the long-term stability of the debates. The future of the debates, I believed, would require the political parties themselves to have a bigger and more public role in convening them. I am an unapologetic believer in strong political parties (though as I wrote in *Voter's Time* in 1969, I do not believe the two-party system necessarily has to be *this* two-party system in which Republicans and Democrats are dominant.)[2] The best way to have a democracy is with two or maybe three strong political parties, a tradition that is part of the stability of our nation. Other countries such as France, Italy, and Israel have multiple parties. It is of course imperative that a two-party system provide opportunities for dissenting voices. Some of the most significant chapters of American history, and some of the country's most important social and political innovations, can be told in the lives of vibrant third parties, a matter I take up further in our final chapter. The Republican Party itself began as a third party. But I believe that once a democracy exceeds a certain number of parties, certainly once the number of parties gets to ten or more, stability is almost impossible. And so after 1984 I began to think that one way the parties could become more important, and more accountable for their actions, would be to make them responsible for the debates.

In that role the parties could put enough pressure on their candidates to compel a debate, even if the candidate did not want to participate. The most persistent and difficult impediment to debates, anywhere, is that the candidate who is ahead in the polls—and particularly an incumbent— will almost never want to debate, and for good reason. That candidate knows he or she would have to share the platform and the audience with an opponent and could likely be hurt by it. The leader's potential for gain is small, while the potential for the challenger is great. Moreover, because of the way the press covers debates, there are rarely any clear winners, but there are always losers. So the incentive for the candidate with a lead *not* to participate is enormous. But I thought the voters benefit from debates and so it was essential to find a way to bring pressure on the candidates to participate. The parties could do that.

After the 1984 campaign, two distinguished national organizations, the Georgetown Center for Strategic and International Studies and the Harvard University Institute of Politics, independently conducted detailed studies of the presidential election process generally and the presidential debates specifically. I took a leave from my law firm to lead the Harvard study, which was funded by the Twentieth Century Fund (today known as the Century Fund). I persuaded a former Harvard law student, Clifford Sloan, to work with me. Cliff had studied at Harvard under my daughter Martha and had served as a law clerk for Supreme Court Justice John Paul Stevens.[3]

The Georgetown and Harvard projects were separate, though as it turned out each group focused on the same four issues: the impact of the debates on the public, the sponsorship of the debates, their format, and the problem of how to fairly accommodate third-party and independent candidates. Both institutions issued reports that recommended finding some way to institutionalize the debates.[4] The report of the Georgetown group, led by Republican Mel Laird and Democrat Bob Strauss, advised that the parties be much more involved in organizing them. Not long after, the respected political communications scholar Kathleen Hall Jamieson urged institutionalizing the debates under party sponsorship because doing so "would minimize the likelihood that the stronger candidate would force the weaker to debate on his or her terms or give up the advantages gained by debates."[5]

Our report followed with much the same conclusion, though we added operational details by which the parties would have responsibility for the debates. Cliff and I drafted a proposal for the creation of a new debates sponsor, and we organized a national conference at Harvard to discuss the plan. We knew that many people would disagree with us on the role the parties should play. Certainly not all the conference participants endorsed our proposal, and Harvard's Institute of Politics remained neutral on our recommendations. But most of the participants believed with us that in 1988 we had a historic opportunity. It would be the first time since 1960 that no incumbent president would be in the debates. Several Republicans were seeking the nomination, and it was by no means a foregone conclusion that George H. W. Bush was going to be his party's nominee. No one knew yet who the Democratic nominee might be. So it was one of those rare moments when the identity of even one of the debaters was not already known and when it would be possible to make significant changes to the debates without the powerful resistance of a sitting president. And, we thought, there was a final factor on our side. It did not appear that there would be a significant third-party challenge for the presidency in 1988. John Anderson was behind us, and Ross Perot was not yet on the horizon. We had no intent to squelch third parties, but we also knew that in the past their presence had served as a pretext for reluctant major-party candidates who wanted to avoid debates entirely.

The country thus had a rare opportunity to institutionalize the debates, and we thought it imperative to take advantage of it. In our report we recommended the creation of a nonpartisan "Presidential Debates Organization" to organize and sponsor the presidential debates. In response, the then-chairmen of the Democratic and Republican National Committees, Paul G. Kirk Jr. and Frank J. Fahrenkopf Jr. respectively, jointly called for the creation of the independent Commission on Presidential Debates

(CPD). The Twentieth Century Fund provided seed funding for the idea, and the Commission was incorporated in Washington, DC, on February 19, 1987, as a private, not-for-profit organization that would "organize, manage, produce, publicize and support debates for the candidates for President of the United States."

Today the Commission is housed in a small office suite that it shares with two other organizations near DuPont Circle in Washington, DC. Except for the busy several months right before the debates, its staff consists of one person, a talented woman named Janet Brown, whom I recommended to run the Commission when it was created and who is still there as the institution's executive director. In election years Brown has two assistants and a receptionist, but that's it. Including its two cochairs, there are currently twelve members of the Commission's board of directors, of whom I am one.[6] Early on most of the board members lived or worked in Washington, but now they are scattered across the country, so we usually talk by phone with Janet and with one another. The full board meets at least once per year, in April, but rarely do we or can we meet together in person; the bylaws allow for the board to meet by conference call. Directors are nominated by a subcommittee of the board and serve four-year terms. We serve with no compensation.

Since the Commission's incorporation in 1987, its board membership has turned over in its entirety at least twice. Kirk and Fahrenkopf, though their terms as chairs of their respective parties ended in 1989, have several times been reelected to the board in the same way as any other board member would be. They have served as cochairs of the Commission since the beginning, for recurring two-year terms. When they eventually step down, they can be replaced either by an existing board member or by someone entirely new to the Commission. The other members of the board of directors can succeed themselves, and several have. None is a member of either the Republican or Democratic national committee, and at least one board member—Dorothy Ridings, a former Knight Ridder newspaper executive and a former president of the League of Women Voters—is not identified with any political party. Most of the board members have other jobs and other board commitments, and frequently they will leave because of real or perceived conflicts of time or interest. Former Missouri senator John Danforth, for example, left the board when he became U.S. ambassador to the United Nations in 2004. After his service at the UN, he returned to the Commission. I was asked to become a member of the board in 1992 to take the place of attorney Vernon Jordan, a former executive director of the United Negro College Fund and former president of the National Urban League. In 2000 I was elected Commission vice chair along with Senator Danforth, and both of us continue in that role today.

The Commission's current board of directors is diverse—six men and four women of different races and ethnicities. But it is fair to ask, for example, whether there should be limits on how many terms any board member can fill. The Commission does its job faithfully and well, in my experience, but it is a self-nominating body with no overseeing public or private authority. For this reason alone the Commission needs to be more transparent, a subject I will return to in chapter 6.

In non–presidential election years, the business of the Commission is threefold. One is advising other countries on debate formats and scheduling. In the last few years Janet Brown has worked with representatives from countries that seek to have political debates.[7] A second activity is advising newspapers, radio and television stations, and civic groups around the United States that wish to organize state and local debates during midterm elections and for state and municipal offices.[8] Budget considerations limit what the Commission can do, but as a source of expertise on the subject of political debates it is without peer.

The third role of the Commission, of course, is to prepare for the next presidential campaign season, and this process is never ending. For the 2008 campaign, for example, the Commission published its site selection guidelines on January 1, 2007, and requested proposals from interested parties by March 1, 2007. As of spring 2004, there were already more than ten sites competing for the 2008 debates and one already in the running for 2012. The Commission requires at least five commitments from any bidder. First, it needs adequate facilities for a debate hall and, separately, a press center for media organizations to prepare and submit stories. Those facilities need to be preexisting and substantial, since the Commission cannot rely on the promises of any bidder to build new facilities just for the debates. Second, the Commission has to be assured that the locale has an adequate number of hotel rooms to accommodate the campaigns and their staffs, political reporters and members of other news media, and observers. Third, there must be adequate air transportation to the site and adequate ground transportation at the site.[9] Fourth, the community must support the idea of hosting the debates, because invariably they interfere with the lives of citizens and the normal activities of local businesses.[10] Fifth, any potential site for the debates must be willing and able to make a sizable financial commitment to them. The Com-

mission itself is a nonprofit organization, so the owners of sites that it se-
lects for the debates are obligated to raise most of the money to pay for
them, at least $750,000. For 2008, the Commission approved a budget of
$1.35 million for each debate.[11]

There is also a sixth, unspoken requirement, says Executive Director
Brown: Any would-be host has to understand that a presidential debate is
not just another big event. It is not a Big 10 football game or a gubernatorial speech or major business convention. Presidential debates have to
be the top priority of any host, at least for a short period of time, or the
Commission will look elsewhere. Not surprisingly, some cities and universities have hosted the presidential debates and then decided that once
was enough—the event requires just too much work, inconvenience,
and expense.[12]

*   *   *

Now, almost twenty years after its creation, the Commission on Presidential Debates has indeed institutionalized the debates, but its reliance
on the two major parties has drawn sharp criticism from people, left and
right, who are critical of the leadership in the Republican and Democratic parties. Steve Forbes, who ran for president in 1996 and 2000, once
called the Commission a "corrupt duopoly." Jesse Jackson has called the
Commission "fundamentally undemocratic." Talking about Perot's exclusion from the debates in 1996, Jackson said, "If this group can arbitrarily
rule that a billionaire who gets 20 million votes and who qualifies for $30
million in election funds can't participate, then God help the rest of us."
Many journalists have added to the complaint. Respected political columnist David Broder has written that the presidential debates "are probably
the single most important part of the contest" but that they are less informative than they could be because the Commission "represents the
two major parties—and only those parties."[13] Political reporter Anthony
Marro described the debates as a "quadrennial sham," complaining that
the intent of the Commission was to give control of the debates to the major parties and that there is only "a small fig leaf of separation" between
the Commission and the parties.[14] Even some people who *like* the debates
are critical: Norman Ornstein, for instance, describes them as both "the
most significant focal point for voters" and a "largely artificial exercise."[15]

Urging a change to this system and endorsing a different organization,
the Citizens Debate Commission, as a new debate sponsor, the *Chicago
Sun-Times* editorialized in 2004 that

things don't have to be this way. They weren't back when the League of Women Voters controlled the presidential debates from 1976 to 1984, and they won't be if efforts to take back the debates from the Republican and Democratic parties are successful. Through a private corporation called the Commission on Presidential Debates, the parties have been able to determine in secret negotiations everything from what questions get asked and who does the asking to what TV cameras are allowed to show and how to configure the seating of the audience.[16]

Sometimes even the candidates themselves have been critical of the debates. Former vice president and president George H. W. Bush, who has participated in more nationally televised debates than any other candidate in history, once told journalist and debate moderator Jim Lehrer, "I'm trying to forget the whole damn experience of those debates. 'Cause I think it's too much show business and too much prompting, too much artificiality, and not really debates. They're rehearsed appearances."[17]

There are grains of truth in these criticisms, but all overlook two critical points. The first is that the organization was *not* set up to represent or reflect the wishes of the two major parties, as I myself had originally proposed. Besides its cochairs, Kirk and Fahrenkopf, none of the other Commission directors are or have been members of either party's national committee. And despite the early language about "bipartisan" organization, from the start the Commission has emphasized *non*partisan rules about candidate participation in the debates. The Commission, in other words, is far more independent than its detractors are willing to admit. I have never heard any Commission director defend the interest of any candidate or party, but only the public interest in providing voters the best information possible before they go into the voting booth.

The second critical point the Commission's critics ignore is this: history shows the choice is not between ideal debates and less ideal debates but between debates and no debates. The critics all underestimate the difficulty and cost of making the debates happen in campaigns that typically involve one hundred or more declared candidates.[18] Further, as explained in previous chapters, it is doubtful that Congress would ever mandate debates by law, and the candidates themselves have great incentives to avoid them. The League of Women Voters' sponsorship was nothing less than heroic, but it did not work well. So the question is not whether the Commission is the ideal solution but whether it has solved problems that the debates have encountered in the past and whether it does a credible job of ensuring that the public gets the information it needs about candidates' political positions and personal character. In the choice of a practical response to these demands, I believe we have to judge what the Commission has done against what happened before its creation, and in that comparison the Commission has been a clear improvement. Can it be improved further? Of course it can—and chapter 6 discusses how to do that.

First, however, it is important to discuss several mischaracterizations of the Commission, and some that I believe are simply wrong. The charges the Commission's critics make—that the Commission conspires to exclude minor-party candidates and that it colludes with the major party candidates to avoid a real debate—deserve an answer. On one matter I agree fully with the Commission's critics: the public knows too little about the Commission and how it works. Much of that is the Commission's fault. As a result it has left itself open to perception that it does not fully take the public's interests into account.

Although there are many fair criticisms people can make of the Commission on Presidential Debates, I believe it has been an effective and fair institution. Debates can happen only when more than one candidate agrees to participate. What the Commission contributes is increased public pressure and expectations to convince candidates to participate—or face the displeasure of the voters. Because of it we have had an unbroken series of presidential debates (and vice-presidential debates) in every election since 1988. That is five consecutive elections, a record that did not seem possible in 1976, after the sixteen-year debate gap. By the election of 1984, the prospect of holding additional debates looked unlikely. Originally, the 1988 debates were to be shared between the Commission and the League of Women Voters—each had announced a separate debate schedule—but it did not happen that way. League president Nancy M. Neuman contended publicly that a choice had to be made between the two sponsors. It was critical to the debates' future, she said, characterizing it as "a contest between the voters and the parties. I think the voters have come to expect that they can see the candidates in a situation that isn't managed by the campaigns."[19] The League's debates for 1988 never materialized, and the League's leaders felt that it had been unfairly pushed aside. According to a statement issued by Neuman at the time, "It has become clear to us that the candidates' organizations aim to add debate to their list of campaign-trail charades devoid of substance, spontaneity and hard answers to tough questions. The league has no intention of becoming an accessory to the hoodwinking of the American Public."[20]

Neuman's charge—that the terms of its creation mean that the Commission can never be a neutral or a trusted sponsor of the debates—has been repeated by many others. In 1992, for example, *National Journal* political writer James Barnes characterized the CPD as "made up of Democratic and Republican politicians,"[21] a reference to its chairmen, Kirk and Fahrenkopf. In editorials, in lawsuits from non–major-party candidates wanting to be included in the debates, and even among the major parties themselves, the Commission is almost always cast as a proxy for the major parties and an impediment to "real debates": the reason the candidates give rehearsed answers to questions, the inflexible barrier to third-party participation in the debates, and the opponent of well-documented public preferences for a more robust exchange between the candidates.

Certainly the presidential debates could be, and should be, more dynamic and informative, but as scholars Kathleen Hall Jamieson and David Birdsell write in their authoritative history on the subject, a golden age of political debate in America never existed. In every age, and long before broadcasting began, "debates have been beset by abusive advocates, fractious crowds, and unbearable tedium. Even when well conducted, they are sometimes difficult to evaluate, yielding results more consistent with the opinions of judges than the character of the arguments."[22]

In nineteenth-century America, presidential debates were typically between surrogates, not the candidates themselves. The stand-ins were often more talented or charismatic than the candidates they represented, and it was in this way that promising young party members gained public exposure, were tested against one another, and were groomed for political careers of their own. Abraham Lincoln, for example, first debated as a surrogate for Whig candidate William Henry Harrison in the 1836 presidential campaign, when Lincoln was only twenty-seven years old. The Whigs fielded three candidates that year in an (unsuccessful) effort to deny Democrat Martin Van Buren an electoral majority, and Lincoln debated South Carolina senator and former vice president John C. Calhoun, who spoke on behalf of Van Buren. In the 1840 presidential election, Lincoln again represented Harrison in a debate with Calhoun (again representing Van Buren). The two men squared off for a third time in 1844, with Lincoln as a surrogate for Whig candidate Henry Clay and Calhoun standing in for Democrat James Polk. Lincoln's last presidential debate came in 1856, when he campaigned for Whig nominee John Fremont.

Two years later, campaigning for the U.S. Senate, Lincoln engaged in perhaps the most famous series of debates in American political history, meeting incumbent Stephen Douglas for seven three-hour debates in Illinois. At the time the debates were controversial because U.S. senators were not elected by voters but instead chosen by state legislatures.[23] Candidates for congressional representative, who *were* chosen by popular vote, were expected to debate, but for Senate candidates the practice was all but taboo.[24] Remarking on the Lincoln-Douglas meetings, one Washington, DC, newspaper wrote, "The whole country is disgusted with the scene now exhibited in the State of Illinois," and went on to say the two men had "violated" the spirit of the Constitution.[25] An Ohio newspaper sniffed that "the members of the coming Legislature of Illinois will be just as free to exercise their own will in the choice of Senator as if neither Mr. Douglas nor Mr. Lincoln had peregrinated the state from lake to river, wrangling over what they are pleased to consider the great national issues."[26] Lincoln lost his Senate bid, but two years later he and Douglas would oppose each other again, this time for the presidency—but for that office there would be no repeat of their debates.

Political spin was also a part of nineteenth-century debates. Newspapers reported on them and reprinted them, and so did partisan pamphleteers and the parties themselves. The candidates and their supporters often rewrote the record of their comments to make themselves sound smarter, better prepared, and more articulate than their opponents.[27]

Perhaps the biggest difference between eighteenth- and nineteenth-century debates and broadcast-era ones, Jamieson and Birdsell write, is that in the prebroadcast era debates were separate from but firmly attached to other forms of public entertainment, such as parades, sporting events, and picnics. Indeed, before the broadcast era politics was the leading form of public entertainment throughout the country. There were few sporting events or traveling shows and no movies. Instead, political parties provided picnics, torchlight parades, rallies, and speeches to attract supporters. Presumably this explains why when George Washington ran for the Virginia House of Burgesses in 1757, his total campaign expenditures, in the form of "good cheer," came to "28 gallons of rum, 50 gallons of rum punch, 34 gallons of wine, 36 gallons beer, and 2 gallons of cider royal."[28] (There were only 391 voters to contest.)[29] Seventy years later, frontiersman and three-time U.S. congressman Davy Crockett found that to get Tennessee voters to attend his political debates "he had to kill coons, trade them for whiskey, and then treat his would-be audience at the bar. In return, the patrons of the bar patronized his speech."[30] In the prebroadcast age, candidates were expected to speak extemporaneously, without notes or other prepared remarks, and to engage their audiences directly. The arrival of broadcasting changed all this because it required the political speech and the political debate to become independent of other events. One result of this change was that by the 1930s political parties and candidates began developing their own radio call-in shows, mock quiz programs, celebrity-endorsement programs, and the like.

The second effect that broadcasting had on political campaigns is well known: it increased the role of advertising and public relations firms in packaging candidates for public consumption, the beginning of a process in which political messages grow ever shorter and less substantive. In 1952, for example, both Dwight Eisenhower and Adlai Stevenson bought commercial time in increments as long as five minutes. By the 1964 presidential campaign, the five-minute spot ad had given way to the sixty-second spot, which in turn evolved into to the thirty-second spot, "time for little more than a slogan, an assurance, an assertion and a smile."[31] In the television age, Jamieson and Birdsell write, political speech of all kinds suddenly had to compete with other, compelling forms of entertainment and to do it in a way that would not alienate viewers and voters. It was a delicate task. In 1952, after one of his televised speeches preempted prime-time network programming, Stevenson received a telegram from an unhappy viewer that read, "I like Ike and I love Lucy. Drop dead."[32]

The modern televised presidential debate is thus unlike anything else before it. It is a hybrid of old and new forms of political discussion, "fusing characteristics of the traditional debate, the staged debate, the question-and-answer session, and the press conference."[33] Presidential debates scholar Sidney Kraus calls the end result a "negotiated" debate and concludes: "Because the format is always a result of political decision-making, it is difficult to conceive of a genuine debate replacing the innocuous question and answer programs."[34]

What the televised debates should not be is formal academic debates — presumably the substance of the criticism that that they are not "real debates," a complaint that began in 1960.[35] In classical debate, opponents argue a stated proposition, for example, "The United States should arrest and deport all illegal immigrants." One side then defends this proposition while the other argues against it. In the nineteenth century, congressional debates often did turn on a single issue. Lincoln and Douglas, for example, argued the same proposition in each of their seven meetings, whether slavery should be extended to the new U.S. territories. As recently as 1948, the nationally broadcast radio debate between Thomas Dewey and Harold Stassen also focused on a single question, whether the Communist Party should be outlawed in the United States. It may be that some issues are so important that discussing them to the exclusion of everything else is a good idea, but anyone who has ever seen an academic debate competition knows that such discussions, while intensely focused and exhaustive in detail, are not much for nuance and not very good for exploring complex policy choices. They are a crush of facts and figures, but to a layperson not very informative or even interesting—precisely what one would presumably not want in the televised encounters between presidential candidates.

In academic debates, judges decide and announce the winner based on which side argues the proposition most effectively—that is on points, not substance. In presidential debates, the real judges are the viewing audience, and their decision comes on Election Day. To the extent the debates affect voters' choices at the ballot box, the standards they use to evaluate the candidates' performances are as varied as they themselves are. Voters mix objective and subjective reasoning, and when they watch a debate, they are often already predisposed toward one candidate or another based on party identification or preference. Who is the "winner" of a political debate can therefore be a matter for dispute (as happened in 1960, for example, when radio listeners thought Nixon got the best of Kennedy in the debates while television viewers had the opposite impression). As scholar David Zarefsky notes, the popular idea that Lincoln won his 1858 debates with Douglas is probably wrong. Lincoln not only lost the election, but in all seven of the Illinois counties where the two men debated, Democrats did better than Republicans on Election Day.[36]

Of course, those 1858 debates also catapulted Lincoln to national prominence, and two years later he defeated Douglas in their contest for the presidency. In the life of a nation, judgments about who "won" or "lost" a debate are ephemeral, and the time frame for the test of ideas can be very long. Academic debate is constrained by the formality of competition, and the end of the contest is the end of the matter. Political debate and public policy rarely work that way. In politics, the constraints of formal academic debate would probably turn off a majority of voters— hardly the strategy any candidate or debate sponsor would want to pursue. Certainly the televised debates can become more substantive, but they should not become formal to the point of exalting rules over the wishes of the public to hear what the candidates have to say on a range of topics. (Indeed, the most common criticism of the debates is that they do just that, and worse, because they replace the equitable and established rules of academic debate with rules that have been chosen specifically to benefit the participants. This is a fair complaint, which I discuss further in this chapter and in chapter 6.)

Where rules do matter in the presidential debates, as in academic debates, is in ensuring that both sides get an equal chance to make their views known and to respond to or rebut the arguments of their opponents. In both cases, for example, participants have to make their arguments within strict time limits. Those limits give each side a fair opportunity to speak, and in political debates featuring incumbents, they give challengers a meaningful opportunity to question their opponents' past performance and to propose alternative policies. That opportunity may not be enough to legitimize unpopular ideas, but it does allow the public to hear and judge them, an important activity in a vital democracy.

The requirement that debates be bound by rules ensures that they do not disintegrate into incoherent and unproductive shouting matches. Reasonable people can disagree about how debates should be structured, and in a series of debates formats can vary (as they do, for example, with the popular "town hall" debates in presidential elections, in which questions come from audience members). But whatever the rules are, they must be determined in advance, accepted by all the debate participants, and made public.

In this respect, the televised presidential debates are actually much *less* structured than formal academic debates, where both sides know what to expect. The candidates may agree to discuss foreign policy, for example, but they do not know what the moderator or any other questioner will actually ask on the subject. Journalist Jim Lehrer, who has served as the principal moderator for several presidential debates, says that out of respect to viewers he not only asks the candidates questions about issues they have chosen to campaign on but also pursues topics the candidates have ignored if he believes there is strong public interest in them. Neither Lehrer nor any other moderator or questioner shares his or her questions with the candidates in advance of the debates. Moreover Lehrer is emphatic that his job is to moderate—to enforce the rules the campaigns themselves have established—not to act as a journalist at a press conference.[37]

Nonetheless, the issue of the debates' rules, how they are determined and who enforces them, has consistently been part of the criticism that the televised presidential debates are not "real." In 1976, 1980, 1984, 1988, 1992, 1996, and 2000, the candidates did their utmost to haggle about dates, places, formats, questions, camera placement, audience reaction shots, even the temperature in the auditorium—seeking advantage for their own campaigns. They entered into "memoranda of understanding," one of which (2004) is included here as an appendix. But in 2004, the Commission asserted its authority by announcing nonnegotiable dates, places, formats, and moderator in advance. In response, President George Bush and Senator John Kerry entered into negotiations with each other, produced a memorandum of understanding, and gave the Commission a deadline to accept it. The Commission rejected the memorandum unanimously.

Commentary on these memoranda of understanding sometimes borders on the hysterical. A recent critic of the Commission is George Farah, a 2005 Harvard Law School graduate, the founder of an organization called Open Debates, and the proponent of an alternative debates sponsor he calls the "Citizens Debate Commission," mentioned earlier in this chapter. Farah's argument is summed up in his 2004 book *No Debate: How the Republican and Democratic Parties Secretly Control the Presidential Debates*, in which he claims that the existing Commission is a "fraud," a bipartisan rather than a nonpartisan organization whose principal concern is insulating the major parties both from challengers and from serious questioning, and which acts in "secret" and "covert" ways to ensure that outcome.[38] In 2004, Open Debates joined with ten other groups—a significant number—to issue a report highly critical of the Commission, "Deterring Democracy: How the Commission on Presidential Debates Undermines Democracy."[39] The report's executive summary argued that

> behind closed-doors, negotiators for the major party nominees jointly draft debate contracts called Memoranda of Understanding that dictate precisely how the debates will be run—from decreeing who can participate, to selecting who will ask the questions, to ordaining the temperature in the auditoriums. Masquerading as a nonpartisan sponsor, the CPD obediently implements and conceals the contracts. . . .
>
> The consequences of such deceptive major party control are distressing. Candidates that voters want to see are often excluded. . . . Issues the American people want to hear about are often ignored, such as free trade and child poverty. And the debates have been reduced to a series of glorified bipartisan news conferences, in which the Republican and Democratic candidates exchange memorized soundbites.[40]

The Commission on Presidential Debates was indeed conceived as a bipartisan organization, and some of the Commission's earliest documents refer to it as such. But those documents also make clear the Commission's concern, from the beginning, for *non*partisan rules for including significant minor-party candidates. The campaigns also negotiate many important details between them, though today they have absolutely no discretion about who is invited to participate in the debates (the subject of chapter 5) or what specific questions are asked. In their negotiations the candidates decide a lot of trivial things. The candidates will argue about the height, style, and placement of podiums, if any; the lighting and temperature in the room; whether the candidates can use notes; if they can, what color paper they must use; whether the candidates can walk around the stage or must stand still; and so on.

In 1976, the Carter and Ford campaigns hammered out what they called the "belt-buckle" principle, which required each man's lectern to intersect his torso at such a height as to make neither man appear taller than the other; in order to work, the agreement required both candidates to wear belts rather than suspenders. (While there was no formal memorandum of agreement between the two campaigns, the League's memorandum on the first negotiations is included here as appendix B. The critical outcome of those negotiations was the candidates' refusal to question each other directly, as the League had proposed.) The single longest negotiation between the two campaigns turned on whether the candidates would stand throughout the debates or could sit in a chair when not speaking. Ford wanted to stand throughout, Carter to sit occasionally.

In 1992, the campaigns of Bill Clinton and President George H. W. Bush negotiated at length over whether the candidates would have glasses of water on stage and, if so, whether the water would be placed on a table or on the floor. After much back-and-forth, the candidates agreed on floor placement until both sides realized that in order for the candidates to actually pick up their glasses they would have to bend over in a most unseemly manner before a national television audience. The water glasses were placed on a table.

Whatever one thinks of the candidates' memoranda of understanding, it is unrealistic to expect the campaigns *not* to negotiate. Even Lincoln and Douglas exchanged letters discussing the terms of their debate. Moreover, participation by the candidates or their representatives in working out the details of debate, even as to format, is consistent with the purpose of having the debates in the first place — to educate the public about the qualities of mind and character of the candidates.

The Kennedy-Nixon experience in 1960 supports this point. Though no written memorandum of understanding from the Kennedy-Nixon debates has ever been found, the two candidates and the networks negotiated extensively before and during the debates, right up to the last one on October 21, 1960. Negotiations began in April 1960, even before Congress suspended Section 315 for the campaign. NBC's Robert Sarnoff offered eight weekly one-hour *Meet the Press* broadcasts to each of the major party nominees. Three weeks later, in May, CBS's Frank Stanton made a similar offer when he testified on the Presidential Campaign Act before Senator Pastore's subcommittee. Neither executive characterized his proposal as a gift but rather as "time over which they, the networks, meant to exercise editorial control."[41] NBC made its offer official on July 27, the night Vice President Nixon won his party's nomination. CBS and ABC followed with proposals of their own for programs with the candidates, as did the Mutual radio network.

By then Nixon had already responded to the idea of debates, in a July 24 interview on CBS with Edward Murrow and Walter Cronkite. He was open to the idea, he said, but on the condition "that the details would have to be worked out so that there would be intelligent and serious discussion of the issues."[42] When the networks made their offers, Kennedy quickly accepted. Nixon responded on August 2, at a press conference in Los Angeles, where he told reporters: "I think what you need is a discussion of the issues without texts, without notes, where the candidates in depth go into specific issues so that the people can learn how they think and how they react to the questions that are raised by each other in the course of the debate."[43] Herb Klein, a Nixon aide, was caught completely by surprise by the announcement. "All the way through," he said, "he told me that he wanted to be certain that I did not say anything which would imply he was going to accept the debate. You had a lot of possibilities that once [the 315 suspension] was passed that you could avoid it through stalling, and I think that he would have. Just two days before he was nominated officially, he told me, 'Be sure you don't bring up the debate. Don't even indicate that I'm going to accept.'" At the Los Angeles press conference, Klein said, "My mouth dropped open as he announced he was going to debate. Eisenhower had urged him not to. I think he felt it was inevitable and maybe that was his chance to come out in a positive way to say it would happen."[44]

A week later, on August 9, representatives from the two campaigns met with representatives of the three television networks and the Mutual Broadcasting System at the Waldorf-Astoria Hotel in New York. It would be the first of twelve meetings in which these various interests, working together and separately, hashed out the schedule and terms of the debates. Both campaigns pressed the broadcasters to let them use as they wished the eight hours already offered to them, but the networks refused; they would retain full editorial control of the programs. At the end of that first meeting, all that was decided was that "debates were desirable, that they should be on all networks simultaneously, one hour in length, end by October 21, and be worked into the candidates' travel schedules by mutual agreement."[45] Fifteen days later, Congress passed the joint resolution suspending Section 315 of the Communications Act, thus making the debates possible.

Throughout August the Kennedy and Nixon campaigns met repeatedly and without the networks' representatives to discuss the number of debates, when they would be held, and the formats they preferred. When the campaigns met again with the networks on August 31, they had agreed to four programs of an hour each. They asked again to use the balance of the eight hours as they wished, and again the networks refused. The campaigns, wrote CBS News president Sig Mickelson, wanted a "press conference format" and "were only interested in broad topics covering general areas."[46] Mickelson and his colleagues at NBC wanted a more traditional and academic-style debate limited to a single proposition. But the campaigns "wouldn't budge an inch. They insisted that there be a panel of interrogators, preferably four at all four shows."[47] The networks did not like the proposal but felt they had to accept it; they certainly did not want to be blamed by Congress or the public if there were no debates. So they relented but insisted that they would choose the questioners from their own news staffs.

The next day, September 1, the campaigns announced the details of the first two debates. The first meeting would be on September 26 and would cover domestic issues; the second would be on October 21 and would cover foreign affairs. At this point, these two sessions were still being billed as "debates"; additional "press conference" programs were scheduled for October 8 and October 13. This raised the question of who would moderate the debates and which journalists would serve as panelists. After considering several prominent nonjournalists as a moderator, both sides settled on CBS reporter Howard K. Smith, but then they argued over the panelists. The networks naturally wanted to use only their own reporters, but the campaigns wanted print journalists included too. The eventual compromise was to include print journalists in the second and third debates and to use only the networks' reporters in the first and fourth programs.[48]

Among the seemingly less important predebate issues to be negotiated between the campaigns concerned lighting and makeup, and both of these would be decided at the last minute. Neither candidate wanted to admit publicly to using makeup, and both refused the services of CBS's makeup expert when she was flown to Chicago specifically to prepare the candidates for their first debate. The use of makeup had already been made a character issue earlier in 1960, when Democrats had charged Nixon with wearing makeup for an appearance on *The Jack Paar Show*. During a primary debate in West Virginia between Kennedy and Minnesota senator

Hubert Humphrey, Humphrey wore makeup for television and was criticized for it. Largely for that reason, wrote Nixon aide Herb Klein, the vice president refused to wear makeup for his meeting with Kennedy. When Nixon arrived for the first debate in Chicago ill, with a temperature of 102, an ABC executive suggested the debate be postponed, but Nixon refused. "People will think I'm chicken," he said.[49] Kennedy, as it turned out, did wear makeup. CBS's Don Hewitt, who directed the program, wrote that Kennedy aide Ted Sorenson had told him that the senator "behind closed doors and out of sight . . . got a light coat of makeup—a light coat to be sure, but makeup nonetheless."[50]

The first serious format issue to be negotiated between the campaigns and the networks was the matter of reaction shots of the candidates—and that took place while the September 26 broadcast was *on the air*. The networks had earlier agreed that each campaign could have two representatives in the production room during the broadcasts, and for the first broadcast Hewitt had made it clear that while the campaign staffers could be there, they could not talk to him. When Hewitt could not get a camera shot of both candidates together, he had to shoot them singly. Nixon's production advisor objected, but CBS left the decision to Hewitt, whose only concession was not to show the vice president while he was wiping sweat from his forehead with a handkerchief. But there were reaction shots of the candidates.[51]

The next quarrel over format came with the third debate, on October 13, which unlike the others did not feature the candidates in the same studio. Kennedy was in New York and Nixon in Los Angeles; the panel of journalists was in a third studio in Hollywood. "What Nixon saw on his monitor that night, but viewers at home did not see, was Senator Kennedy standing at his podium during the broadcast with a couple of pieces of paper on the top of it," writes historian John Self.[52] After the program, Nixon said he was "shocked" by Kennedy's use of notes, and Nixon press secretary Klein said both sides had had an informal agreement not to use them. Kennedy press secretary Pierre Salinger replied that the "memorandum of agreement on ground rules makes no mention of notes whatsoever,"[53] and Kennedy said the papers were not notes but public documents he wanted to quote. ABC News president John Daly, who had supervised the program, issued a statement saying that the candidates' oral agreement did not allow the use of notes but were vague on the use of "verbatim texts of public documents."[54]

The controversy over notes was quickly overshadowed by a proposal from Senators John Pastore, Warren Magnuson, and Mike Monroney for a fifth debate. NBC agreed and Kennedy accepted, but Nixon's aides said four debates was enough. If anything, Nixon said, the fourth debate scheduled for October 21 should be expanded from one hour to two, with the first hour a debate between the vice-presidential candidates. The campaigns met in Washington on October 15 to discuss the various proposals and counterproposals but resolved nothing. Two days later, Nixon offered a twist on his earlier proposal, this time urging a second presidential debate to follow immediately after the first on October 21. Kennedy did not accept the offer until the day of the debate, and by then it was too late.[55]

The campaigns' representatives met for several days in late October to discuss a fifth debate and on October 26 announced they had "made progress."[56] The networks began planning for a fifth broadcast, to be produced by CBS, but the negotiations between the campaigns collapsed when the negotiator for the Kennedy campaign publicly accused his Republican counterpart of "bad faith."[57] Nixon's negotiator responded in kind, saying he doubted "whether or not the Democrats really wanted a fifth debate."[58]

In the end, the negotiations surrounding the 1960 debates established several precedents. The most important by far was the agreement to debate. Never before had the leading candidates for the presidency faced off in public, and certainly not with the entire nation watching. The second precedent was the campaigns' involvement in the debates. The candidates sought to set the terms, then did their utmost to force those terms on the debate sponsor, the networks. That process has continued ever since, and it would not be until the elections of 2000 and 2004 that a debate sponsor—the Commission on Presidential Debates—would effectively resist, refusing in 2004 to sign the agreement negotiated by the Bush and Kerry campaigns or even to show it to the debate moderators. The third precedent was of journalists' participating in the televised presidential debates, acting as questioners so the candidates would not have to. In 1960, the networks explicitly did not want a role beyond producing and broadcasting the programs. The network news divisions did not want to be seen as manipulating a news event they were covering. They accepted a larger role as participant against their own news judgment, fearing a backlash from Congress and the public if the candidates backed out. Don Hewitt said years later that "to have news people in debates is like a sportswriter leaving the press box to come down and get in the scrimmage. We don't belong there."[59] The fourth precedent from 1960 also concerned format: the original plan to have two "press conference"–style debates and two formal academic debates was abandoned. All four meetings between Kennedy and Nixon were question-and-answer programs.

Much of what critics find to fault in the televised presidential debates, then, has nothing to do with the Commission. Rather it is the legacy of the many historical, political, and legal impediments that once made the debates impossible. But there is another, more important aspect of this legacy. The League of Women Voters and later the Commission spent many years negotiating with the campaigns from a position of weakness. But their combined success in sponsoring the debates for more than a quarter-century has now put the Commission in a position of relative strength vis à vis the campaigns. The campaigns will always want to negotiate terms prior to the debates, but those negotiations are not as important as they once were for a simple reason: the candidates can no longer refuse to debate, so there are limits on the conditions they can place on their participation. The Commission now has the opportunity and the obligation to assert its authority over the debates in ways that will most benefit the public.

The Commission declared its independence in 2004 by announcing that the dates, places, formats, and moderators for the debates were nonnegotiable. The Commission refused to sign a memorandum of agreement prepared by the representatives of the Democratic and Republican candidates. From now on, it was saying, the Commission is in charge.

5 ‖ *The Dilemma: Who Debates?*

The most serious criticism of the Commission on Presidential Debates is that it conspires with the major parties to deny candidates other than the Republican and Democratic nominees the opportunity to participate in the debates. Having exhausted their legal arguments before the Federal Communications Commission, minor-party candidates have now taken their legal challenges elsewhere, to the Federal Election Commission and the Internal Revenue Service. (Readers who want more detailed explanations of those challenges will find them in appendix D.) The new approach is to argue that the Commission on Presidential Debates is a "bipartisan" rather than "nonpartisan" organization and is therefore illegal. The distinction may not sound like much, but it is crucial. If the Commission were a bipartisan organization—nothing more than an extension of the Republican and Democratic parties   then the various corporate contributions to the Commission (which as a nonprofit organization depends on donations for operating and program revenue) would amount to illegal campaign contributions to the candidates under federal election law.[1]

In 2000 and 2004, Green Party candidate Ralph Nader made this charge repeatedly. That he was able to do so effectively owes in part to his rhetorical gifts, but even more to the controversy surrounding Reform Party candidate Ross Perot in 1996. To most Americans, I think, it made little sense that Perot could have been qualified to participate in all of the 1992 televised debates but none of the 1996 debates, an argument Perot pursued in court and in the court of public opinion. Perot's experience and Nader's attacks on the Commission for Presidential Debates for excluding him from the debates focused public attention on the most critical question of all: what qualifies a candidate to participate in the debates?

This question is part of a larger discussion that confronts all democracies: how are television and radio broadcasting to be used in a way that serves the public interest? In the United States, broadcasters are required by law to serve the "public interest, convenience and necessity." The Equal Opportunity rule discussed in chapter 3 is part of that requirement. Any democracy you care to name—Canada, Chile, the United Kingdom, Holland, Germany, Poland, Japan, Australia, Indonesia, South Africa—also regulates broadcasting in ways it believes, consistent with its cultural and political values, advance the public interest. And all regulate political broadcasting in some fashion, usually to ensure that candidates and parties get access to the airwaves so they can explain their views to voters.

Televised debates are one way of providing such access. In addition to the United States, most of the countries of the European Union now hold televised debates. One of them began before the United States—Sweden, in 1956.[2] Australia and New Zealand have held presidential debates since 1984; Canada has organized federal leaders' debates since 1968. The lone, conspicuous holdout in the democratic world is the United Kingdom, whose voters have yet to witness a televised encounter between rival party leaders contending to become prime minister. The lack of debate is not the fault of the British Broadcasting Corporation, which has pushed since 1964 to organize national debates against the formidable resistance of the parties. Former prime minister John Major once explained to a BBC interviewer his unwillingness to debate his opponent: "We hold televised debates in the House each week," he claimed, thereby missing (or dodging) the point of the question entirely.[3] The weekly *Prime Minister's Questions* is indeed televised, but the format is hardly a debate: one side *only* asks questions, the other side only answers them.

What Britain does do—what virtually all democracies except the United States do—is provide public-service airtime to parties or candidates free of charge in the weeks and days leading up to an election. The United Kingdom, which has no First Amendment, also prohibits both parties and candidates from buying time and airing commercials. (This would raise constitutional issues in the United States.) It thus avoids much of the corruption and public distrust that result from campaign financing in the United States, the lion's share of which goes to buy television time.

The dilemma of deciding who gets access to broadcast time in national referendums and elections for public office is a novel one in the many parts of the world, from Central Europe to Latin America, Southeast Asia to southern Africa, where democracy itself is either new or newly reborn. This seemingly straightforward question, presumably critical to the quality and quantity of public participation in governance, leads to countless other questions with no single satisfactory "democratic" answer:

- Do candidates or parties or both get access? Do all candidates get access, or only some? If there are multiple candidates, what threshold requirements, if any, must they meet to qualify for broadcast time?
- Is airtime free to the candidates? If it is, who bears the cost of production? Are broadcasters compensated in any fashion for candidate time, especially if there are several or even dozens of candidates?
- Do candidates get equal time, or are specific times and length of time allotted by formula? If so, what formula, devised by whom? How should the formula deal with minority parties?
- May broadcasters sell time? If so, on what terms? Must they sell time to any and all candidates for office — in effect compelling broadcasters to associate with ideas and with people with whom they may strongly disagree — or may they exercise their independent editorial judgment (presumably a cornerstone of any system of free expression) and choose not to sell time to some candidates?
- What about content requirements? For example, whether the airtime provided to candidates is unpaid or paid, must candidates appear on their own behalf, or can others represent them? Must candidates identify themselves in any way with promotions aired on their behalf? Can political advertising be bound by time restrictions that specify a minimum or maximum number of seconds, minutes, or hours? If candidates are allowed to purchase airtime, must they disclose the source of their funding?

All of these questions apply as well to the possibility that members of the public — individuals, civic groups, trade associations, unions, for-profit and not-for-profit firms, representatives of racial and ethnic minorities, political action committees, the expatriate community, and so on — are also entitled to airtime (free or otherwise) during elections. A final regulatory difficulty is how to make principled and understandable distinctions between candidate time, of whatever type, and legitimate news coverage of candidates and their activities and policies. Broadcasters and politicians everywhere understand that "objective" news stories about "newsworthy" events — many of them "pseudo events" created by politicians themselves — are more essential than political advertising to electoral success. Incumbents especially enjoy an enormous advantage in this respect, since presumably their regular participation in public events of all kinds is newsworthy. Conversely, both broadcasters and politicians understand that the decision by a broadcaster to portray a candidate negatively, or worse, simply to ignore her, can effectively kill her campaign — and her political career.

Where televised election debates are held, they now often follow the American format — nonconfrontational, evenhanded, with the candidates rarely addressing one another directly. Countries resort to American-style debates because they provide a reliable, tested model. (As mentioned, a major part of the work of the U.S. Commission on Presidential Debates now consists of advising other countries how to organize these events.) Some countries have followed this format for decades; others are just beginning to shift away from a more volatile format. What is still not clear in many countries is whether debates have a firm place in their political culture. The debates tradition has been growing, but voters can still accept the idea of an election without them. In 2006, for example, Ehud Olmert rose to victory in Israel with his new Kadima Party after refusing to debate opponents Benjamin Netanyahu and Amir Peretz, the leaders of Israel's more established parties. About the same time, Italian prime minister Silvio Berlusconi lost to opponent Romano Prodi after the two appeared together in two American-style debates, new to Italian politics.

Everywhere debates are held, politicians, journalists and the public alike express the desire to get more out of them. No consensus exists, however, on just how to do that. With some exceptions, the culture of leader debates everywhere has a few things in common. The first is that reporters tend to cover them not for substance but as strategic gambits or as political theater. Newspaper and TV coverage of debates throughout the world overwhelmingly emphasizes the same questions: Who won the debate? Did anyone make a major mistake? Will the debate change the candidates' standing in the polls? In Australia and New Zealand, for instance, debate coverage revolves around the "worm," an on-screen gimmick that registers the instantaneous reactions of various focus groups to the debates and that has been known to sink otherwise strong campaigns.[4] A second common aspect of debates is the view among scholarly, political, and media observers that debates more often confirm voters' choices than shift them. Candidates themselves believe otherwise, and both anecdotal and scholarly evidence suggests that at least in some instances they are right. Israeli scholars Shoshana Blum-Kulka and Tamar Liebes found in a study of the 1996 debate between Benjamin Netanyahu and Shimon Peres that a debate can change public opinion if it brings out a side of a candidate that the rest of the campaign does not. Before they met on television, Peres and Netanyahu both tried to hew to the middle. Their debate revealed significant ideological differences between them, however, and Blum-Kulka and Liebes believe that revelation influenced the poll shift that followed.[5]

A third common feature of political debate culture is that confident incumbents will try to avoid debating their opponents—and in most democracies they get away with it. Jacques Chirac debated his opponents in 1988 and 1995, as a challenger. In 2002, as president of France, he refused to debate Jean-Marie Le Pen and tried to turn this to his advantage, announcing that he would not accept a "transaction with intolerance and hatred." In Israel, Olmert and the Kadima Party also took a self-righteous line in their refusal to debate in 2006: "Kadima will not be a partner to [Likud Chairman Gideon] Sa'ar's attempt to save the Likud from the worst-run political campaign in history," a Kadima spokesman told the *Jerusalem Post.* The same year, in Brazil, President Luiz Inacio Lula da Silva took self-regard to new heights when he declined to debate his opponents after publicly comparing himself to Jesus Christ and saying that "some adversaries" were out to get him "in a game with cards that are marked."[6] Russian president Vladimir Putin rejected debates and won reelection in 2000 and 2004, though in 2000 his opponents held their own debates without him. In 2004, Putin dismissed the idea of debating, telling ITAR-TASS News Agency that debates were pointless: "All I could have said is what I accomplished over the past four years. I also knew pretty well what the other candidates would say. It would've been a foolish game or shadow boxing, when the end result is known in advance."[7]

Chirac and Olmert at least made a pretense of turning their rejections into principled stands. Lula chose divinity and conspiracy as his way out. Putin simply asserted that the voters already knew what they need to know; he ignored the fact that in a debate he would almost certainly have been required to tell voters what he planned to do *after* reelection. If disingenuous, Putin nonetheless hinted at a commonly heard complaint: debates rarely tell voters anything they could not learn from campaign materials or news coverage of the candidates. The constant complaint about American-style debates, for example, is that they're emasculated "joint press conferences" in which candidates, rather than engage each other, recite the same sound bites they use on the campaign trail.

On the other extreme are debates that devolve into chaos. Before attempting American-style debates in 2006, for example, Italy's debates were better known for theatrics and wild accusations than for policy or ideas. In 1994, the Associated Press quoted an exchange between Berlus-

coni and Achille Occhetto in which the former called his rival a "Stalin-
ist" and the latter retorted with "demagogue." Even with the change to a
moderated format, the 2006 Italian debates were notable for their insults
and lack of substance. In the second televised debate, on April 3, challenger Prodi called Berlusconi a "drunkard" and a political criminal. Berlusconi shot back, calling Prodi a "useful idiot" for the Communist Party
and any Italian who voted for him a "dickhead."[8] Neither candidate said
anything about Italy's zero percent economic growth, the issue most important to voters.[9] Canada in 2006 shifted to a nonconfrontational debate
format after having tried different combinations of moderator and audience questioning that always seemed to get out of control. A 1997 debate,
for example, called for candidates to give sixty-second answers to journalists' questions followed by a thirteen-minute "free-for-all" and questions from audience members; the result was an incoherent shouting
match among the five participants.

As in the United States, it is not all that unusual for candidates to
engage in public squabbles over debate formats or even whether to have
debates, but it is rare for those battles to turn into live, televised con-
frontations. In Mexico's 2000 election, plans for a debate among the three
leading presidential candidates broke down temporarily when behind-
the-scenes negotiations failed. In an effort to save the debates, the three
candidates organized (what else?) a televised debate to discuss the format
and timing of any subsequent debates. The meeting boiled over into argument when President Vicente Fox said that he wanted to "debate alone,"
but somehow, out of the public eye, the three did manage to arrange a debate a few days later.

Britain, doing things its own way, offers in lieu of debates a rough-and-
tumble compromise in the form of the BBC program *Question Time*.[10] In a
series of special broadcasts of the program in 2005, three candidates—
Tony Blair, Michael Howard, and Charles Kennedy—each had a half-
hour, alone on stage, to answer questions from a studio audience and a
moderator. The advantage of this format was that the candidates could
not get into shouting matches with one another, and each had ample opportunity to explain his views—perhaps more than any of them would
have liked. On each program, the candidate faced audience questioners
who were aggressive and often angry and who constantly interrupted
when he attempted to explain his positions. Rather than shield the candidates from this interrogation, the program moderator pressed each repeatedly when he tried to evade the audience members' questions. The
format allows audience members to make false assertions and to sling in-

sults that do not really further the discussion, but most of the questions are civilized and well informed, if hard edged. Of course even this format does not force a candidate to break from his script, but the aggressive questioning can throw an inadequate answer into sharper relief.

Germany has also found a compromise between the American approach and something more vigorous. In the country's first televised debates since reunification, Chancellor Gerhard Schroeder and rival Edmund Stoiber held two televised debates in 2002. The first stuck closely to the U.S. question-and-answer format, with journalists asking the questions. The second allowed the candidates to confront each other directly; in fact, after the first debate, Schroeder demanded a rule change that would allow him more time to reply to Stoiber, not just to the moderator.

The world's new democracies have fared no better or worse in their approach to debates. In the aftermath of its Orange Revolution and a fraudulent runoff election, Ukraine witnessed a 2004 televised debate between candidates Viktor Yushchenko and Viktor Yanukovych in which the candidates stood facing each other at a distance of about six feet, jabbing fingers and trading accusations of criminality and cronyism. In 2005, Kyrgyzstan, which has a weak democratic tradition, and Chile, which has had democratic governments interrupted by dictatorship, held their first presidential debates. Kyrgyzstan required the candidates to use their free television time to debate one another. State broadcasting scheduled a series of four—three between different combinations of candidates and a final one among all seven. BBC excerpts from the first debate, between Jypar Jeksheyev and Toktayim Umetaliyeva, showed a mix of questions from a moderator and audience members. The candidates answered the questions and apparently did not get into arguments with each other. In Chile, all four registered candidates participated in two debates, also nonconfrontational, in which they were given equal amounts of time to answer journalists' questions. In other new democracies the experience has been less positive. A debate in the 2004 Slovak presidential election, for example, was clouded by a personal dispute between the candidates, who had formerly been colleagues. The Czech News Agency quoted several exchanges like this:

> "First, you kiss someone's behind and then you slander him," Meciar said today.
> "You're lying as you always have. That's you all over—a liar from beginning to end!" Gasparovic responded.[11]

On the nettlesome question of which candidates to include in a debate, each country, party, candidate, TV network, and broadcast group appears to have a different solution. Canada's 2006 round of debates in-cluded four candidates, but Canada's Green Party complained about its exclusion. In the past, Canada's debate organizers had struggled with whether and how to include the Bloc Quebeçois and Ralliement Creditise candidates. Some of these candidates speak only French, and often these parties run candidates only in Quebec. In Japan, six candidates, includ-ing a Communist, participated in the country's 2005 debate—a seventh would have participated but said he had to attend to his duties as a prefect governor. Holland traditionally holds separate debates for major- and minor-party candidates. France includes only the two candidates who make it to the election's second round. The first televised debate in Aus-tralia's 2005 election included eight candidates. Network TV3 wanted to include only six but included the last two after a judge said exclud-ing them would be arbitrary. In most cases, the dispute over inclusion takes place in negotiations—usually not public, or only partially so—among the candidates and their parties, the government, private corpo-rations, and nonprofits.

When every attempt at compromise fails, or when a powerful incum-bent refuses to debate, it is the public that is cheated. In the 2006 Israeli elections, the Federal News Service held roughly equivalent one-on-one interviews with Olmert and Netanyahu in Hebrew during the weeks be-fore the election; the published interviews read more or less like halves of an American presidential debate, though with a little more interruption and pushing from the interviewer and none of the spontaneity or inter-action of a live meeting. In 2004, Spain's Canal Plus television network took a satirical approach when the country's ruling Popular Party repeat-edly turned down offers of a debate between its leader, Mariano Rajoy, who was far ahead in the polls, and José Luis Rodríguez Zapatero, his So-cialist rival. Canal Plus staged a debate anyway—using hand puppets. The mock sock-and-button candidates stabbed each other with Spanish flags, made wild election promises, and stole each other's best ideas.[12] In the end, Rajoy lost his lead and Zapatero was elected Spain's prime minister.

*   *   *

In the United States, the problem of whom to include in a televised de-bate has been with us from the beginning. In 1960, for example, fourteen legally recognized candidates ran for president, including representatives of the American Beat Consensus and the American Vegetarian parties. The third-party candidate who garnered the most votes that year was Arkansas governor Orville Faubus of the National States Rights Party, with 214,541 votes, followed by Eric Haas of the Socialist Labor Party, with 47,522 votes. Kennedy and Nixon combined received more than 68 million votes. When the televised debates finally resumed sixteen years later, in 1976, more than 160 candidates were seeking the presidency, and several of them wanted to participate in the debates: independent Eugene McCarthy, Lester Maddox of the American Independent Party, Thomas Anderson of the American Party, and Peter Camejo of the Socialist Workers Party.[13] Both McCarthy and Anderson sued to be included, claiming their First Amendment rights had been violated, and both lost.

The League of Women Voters chose to invite none of the third-party candidates and later explained its decision this way: "To invite every legally qualified candidate was a patent impossibility; to select one or two of the major 'minor' contenders would have been arbitrary and less defensible than the course we chose. The solution to the third party dilemma was, and is, beyond the League's problem-solving abilities."[14]

America magazine, among others, opined that the League's exclusion made sense, writing that while both McCarthy and Maddox were "bona fide" candidates for the presidency and both would surely have brought "an added point of view to the national discussion of issues that should accompany an election," a decision to have included them would almost certainly have led the major-party candidates to cancel.[15] The important thing, the magazine said, was to give voters a good view of the candidates who had a realistic chance of winning the contest. "Providing a forum for all," it said, "would reduce the debate format to a telethon from Babel."[16] The League said publicly that the decision about whom to include in the debates was a matter best left to Congress, the courts, and the Federal Election Commission.[17]

In truth, the problem of whom to include is beyond anyone's ability to solve perfectly. The dilemma is a classic example of what social scientists know as the "impossibility theorem," which won Stanford professor Kenneth Arrow the 1972 Nobel Prize in Economics. Arrow's theorem comes down to this: in any situation offering more than two choices, there is no rule that will take people's individual preferences and aggregate them into a single, identifiable preference. Put another way, there is no such thing as "the public interest"—at least not in the terms known to economists. What Arrow was trying to do in his own work was not unlike what the Commission on Presidential Debates is expected to do every four years: create a selection system that is consistent and fair and that will lead to orderly and rational group preferences when there are more than two options to choose from. Not only could Arrow not create such a system, but in the process he proved that such a system was impossible unless we are willing to impose some kind of restraint on the choice—for example, the restraint of majority rule—or to violate basic norms of fairness.[18]

So what does this mean for debates? First, it means every method of selecting candidates to participate in them will be imperfect, and though each method will have its advantages, each is *guaranteed* to have some of the disadvantages—that is to say the sometimes less than ideal results—predicted by Arrow's theorem. No matter how scrupulously fair and transparent the Commission on Presidential Debates may be in organizing the debates, someone is bound to cry foul. The critical point is that the same would be true for *any* selection scheme envisioned by *any* debate sponsor.[19] The challenge in every case is for policy makers and citizens to choose the system whose outcomes are most widely perceived as just and fair.

What does such a system look like? Arrow himself recommended the test proposed by the philosopher John Rawls: a just system is one in which any of us would be willing to take our chances and be thrown into it at random, not knowing where we might end up. If that is the test, I believe we can assume that two principles should govern any selection process. The first is that whatever the rules are, they should be clear and established well before the general election is under way. As with any contest, the rules cannot be devised in the middle of the game, nor can they be subject to the tactical calculations of the campaigns. The second rule is that the selection criteria be as specific and objective as possible, so that whoever applies them reaches a consistent, replicable, and indisputable result. The system should allow little or no room for discretion on the part of the debate sponsor or the candidates themselves about who gets included and why.

*   *   *

On October 1, 1987, more than a year before the Commission on Presidential Debates sponsored its first debate, it brought together a special advisory panel to guide it on several issues, chief among them how to deal with non–major-party participation in the debates.[20] I served on that panel, and the problem we had to solve was not abstract but urgent. The Commission's activities could be construed as legal under existing campaign finance law only if it chose participants using nonpartisan criteria. The panel appointed a special subcommittee to investigate the problem and make recommendations, and it appointed as its chair the late Richard Neustadt, a professor at and founder of Harvard's Kennedy School of Government. A little more than a month later, on November 20, the subcommittee recommended to the Commission that the selection criteria for candidates to be included in the debates focus on three major factors: evidence of a national organization, signs of national newsworthiness and competitiveness, and indications of national public enthusiasm or concern.

Nothing in these criteria contemplated any kind of quantitative threshold for inclusion in the debates, something the Commission would not do until the election of 2000. On February 4, 1988, the CPD board unanimously adopted the Neustadt subcommittee's proposals and, applying them, concluded that no non–major-party candidate should be invited to participate in the 1988 debates, which would feature three encounters between Vice President George H. W. Bush and Massachusetts Governor Michael Dukakis, and one vice-presidential debate between Indiana senator Dan Quayle and Texas senator Lloyd Bentsen.

In 1992, the advisory committee applied substantially the same qualitative criteria it had used in 1988 and concluded that no non–major-party candidate then seeking the presidency had a "realistic chance" of winning. The "realistic chance" standard, Neustadt explained later, required that "the chance need not be overwhelming but must be more than theoretical."[21] In other words, a candidate had to have more than a purely mathematical prospect of winning the Electoral College vote. The subcommittee met on September 9 and examined all of the one-hundred-plus declared presidential candidates. It did not consider Ross Perot, who had withdrawn from the race in July. On October 1, however, Perot reentered the race, and when the subcommittee reconvened four days later it decided that he satisfied the criteria for inclusion.

Perot's candidacy was unique both in the levels of popular support he enjoyed and in the level of personal financial resources he devoted to his campaign. Public opinion polls gave Perot support of nearly 40 percent at the time he withdrew from the race in July, and when he reentered polls showed him with diminished support, ranging from 9 percent to 20 percent. But he had the money to buy huge chunks of television time and was clearly willing to do so. The advisory committee could not predict the consequences of that combination and thought the prospect of Perot's winning unlikely, but it also thought that the possibility was not unrealistic. Though the chances were "incalculable," the subcommittee concluded,

Perot could win if no candidate received a majority of the Electoral College votes and the election were determined in the House of Representatives. On that basis the Commission extended an invitation to him and
his running mate, Admiral James B. Stockdale, to participate in the first
two 1992 debates. It immediately became clear to us that the already-
determined schedule for the debates—four of them over the course of
eight days—would make it impossible to reexamine Perot's eligibility to
participate, and so the CPD extended its invitation to him to include
all four debates. Perot finished the campaign with 18.7 percent of the
popular vote.

In September 1996, the Commission's advisory committee applied its
criteria to more than 130 candidates for the presidency, as well as to the
two major-party candidates, Senator Bob Dole and President Bill Clinton.
Ross Perot was running again, but this time his funding was limited by his
acceptance of a federal subsidy. As Neustadt explained the situation in a
letter to the Commission's chairs, "Mr. Perot has no realistic chance either of popular election in November or of subsequent election by the
House of Representatives, in the event no candidate obtains an Electoral
College majority. None of the expert observers we have consulted thinks
otherwise. Some point to possibilities of extraordinary events later in the
campaign, but grant that those possibilities do not change the likelihoods
as of today." In addition to Perot, Neustadt wrote, three other minor-party
candidates had a "theoretical chance" of election by virtue of their placement on enough state ballots to produce an electoral majority, but in no
case, he said, was election a realistic possibility.[22]

The subcommittee therefore recommended inviting only Dole and Clinton, who debated twice, and vice-presidential candidates Al Gore and Congressman Jack Kemp, who debated once. For excluding Perot, the Commission took a beating from the press. The New York Times editorialized
that "by deciding yesterday to exclude Ross Perot from this year's debates,
the Commission proved itself to be a tool of the two dominant parties
rather than guardian of the public interest. This commission has no legal
standing to monopolize debates, and it is time for some more fair-minded
group to get into the business of sponsoring these important events."[23] In
Florida, the Sun-Sentinel newspaper was even harsher in its criticism: "In
dictatorships, it's common for political insiders to hinder or even silence
non-establishment challengers. To do that in America, which supposedly
champions open elections, is outrageous and intolerable. But that is just
what the Commission on Presidential Debates has done."[24] Clarence Page

of the *Chicago Tribune* wrote, "We really ought to stop trying to manipulate history before it's happened."[25]

*   *   *

In 1999, a year after the Federal Election Commission rejected Perot's complaint, I led a Century Foundation study into the Commission on Presidential Debate's policy on whom to include in the debates. My colleagues in the study were Clifford Sloan and Carlos Angulo, a Washington lawyer. Perot's challenge may have failed in court, but it dealt a public relations blow to the Commission. After all, 1996 marked the first time a third-party candidate was *ever* awarded federal funds for the general election, and yet that candidate was excluded from the televised debates. The same candidate participated in the 1992 debates despite not receiving any federal funds, and in that election he received historic levels of public support. Four years later, in 1996, Perot wound up getting 8 million votes, or just over 8 percent of the total, making his exclusion from the debates all the more difficult to understand. As a legal matter, it all made sense. But legal matters aside, this result appeared unfair and confusing to many people, if not simply wrong.

In our report for the Twentieth Century Fund, we urged the Commission on Presidential Debates to revise dramatically its selection criteria. We realized that no criteria would satisfy everyone, that every method of choosing participants for the debates had one or more weaknesses, but that the key was to find some criteria or criterion that was as objective, concrete, understandable, and fair as possible.

There were three critical matters as we saw it. The first was finding some way of selecting debaters that would be resolved *in advance of* the nomination of candidates. We knew for certain that it was unacceptable and unfair to be publicly arguing about the rules in the middle of the game. Doing so had hurt the League of Women Voters' credibility in 1980, and it hurt the Commission for Presidential Debates in 1992 and 1996. In each instance, the negotiations took too little account of the wishes of voters. While we were sympathetic to the work of the Commission in our report, in the end we also thought that the standards it had been using were too vague, too confusing, and too susceptible to second-guessing. They also gave too much power to journalists, pundits, and academics. A Federal Election Commission report, for example, noted that the CPD measured "signs of national newsworthiness and competitiveness" by collecting

"the opinions of Washington bureau chiefs of major newspapers, news-
magazines and broadcast networks; the opinions of professional campaign
managers and pollsters not employed by the candidates; the opinions of
representative political scientists specializing in electoral politics; a comparison of the level of coverage on front pages of newspapers and exposure on network telecasts; and the published views of prominent political
commentators."[26] It relied, in other words, on the opinions of political insiders, not the public. Another criterion, which the CPD had used since
1988, did require "indicators of national public enthusiasm," and though
it included "the findings of significant public opinion polls," it set no
quantitative threshold. Instead it relied on another subjective measure,
"reported attendance at meetings and rallies across the country."[27]

When we studied the CPD's criteria for selection, we did not do it because they posed a legal problem but because they posed a fairness problem. Four years earlier, in 1996, Perot's Reform Party had challenged the
Commission's criteria at the FEC. The FEC found them acceptable, despite their subjective character, and found no evidence that they were
"designed to result in the selection of certain pre-chosen candidates."[28] In
fact, it was a matter of public record in 1996 that the Clinton/Gore campaign wanted Perot in the debates and had urged the Commission on
Presidential Debates to include him.[29]

But this was also part of the problem. Though the Federal Election
Commission dismissed Perot's complaint, the agency's general counsel
found much to criticize with respect to the role of the major party campaigns in selecting debate participants. It questioned whether the Commission on Presidential Debates' criteria were really "pre-established" or
"objective" and suggested that other, subjective factors had a lot to do
with its decisions about whom to include and whom to exclude. The FEC
general counsel was particularly critical of the idea that "signs of national
newsworthiness and competitiveness" was an objective standard, calling
it nothing more than the "accumulated subjective judgments," personal
preferences, and biases of Washington insiders with whom "rational
minds could certainly disagree." Making matters worse, he said, the CPD
reserved for itself the decision about which experts to consult, only adding
another layer of subjectivity that made the whole process so "vague and
undefined" as to be *incapable* of objective application.[30] Finally, the general counsel's report argued that the CPD's inclusion of the major-party
candidates for reasons of "historical prominence" and "sustained voter
interest" were technically illegal (an argument the agency's commissioners apparently found unpersuasive).

The second concern of the Twentieth Century Fund study followed from the first: any selection criteria for the debates had to command the greatest possible consensus among all those wishing to participate in the debates, and the criteria could not be so complex and legalistic as to be incomprehensible to voters. The third essential matter was finding a set of selection criteria that would not be so narrow or mechanical as to undermine the serious purpose of the debates: allowing the American people to make a final decision about the candidates with realistic chances of winning the election.

There were three major options for change, as we saw them: First, allow debate participation based on a candidate's presence on a sufficient number of state ballots to permit an Electoral College victory. Second, admit candidates to the debates who qualified for federal matching funds or who met some other fund-raising standard. Third, invite candidates to debate based on their standing in public opinion polls taken before the debate.

The first two had much to recommend them but suffered from critical drawbacks. Ballot eligibility, for example, greatly narrows the field of debaters simply because too few candidates appear on enough state ballots to have even a theoretical chance of winning an election. At the same time, we thought, the debates are not theoretical exercises in democracy building; rather their purpose is to give Americans the opportunity to consider seriously and at length those candidates who have a *real* chance of winning the election. The debates are the end of a long process, like the Super Bowl after the season and playoff games are over, by which candidates establish their policies and develop public support, and obscure candidates should not be allowed to use them as a springboard to public prominence. Moreover, if ballot eligibility alone were the deciding factor in who gets to debate, that would become the focus of all non–major-party candidates, with the result that the number of qualified debaters would grow to an unmanageable number. So while ballot eligibility has the advantage of being specific and predictable, we believed that by itself it was too low a bar, a necessary but not a sufficient condition for inclusion in the televised debates.

Using federal funding as a criterion for inclusion in the debates is also predictable and easily quantifiable. Among other things, it is tied directly to a democratic decision by Congress to recognize candidates who performed well in previous elections by giving them federal financial support (although it is true that third-party candidates get federal funds at a level much lower than that received by the two major parties). Additionally, the number of presidential candidates who qualify for federal funds is historically so tiny as to sharply limit the number of candidates eligible to debate—usually, in fact, to the two major-party candidates. But the problem with federal funding as a debate criterion, we thought, is a fatal one: it is all about how a candidate did four years ago—an eternity in politics—and not about the present. As a result, a federal funding criterion is *underinclusive* because it excludes candidates with strong public support who did not run in the last election, and it is *overinclusive* because it includes candidates whose party did well in the last election but who four years later have little or no public support. By such a standard Ross Perot would never have debated in 1992, and certain parties—George Wallace's Independent Party in 1972,[31] John Anderson's party in 1984, and Perot's Reform Party in 1996—would have been guaranteed a place in the debates even if they had no public support.

In the end we recommended the use of public opinion polls to determine debate eligibility because it was the measure most closely tied to the contemporaneous wishes of voters and the least susceptible to skewed, nonsensical, or even unjust results. We made the recommendation fully recognizing the problems with polls and concerned about politicians' overreliance on them in making policy. We were very aware of the blistering criticism that the League of Women Voters had received in 1980 from pollsters themselves when the League used polls first to include Anderson in the debates and then to exclude him. The pollsters argued that to use poll results in this way was to rely too much on their accuracy and validity, to the point of misusing them. We were aware also that part of the beauty of the American political system has been its historical unpredictability. What American has not seen the famous picture of Harry Truman holding up a copy of the *Chicago Tribune* with the headline "Dewey Defeats Truman"?

Still, the use of polls did not have the same shortcomings as the other two options. We urged that the Commission use the cumulative results of several polls rather than just one, and we recommended that an organization other than the Commission itself, such as the impartial National Council of Public Polls, evaluate the poll data. The Commission has taken that advice, wisely deciding not to do its own polling because it does not have the expertise or resources to do it. In 2000 and 2004 the Commission relied on the same five polls to determine candidate eligibility: ABC/*Washington Post*, NBC/*Wall Street Journal*, CBS/*New York Times*, Fox News/Opinion Dynamics, and CNN/*USA Today*/Gallup. To evaluate poll results, the Commission retains as a consultant Frank Newport, the editor-in-chief of the Gallup Poll.

Critics of this poll-based selection system charge that it is too imprecise, with margins of error that could unfairly exclude a third-party candidate hovering in the 15 percent range of public support. That is certainly plausible, but there is no *more* precise way to measure support, and the risk of error is the reason the Commission takes the average of five polls rather than relying on just one or two. Any third-party candidate who gathered anywhere near 15 percent support would be very newsworthy — the subject of constant polling. It is hard to imagine such a candidate's poll numbers not getting the benefit of heightened scrutiny. A second criticism of polls is that they exclude third-party candidates from their surveys and thus do not accurately reflect public support for them. But public opinion surveys do not simply provide a list of candidates and ask for voter responses to them. Instead they measure public support by asking one of two questions, or both of them. They will ask respondents to rate presidential candidates based on their own judgment of the candidates' strengths; and they will ask the open-ended question, "What candidate do you support?"

Finally, we argued in 1999, and I believe still, that a candidate whose public support qualifies him or her for participation in the *first* debate should be allowed to participate in *all* the debates, irrespective of how the polls rise or fall thereafter. The League's decision to drop John Anderson after the first 1980 debate, I believe, was a mistake. It hurt the League's credibility, despite its attempt to explain its decision, by encouraging the perception of the debates as monopoly of the two major parties. Once a candidate has qualified for participation in the debates, he or she should stay in to the end. Similarly, if a non–major-party candidate should reach the required percent threshold at any point after the debates have begun, that candidate should be included in the remaining debates. Presidential debates are not vaudeville acts in which a faltering performer gets the hook midway through the show, and to treat third-party candidates that way is to cut off the larger public debate about the country's future. Including a qualifying non–major-party candidate in all the debates also gives those parties a realistic chance to establish themselves and their ideas.

In January 2000, the Commission adopted new standards that were clearer and improved for judging candidates' eligibility for participation in the debates. The new criteria were virtually identical to those once used by the League of Women Voters, which in August 1980 had required a candidate to meet the constitutional requirements for presidential eligibility (under Article II, Section 1), to be on a sufficient number of state ballots to "have at least a mathematical chance of securing an Electoral College majority," and to show a level of support of at least 15 percent of the national electorate "as determined by five selected national public opinion polling firms, using the average of those organizations' most recent publicly reported results at the time of determination."[32] The one difference between the Commission's requirements and those the League had used was that the League had allowed that a non–major-party candidate could participate if, instead of showing 15 percent support, he or she enjoyed a level of support "at least equal to that of a major party candidate."[33] Compared to the old rules, the Commission's 2000 criteria were more explicitly nonpartisan. Indeed, they are the same selection criteria the Commission uses today, with the first determination of public support coming shortly after Labor Day, well in advance of the first debate.[34]

The most controversial eligibility requirement is the 15 percent rule. When the League of Women Voters used the 15 percent standard to include John Anderson in the first 1980 debate and then to exclude him from subsequent debates when his public support fell, Anderson said the decision destroyed his candidacy: "It was devastating. The only thing I could think of was that on the television set as people across the country watched that debate, it was a two-man race. If I had been important, if I had really been other than simply tangential to the whole process, I would have been there. [The public] didn't know about all of the back-and-forth and the efforts that we had made to get into the debate. They couldn't possibly know the disappointment. It was absolutely crushing."[35]

Some critics thought the 15 percent figure arbitrarily high (Anderson among them), while others thought it too low. Even some pollsters questioned the use of polls, noting problems of sampling error and variation in techniques. Democratic pollster Peter Hart wrote in the *Washington Post* that "the use of survey research to determine who should participate in the 1980 presidential debates is a perfect example of misuse of the tool of survey research."[36]

The League countered this criticism by arguing that there was no fairer way to gauge voter interest.[37] The League's advisory committee that settled on the 15 percent figure had discussed and at one time preferred a higher figure, 25 percent, but settled on the lower and "admittedly arbitrary" 15 percent when it concluded that "any non-major party candidate who, despite the odds such candidates face, received even a 15 percent level of support in the polls should be regarded as a significant force in the election."[38] Still, in response to criticism, the League used the data produced by eight national polls (including Gallup and Harris), rather than the current five used by the CPD, and it argued publicly that despite their different sample pools and sample sizes, survey instruments and techniques, the polls produced a "consistency of data"[39] that supported their claim that relying on polls was objective. At the same New York press conference, League president Ruth Hinerfeld announced that the League reserved "the right to reassess participation of non-major party candidates in the event of significant changes in circumstances during the debate period"[40] and that it would extend or withdraw invitations accordingly.

Today the challenge to the 15 percent rule is a legal one, and the thrust of the challenge is that the rule is neither "preexisting" nor "objective." The argument is on the one hand quantitative: that the polls the Commission uses have significant margins of error that make it difficult to determine public support with any useful precision, and that the five polls use different sample sizes and target different populations, such as "eligible voters" and "eligible voters likely to vote." The other objection is qualitative: that the Commission gives complete discretion to the polling organizations to decide whom to poll, what questions to ask, and which candidates they will ask about.

The point of these complaints, of course, is that the threshold for participation should be something less than the 15 percent it is now (an issue I discuss further in the next chapter). Some—the Reform Party and the Natural Law Party, for example—want the basis for inclusion to be whether a party received 5 percent or more of the popular vote in the previous election. The group Fairness and Accuracy in Reporting (FAIR) says the standard for inclusion should be 5 percent public support or that the debates should include any candidate whom 50 percent or more of eligible voters say they want to see included. The group Reclaim Democracy urges that any candidate who appears on enough state ballots to have a mathematical chance to win the Electoral College should be included in the first debate of the general election irrespective of popular support, a proposition that the organization says would typically yield from four to seven candidates. After that first debate, Reclaim Democracy says, "the field could be narrowed fairly with more stringent criteria," though it offers no further guidance on how to do this. Others have argued that a more objective criterion (if a manifestly unfair one) would be the amount of money a candidate or party has spent on his or her campaign by a specified date prior to the first debate.

Still others urge criteria that are undeniably subjective. In 2000, for example, the *New York Times*, having blasted the Commission for excluding Perot in 1996, supported the exclusion of both Ralph Nader and Patrick Buchanan from the debates because "neither . . . has yet reached the status of a candidate with demonstrated national support. Should that change as the campaign progresses, the commission can respond accordingly."[41] The same year, the *Washington Post* criticized the 15 percent bar as too high and urged the Commission to include "candidates with smallish followings . . . because the race is close, so they may decide the election even if they cannot win it."[42] Including Nader and Buchanan, the *Post* said, would also boost voter interest in the debates and put "important issues on the table" that the major-party candidates were not talking about.

Some of these are good reasons for including minor-party candidates, but without some kind of organizing principle they would wreak chaos on the debates. Under the *Times*'s proposal, what organization would determine "national support"? Under the *Post*'s proposal, which of the hundreds of candidates for president would *not* be eligible to participate in the debates? And how is either proposal to be defended as "fair"?

6 How to Improve the Presidential Debates

The 150th anniversary of the 1858 Lincoln-Douglas debates is in 2008. The 2008 presidential election is the first in fifty-six years—since Dwight Eisenhower ran against Stevenson in 1952—that American voters do not have a choice on their ballots that includes a sitting president or vice president. The election occurs in the midst of a communications revolution in which more than 70 percent of American households have Internet access and 90 percent of U.S. Internet users are registered voters.[1] They can get their news and political information from Web sites maintained by television and cable news organizations, candidates, political parties, advocacy groups, and nonpartisan voter education groups. My daughter Mary has showed me how they can get it from political blogs, of which there are tens of thousands; peer-to-peer networks such as Limewire and BitTorrent, online video sites like YouTube, Brightcove, and Maven; virtual reality sites like Second Life; social networking sites like MySpace, Friendster, and Facebook; and simple e-mail lists. Perhaps the most dramatic change is the phenomenon increasingly referred to as "Web 2.0," which draws on users to create and comment on content. Citizens can organize virtual communities of interest; participate in electronic town meetings; attend congressional hearings; view, save, and print government documents; propose and critique referenda or legislation; monitor their representatives' activity; and e-mail them their views anytime, all the time.[2]

In 1996, the first presidential election year in which the Internet was widely available, 10 million households in the United States subscribed to some kind of online service, and about 30 percent of households owned a personal computer. That year, Republican Bob Dole was the first candidate to urge people to visit his campaign's Web site during his nomination acceptance speech. Four years later, Republican Steve Forbes announced his presidential candidacy on his Web site. Democratic candidate Al Gore's Web site featured several live "town hall" meetings in which he answered voter questions submitted by e-mail. In 2003 an Internet campaign resulted in the recall of California governor Gray Davis, and another online effort launched the 2004 presidential campaign of retired army general Wesley Clark. In 2007, New York senator Hillary Rodham Clinton, among others, announced her 2008 presidential run on her Web site. Illinois senator Barack Obama announced his candidacy before a crowd in Springfield, Illinois, but won praise from reporters for his campaign Web site, which had several social networking features that allowed his supporters to communicate with one another and to organize.

In 2006, 50 million Americans were using the Internet for news everyday, almost twice the number that did so in April 2002. Nearly one-fifth of Internet users spent some time reading about politics, and almost half of "likely voters" (43 percent) said they did so in the weeks right before the November elections.[3]

Will the Internet make our politics more informative or less? Both, especially as increasing numbers of Americans go online using broadband connections.

Without question, the Internet has the potential to improve the character of our politics by providing more and better-quality information to more people. Democracy, after all, depends on access to multiple and competing sources of information, an underlying assumption of the First Amendment.[4] Many nonpartisan Web sites seek to meet that need, one of the best of them the League of Women Voters' Democracy Network, where voters can learn about virtually any campaign, candidate, ballot measure, or referendum in any state.[5] Even more useful, voters can get details about local polling places and times, state eligibility identification requirements, absentee and provisional voting, voting machines, and almost anything else they need to know to make their votes count.

But if historical experience is any guide, Internet use by itself will not produce "better" democracy or "more informed" citizens, either in nation-states or globally. In their time, telephony, radio, and television were all heralded as technologies that would make democracy more inclusive and dynamic.[6] But with radio and television we failed as a nation to honor our best hopes, as we allowed political broadcasting to become a cynical and relentlessly negative money game played by campaign consultants. The Internet, according to political reporters Mark Halperin and John Harris, has further fueled this "freakshow."[7] But the Internet has also brought changes. As political scientist Michael Cornfield writes, today's candidates "must continuously monitor YouTube—along with googling and wikepedia-ing themselves—to see what citizen media-creators have wrought."[8]

For many political observers, 2006 became known as the year of the "YouTube election." YouTube, a video-sharing site, did not exist in 2004, but when Google bought the business for $1.65 billion in fall 2006 YouTube was attracting 20 million visitors monthly, and in 2006 the site made its presence felt in elections in a big way. The most notorious YouTube moment came when Virginia senate candidate George Allen confronted a young man working for an opponent and filming Allen's campaign appearance and called him a "macaca." The video immediately showed up on YouTube, where overnight it went to the top of the site's most-viewed list. From there it went to the front page of the *Washington Post*, and from there to cable and to network television news.[9]

Some scholars argue that the Internet simply reinforces traditional patterns of social and political life.[10] Others argue that digital democracy will be "decentralized, unevenly dispersed, even profoundly contradictory"[11] and that any increased pluralism that results from Internet use (if that's what it is) may simply make our politics more fragmented, partisan, and unstable.[12] To the extent the Internet creates new kinds of political relationships, they may be weaker than what a strong democracy requires. The Internet generally does not develop what sociologists call "thick" community. Its celebration of spontaneity and anonymity (and even deception) does not promote the development of broadly shared norms and values, nor does it do much to build social trust. The Internet is characterized by fluid and ephemeral relationships, a constant reshuffling of identities and associations. Thick community, by contrast, is characterized by stable, long-term relationships. Indeed thick community relies on the kind of social pressure that is made possible only through face-to-face contact. In theory, at least, such contact builds empathy, avoids or alleviates conflict, and makes speakers assume responsibility for their words and actions—all things the Internet generally does not do.[13]

The critical consequence of all this—and the irony—is that the Internet may make voters *less* informed rather than more so.[14] In his analysis of Internet use in the 2000 presidential campaign, political scientist Bruce Bimber found that voters did not use candidates' Web sites to help them decide whom to vote for. Instead, Bimber said, "people tend to go to the Web sites of the candidates they support, and they tend to come away feeling ever more strongly about them than they did going in. Some optimists thought that people would sample each candidate's Web site, gather information and make up their minds, but it doesn't work that way."[15] Michael Cornfield made a similar observation after the 2006 midterm elections, wondering if Internet politics "only hardens our views, polarizes our politics, and contributes to the nation's red and blue divides."[16]

Ancient Athens, the best known of the many early Greek experiments in *demokratia*, never had more than about thirty thousand full citizens, and of these about five thousand might regularly attend the meetings of the city Assembly. The Athenians believed that productive debate was possible only among the number of people who could all hear one speaker at the same time. Similarly, the American revolutionaries thought the North American continent was too vast, its people too widely dispersed, for democracy to exist under a single polity. Instead they envisioned a continent of many small, allied republics. In the twentieth century, broadcasting increased exponentially the size of the audience that could see and hear simultaneously. The Internet increases exponentially the size of the audience that can speak.

It would be foolish to think that all speakers are politically, socially, or economically equal. But we can all now speak, either for ourselves or in concert with others. Israeli prime minister Shimon Peres once said that television makes dictatorship impossible but democracy intolerable. And the Internet? At best it makes democracy more egalitarian and dynamic. At worst it can make democracy dysfunctional.

In this new media and political environment, there is one thing of which I am certain: the televised presidential debates are more important than ever before, for three major reasons.

Most important is that, whatever their shortcomings, the debates are the *only* time during presidential campaigns when the major candidates appear together side by side under conditions that they do not control. For voters and for the nation, they are the only simultaneously shared experience of the campaign. Second, the debates *are* substantive. They are overwhelmingly about issues and contribute enormously to viewer learning.[17] Second, the debates reveal the differences between the candidates—a particularly important function in a system like ours, where presidential candidates are much more independent of their parties than are candidates in parliamentary systems. The debates stimulate voter interest and lead to greater voter participation, and they reveal candidates' views and positions in a way no other event or communication of the presidential campaign does, including candidate speeches and advertisements.[18] As Kathleen Hall Jamieson and David Birdsell write, "Viewers turn to debates to provide sustained analysis of issues and close comparisons of candidates. 'Debate' has become a buzzword for 'serious politics.'"[19]

Third, the debates have symbolic importance, especially in an age in which political communications are targeted to ever more narrowly segmented slices of the electorate. Viewers get the chance to compare the candidates' personalities and character, to decide if they trust or do not trust the person who may become their president. As we navigate the chaotic world of digital communications and Internet politics, what we need more than ever are real debates—face to face, live, and in the full view of everyone in the country—not virtual ones in the remote corners of cyberspace.

Long-time debate moderator Jim Lehrer says it best: "I have a very simplistic, old-fashioned view of this. It doesn't matter what the format is, it doesn't matter who the moderator is; anytime you get the candidates for president of the United States on the same stage, at the same time, talking about the same things, it's good for democracy."[20]

What then, can be done to secure the presidential debates for the future, to make them more substantive and useful to voters? I have five recommendations.

1. *To better serve voters, the televised debates should be less formal and more spontaneous—without canned speeches, and with opportunities for the candidates to question one another and for citizens to question candidates directly.* When asked, voters urge this change to the debates more than any other. The Commission in 2004 managed to take away from the campaigns control over debate topics, questions, moderators and questioners. It did not succeed in opening up direct questioning by the candidates themselves. The public overwhelmingly wants greater say in the questions that get asked and longer and deeper discussion of major issues, and they want candidates to be able to address one another directly and not merely with rhetorical questions—all things the campaigns resist.[21] As I explained in chapter 4, the Commission declared its independence in 2004 when it refused to sign the thirty-two-page memorandum of understanding negotiated between the Bush and Kerry campaigns (the memorandum is included here as appendix A).[22] The Bush campaign threatened to walk away from the debates if the Commission made no commitment to enforce the memorandum agreements, but it did not.

In fact, it would be illegal for the Commission to sign any memorandum negotiated between the major parties: doing so would violate the requirements for nonpartisanship. If the candidates want to primp and pose for each other by arguing over makeup, podium heights, coin flips, handshakes, water glasses, pencils, and notepaper, fine. The Commission cannot and should not do anything about these matters. But on issues of debate format and substance, the Commission should work only with its own moderator(s) and, wherever possible, with voters themselves.

The question of format is important only so long as it makes the debates more informative and allows the candidates to speak at greater length and directly to each other.[23] Scholars Kathleen Hall Jamieson and David Birdsell, for example, recommend at least one "direct confrontation" format in which candidates pose the questions while a single moderator keeps time and intervenes only if a candidate veers from the agreed-upon topic. They propose that debates begin with eight-minute opening statements from each candidate, followed with six-minute segments for restatement and rebuttal, and then two four-minute segments for elaboration.[24]

In the United States and around the world, there are usually six basic debate formats. The podium style is the most traditional and probably the most formal and least open to spontaneity. The town-meeting style has the advantage that citizens ask the questions and for that reason is most popular with the public; the disadvantage is that questions can be narrow or repetitive and may not cover a broad range of topics. The roundtable conversation style is also informal, with the candidates seated at a table alongside the debate moderator, and was used by the CPD once during the 2000 debates. The multicandidate style is used mostly in primary elections in which several candidates are contesting a nomination; the problem with the larger number of candidates is that none can talk at length, fewer topics are covered, and fewer are covered in any depth. In the interview style, used by the BBC, candidates are seated on chairs next to a host who asks questions. Finally, the television remote interview style has candidates seated in separate studios, sometimes thousands of miles apart, and viewers see the participants on a split screen; the "talking head" approach is not conducive to give-and-take between the candidates.

There are other format possibilities, of course. After the 1960 debates, journalist and historian Theodore White urged that future debates be held before a joint session of Congress.[25] More recently, *Washington Post* columnist David Broder suggested that candidates not be allowed to mention each other's name during the debates. Theoretically the candidates then would be forced to explain their own views rather than caricature their opponent's. *National Journal* founder Neal Peirce has proposed that a single moderator lead the candidates through hypothetical scenarios, much as journalist Fred Friendly once did in his televised seminars for public television. In 1987, my daughter Nell and I wrote an essay for the *Christian Science Monitor* in which we urged an "Oregon-style" debate, "with some questions posed by voter groups, students, state legislators, mayors and governors, and the public at large." We also suggested that living former presidents be invited to ask questions, or that there be Oxford-style debates, with the candidates alone asking and answering the questions.[26]

All of these choices have their advantages and disadvantages, and each raises different issues of fairness and program discipline—and plausibility. The important issue for the future, I believe, is that the Commission work harder to allow, in at least one of the debates, questions by the candidates themselves and by citizens. The moderated format has worked well, thanks to Jim Lehrer. Many fine reporters have served as panelists on the debates over the years (including my friend and college roommate Sander Vanocur, a panelist on the first 1960 debate in Chicago), but I nonetheless believe having reporters asking the candidates questions is the wrong way to go. Reporters have an interest in, and bias toward, creating controversy. It helps them write a story. Not surprisingly, they will often have a "gotcha" approach to questions. They try to come up with questions that will hurt a candidate with some part of his or her constituency, since that will cause the candidate to squirm. And of course journalism is a competitive business. Journalists asking questions at a presidential debate are aware that they may get only one bite of the apple—a place in history—so they want to make it a good one. They may try to anger a candidate, or they will give speeches in the form of questions, or they will ask rhetorical questions: "Candidate X says you are a liar—what do you have to say?" Of course nothing prevents citizens and candidates from grandstanding in this way, but they have less incentive to do so. In any case, debate formats should encourage informality and spontaneity.

The debates are now de facto mandatory. The Commission and the League of Women Voters have given the nation an unbroken series of eight debates. Presidential candidates who today refused to participate would demean themselves in front of their supporters, the nation, and the world. I understand that some will question whether this is really so. After all, if a candidate does not want to debate, why would she do so? Why would her party pressure her to do so? *Because both the candidate and the party want to win.* The voters now *expect* debates, and a candidate will not risk their displeasure by refusing to participate in a national tradition. It may be here that the Internet will prove most powerful as a political force. For the candidate who refused to debate there would be no place to hide. In 1992, when George H. W. Bush balked at debating Bill Clinton and Ross

Perot, citizens dressed in chicken suits heckled him at every public appearance. Today, with all that is made possible by digital communications technologies, a candidate who refused to debate would see his or her candidacy pecked to pieces by millions of virtual chickens.

2. *For voters, remember that you cannot learn all you need to know in a ninety-minute broadcast—or even four of them.* The televised presidential debates may be the most important, substantive, and revealing moments of the presidential campaign, but they are not enough. There are many fine print and online sources of political information, much of it nonpartisan and far more detailed than can be provided in even the best debate. Remember when you watch the debates that the debate moderator's job is to moderate, not to cross-examine the candidates. That job should be for the candidates and the voters themselves.

Finally, after you watch a televised debate, turn your television set off and do your best to avoid the torrent of spin that follows. Give yourself the time—a day, if you can manage it—to talk about the debate with your family, coworkers, friends, neighbors. Then, if you want, go see what the pundits have to say—and whether you think they got it right. In the 2000 debates, for example, most Americans thought Al Gore won his first debate with George W. Bush. But after forty-eight hours of news coverage and political spin about Gore's audible sighing and exasperated facial expressions during the debate, perceptions changed and Gore's "victory" disappeared. Viewers, not pundits, should decide who makes the better case in a debate. In the end it will be your voice that counts, not theirs.

3. *Require television and radio broadcasters to provide public-service time to qualified candidates for the presidency in the six weeks before the election. Further, one half-hour of public-service time should be allotted to each candidate on the night before the general election. The nation's public television stations should take the lead in this effort.* Almost forty years ago, I served as chairman of the Twentieth Century Fund's bipartisan Commission on Campaign Costs in the Electronic Era. Our task was to examine the quantity and quality of political information provided to voters in national political campaigns. Among the conclusions in our report, *Voters' Time*, was this: "The sharply rising use of television and radio broadcasting by presidential candidates in the United States poses serious problems that affect politicians, the parties, the voters, and the very fabric of our democratic process. . . . It is the task of policy makers to ensure that technology itself

does not alter our fundamental policy principles, that men remain the masters of technology and not the other way around."[27]

In the intervening decades, our nation has failed terribly at this task. The quantity and the quality of political news on broadcast television has steadily diminished. (It is true that there are many more political *discussion* programs today on cable and talk radio, and many of these include audience commentary and opinion. Rarely, however, do any of these programs feature any original reporting, nor do they include points of view other than those favored by their hosts. Few give any serious consideration to opposing views.) In 1968, the average sound bite of a candidate speaking on the evening news was forty-two seconds long. By 1988, the average candidate sound bite had dropped to ten seconds in length, and by 1996 to eight seconds. Today, for every few seconds we see candidates speaking on television, there are endless hours of reporters, anchors and outside "experts" doing their own analysis of the candidates' views and telling us what they "really" mean.

For candidates in our political system, there is only one sure way to get their views in front of voters; for five decades now campaign expenditures have been driven relentlessly upward by the rising cost of television advertising. In 1960, in the first presidential campaign to make wide use of television, Democrats and Republicans together spent $14.2 million on radio and television commercials. In 2004, the campaigns of George W. Bush and John Kerry, combined with so-called 527 groups aligned with both sides, spent $587 million on television advertising.[28] (527 organizations, named after a section of the federal tax code, are not regulated by the Federal Election Commission and are not subject to the limits on contributions that apply to political action committees.) Local television stations in the nation's top one hundred markets collected a total of $1.6 billion in political advertising revenue in 2004, more than double the $771 million they received in 2000.[29] Two years later, in the 2006 midterm elections, political spending on broadcast television advertising broke all existing records to total more than $2.1 billion.[30] According to news reports, many stations had such high demand for political ads that station managers were able to charge top dollar for them and pulled other less lucrative commercials to free up time. As one station manager told Bloomberg News, "We start them out at the top rate, which nobody pays by the way, then we double it. It will triple in the final week. They will pay it if they want to get on."[31] (Readers who wonder how broadcasters can circumvent the apparent requirement of the law can find the answer in appendix C.)

There is a colossal irony here: Citizens who want access to the public officials who work for them buy that access with money contributions. And politicians need that cash so they can buy access to something that we, the citizens, own: the public airwaves used for broadcasting. Put simply, we pay our politicians to listen to us, and they use our money to pay broadcasters so we can listen to them. This is harebrained public policy, and, more important, it is corrosive to our democracy.[32]

And that's not the worst of the story. Local stations throughout the United States increasingly choose *not* to cover federal, state, and local political campaigns, *compelling* candidates to buy advertising time if they want to get their views in front of voters.[33] And what kind of ads do voters see? Relentlessly negative, outrageously offensive, and even false ones.[34] Political scientists who study campaign commercials will often argue that negative ads are, on the whole, more informative than positive ones. This is like saying Lake Michigan has less toxic waste in it than Lake Erie. It is an insight without context, and certainly unhelpful to voters.[35] As journalist Michael Kinsley writes, "Candidates and partisan commentators strike poses of outrage that they don't really feel, take positions that they would not take if the shoe was on the other foot, feel no obligation toward logical consistency. When we vote after a modern political campaign run by expensive professionals, we have almost no idea what the victor really believes or what he or she might do in office."[36]

Those who disagree with my characterization of the modern presidential campaign, and even some who agree with it, will argue that all of the problems I have described—negative and false advertisements, candidate posturing and inconsistencies, vapid cable and talk radio campaign coverage—are also protected by the First Amendment. That is an incomplete response. As Supreme Court Justice Potter Stewart once said in a different First Amendment context, there is a difference between the right to do something and the right thing to do. If little can be done constitutionally to deal with these problems, what constitutionally and *positively* can be done, in addition to the debates, to contribute to better campaigns?

One proposed remedy is to require by law that television and radio broadcasters provide no fewer than thirty minutes each week of public-service time to presidential candidates in the six weeks before the election.[37] My friend and former chief counsel at the Federal Communications Commission, Henry Geller, suggests that in the last three weeks before the general election there be four thirty-minute programs on the great issues of the day—at the time of writing, for example, these might be Iraq, entitlements or Medicare, immigration, the environment—carried by all the broadcast networks. Each candidate would get fifteen minutes (or if there are three candidates, ten minutes) to explain his or her views on the designated issue. The audience for these programs would be much smaller than those for the debates, but such programs would complement the debates by contributing to more in-depth understanding of the candidates' positions on key issues. Over this same three weeks, Geller proposes, candidates could prepare two-minute presentations on these issues that would be presented in four-minute segments in between regularly scheduled programs. Under current law, Geller says, these short programs would not be subject to Section 315's equal time requirements.[38]

The issues of who gets time and how the candidates or parties may use that time could, in many cases, be determined by the FCC, but I believe these decisions should be for Congress and Congress alone. We are dealing with campaigns of the highest importance. I agree with Geller that short political programs and mini-debates are a good idea. The presidential candidates themselves—not surrogates or supporters—should be required to appear on their own behalf.[39] In at least half of their public-service time, candidates' appearances should be live, without the benefit of after-the-fact editing and enhancement in the production room. And on the night before the general election, each candidate should get an additional half-hour of primetime to summarize his or her views.

I do not suggest that these proposed reforms to our current use of television in campaigns will solve all the problems of money in campaigns and negative advertising. Personally, I would go further and, as the British do, ban paid political advertising on television entirely, but I do not believe that proposal would be politically feasible, and it would raise constitutional arguments.[40] But the United States stands almost alone in the democratic world in not requiring some form of public-service broadcast time for candidates in national election campaigns.[41] It is time to change that policy. Today the average broadcast television station is on the air for about twenty-nine thousand hours over a four-year period. If a station gave six hours of public-service time to the two major-party presidential candidates, that would come to a negligible 0.0002 percent of its overall programming time over that four-year period. Is that asking too much?

There are obviously many other important policy questions about public-service time, and my concern here is presidential elections only, not congressional elections, not primaries, not state and local elections. The biggest question, of course, is essentially the same as with the debates: Both television time and audience attention are limited, so which candidates are eligible to receive time? Surely not everyone. When Czechoslovakia held its first post-Soviet democratic election in 1990, it decided to give each of the two dozen parties contending for election four hours of free time during the forty days before the election. The Poles did the same, dividing forty hours of time among six presidential candidates in the month before the election. In both countries, voters were overwhelmed and lost interest in what, for almost all of them, was their country's first free election in memory.[42] Whatever method one uses to award and assign time, it should be as fair and objective as possible and presumably would rely at least in part on a quantitative test of the kind used by the Commission on Presidential Debates.

In 1996, after a push led by journalist Paul Taylor and a consortium of reform groups (which included Presidents Ford and Carter), the major U.S. broadcast networks and several cable news channels engaged in a public-service time experiment in the last two months of the presidential campaign, providing candidates time in segments that ran from one to five minutes in length.[43] A subsequent study of the experiment by the Annenberg Public Policy Center at the University of Pennsylvania was optimistic but critical. Voters who saw the candidates' segments found them "more useful" than the candidates' paid advertisements, but only 20 percent of the public ever saw or heard the ads, largely because the news organizations involved provided almost no publicity for them. Newspapers did not include them in their programming schedules, and they aired at too many different times, often embedded in regularly scheduled programs. Even many journalists did not know about them.[44]

I recognize the First Amendment issues related to whether Congress can constitutionally require broadcasters to provide public-service time. I believe it can. The public trustee concept for broadcasting has repeatedly been found constitutional by the Supreme Court, in 1943, 1969, 1994, and again in 1997.[45] In 1996, Congress passed and President Bill Clinton signed the 1996 Telecommunications Act, which carried the public trustee concept into the age of digital television.[46] In March 1998, President Clinton appointed a special commission to advise him, the Congress, and the FCC on the public-service obligations that should attend this spectrum grant. I served on that commission, led by Vice President Al Gore. We provided a thoughtful and wide-ranging set of recommendations. Neither Congress nor the FCC did anything with them. The question is still before us more than a decade later: What should be the public interest obligations of digital broadcasters? Is it too much to ask that candidates for president of the United States be granted public-service broadcast time to speak to the American people, using a resource the American people themselves own?

To give this proposal a strong start, the nation's public television stations should take the lead in offering public-service time to the qualified presidential candidates and other candidates for major public offices. While some public television stations are exemplary in this regard—most famously WTTW-TV, in my hometown of Chicago—the country's 356 Public Broadcasting Service (PBS) stations as a whole do just about as bad a job as their commercial counterparts in carrying local campaign debates for the races in their markets. More than 90 percent of the nation's gubernatorial, House, and Senate race debates are not carried at all by the public or commercial television stations in the markets where the races are happening—a shameful record.

4. Maintain the existing 15 percent public-support criterion for debate inclusion because it has worked well and has been approved repeatedly by the federal courts and the Federal Election Commission. However, once a candidate meets the standard for inclusion, he or she should be included in all the debates that follow irrespective of poll numbers. This issue is perhaps the most contentious of all concerning the debates, and as I have explained there is no perfect solution to it. The prevailing view at the Commission on Presidential Debates and supported by the Federal Election Commission is that only candidates who poll at least 15 percent public support and who are on enough state ballots to win the Electoral College vote should participate in the debates. Every election year, there are two hundred or more people who declare as candidates for the U.S. presidency. Of these, perhaps a dozen are on enough state ballots to win an Electoral College vote, though the last independent candidate to win *any* electoral votes was George Wallace in 1968: his American Independent Party won a block of five southern states and a total of 46 electoral votes. A line must be drawn somewhere. The purpose of the debates is not to springboard obscure candidates to national recognition but to present to the country the real choices to be made on Election Day.

Opponents argue that it is unfair as a matter of principle to exclude any candidate because in a democracy each has the right to be heard and every voter has the right to hear every candidate. A second objection is that denying minor-party and independent candidates an opportunity to debate is to deny them both credibility and an opportunity to build public support.[47]

It is true that third-party candidates in the United States face substantial obstacles to building public support, but those obstacles have nothing to do with the Commission on Presidential Debates. Federal law makes it much more difficult for third-party candidates to qualify for federal campaign funds,[48] and third-party candidates also have to negotiate ballot-access requirements on a state-by-state basis (to have a mathematical chance of winning the electoral vote). At a minimum that usually means collecting signatures on nominating petitions, a process that is time and labor intensive and potentially very costly. In 1992, for example, it cost Ross Perot $18 million to get on the ballot in all fifty states and the District of Columbia.[49]

Despite these and other obstacles, third parties have played an important role in American political history. In the twentieth century, the single most popular third-party movement was Theodore Roosevelt's progressive Bull Moose Party, which in the 1912 election won 27 percent of the popular vote with the immensely popular former president as its candidate. Six independent presidential candidates would have met the 15 percent public support criterion for debate inclusion required first by the League of Women Voters and today by the Commission for Presidential Debates: Roosevelt in 1912, Robert LaFollette in 1924, Henry Wallace in 1948, George Wallace in 1968, John Anderson in 1980, and Ross Perot in 1992.[50] Of course, none won office. As democracy scholar Robert Dahl once observed, the electoral record of third parties in America is one of "nearly total failure."[51]

From a broader historical viewpoint, however, electoral success is not the issue. Rather, the best argument for including third-party candidates is that third parties were the first to introduce many political innovations that Americans now take for granted: the direct election of senators, women's suffrage, the graduated income tax, railroad and utility regulation, high standards for civil service, and the legitimacy of labor unions and cooperatives, to name a few. Many of the programs that Franklin Roosevelt introduced in New Deal legislation had been first developed in the Progressive Party platforms of preceding decades.[52] Such profound changes to the electoral system, wrote historian John Hicks in 1933, "would seem to indicate that [a vote for a third party] is probably the most powerful vote that has ever been cast."[53] More recently, third-party candidacies of defecting southern Democrats, most importantly Wallace in 1968, transformed the platforms and composition of both major parties and helped launch the modern conservative era. However one chooses to read this historical record, it would be wrong to dismiss third parties in American politics as having no lasting legacy.

Third-party and independent candidates usually run in the first place to introduce ideas they believe the major-party candidates are ignoring. Some minor parties quite legitimately regard proselytizing, rather than vote getting, as their principal objective, and they participate in the electoral process for that purpose. When their ideas and proposals win public support, the major parties have historically adopted them as their own, with the result that the third parties thereupon have disappeared.[54] Perot, for example, transformed the 1992 presidential race by his singular focus on the budget deficit, which compelled both President Bush and Bill Clinton to take up that issue in their campaigns.[55] Wallace prompted Hubert Humphrey and Richard Nixon to talk about busing and racial segregation. Anderson gave a central place in his platform to energy policy and social security reform, issues that have grown more urgent since 1980. Including third parties in the debates, therefore, can push the major party candidates to address issues they might well prefer to avoid, prompt them to clarify their policies and programs, and require them to answer for their past decisions.

If poll results are to be believed, third-party participation in the debates will also energize an electorate in which large majorities say they are dissatisfied with the major-party candidates and want to see a viable third-party candidate emerge.[56] Turnout in presidential elections has consistently declined over the decades, and at least part of that decline is the result of voter dissatisfaction with the major parties.[57] Public opinion data show, for example, that between 1990 and 2000, even people who identified themselves as either Republican or Democrat never rated their party higher than 55 on a 100-point "feeling thermometer." Americans have as many negative as positive things to say about both of the major parties. In 2000, the American National Election Study examined public attitudes toward the major parties and could not find a majority who supported maintaining the two-party system (42 percent of the ANES sample identified themselves as independents). Only 38.3 percent of those polled wanted the system to remain unchanged, while just under 34 percent said they "wanted more parties to effectively challenge Democrats and Republicans." Another 30 percent, when asked, preferred candidates to run without party labels.[58] A 2002 telephone survey of 191,000 voters nationwide found a majority—53 percent—saying candidates from third parties should "always" be included in presidential debates. Ninety percent of the sample thought third-party candidates should have "at least some access" to presidential debates.[59]

So when and on what basis should third-party and independent candidates be included in debates? There are many counter-proposals to the Commission's 15 percent rule, but the most commonly suggested, discussed in the last chapter, is to base inclusion on a candidate's past election performance (and usually on their qualifying for federal funds as the result of having won 5 percent or more of the popular vote). Again, the Commission (and the League of Women Voters before it) has viewed that choice as both underinclusive and overinclusive because it rewards candidates for past performance instead of present popularity. By that standard, for instance, Perot would never have been included in the 1992 debates, even with his public support exceeding 40 percent.[60] Choosing instead to include candidates based on current public support gives voters a chance to get behind a candidate and actually make a difference to the campaign.[61]

It is important to note in this regard that many political professionals believe a significant third-party movement will emerge in the next few years, the result of voter dissatisfaction with the two major parties and the ability for a political movement to organize, raise funds, and build support online.[62] In June 2006, a virtual organization called Unity08.com opened shop on the Internet, its avowed purpose to nominate a third-party candidate for president in 2008 and get him or her on the ballot in all fifty states.[63] Unity08.com is the creation of Democrats Hamilton Jordan and Gerald Rafshoon (both from Jimmy Carter's 1976 campaign); Doug Bailey, a former media adviser for Gerald Ford and the founder of the political publication *Tip Sheet*; and Angus King, the former independent governor of Maine. According to Unity08's web site, "the leaders of both major parties are well intentioned people trapped in a flawed system. The two major parties are today simply neither relevant to the issues and challenges of the 21st Century nor effective in addressing them. As a result, most Americans have not been enthusiastic about the choices for President in recent elections, the key issues they ran on, or the manner in which the campaigns were conducted. A Unity ticket in office for one term or even taking part in just one election can bring new ideas, new integrity and new leaders to the fore."[64]

Unity08's plan is to convene an online third-party convention in early to mid-2008, following the first primaries. Any registered voter can be a delegate, and Unity08 will confirm delegates' identities by checking them against voter registration rolls. This virtual convention will have a centrist platform and nominate a bipartisan ticket. Unity08's goal is to enlist the support of 20 percent of the voting public on the theory that a group that large can determine who wins the 2008 elections.[65]

I believe that a viable independent candidate eventually will challenge the major-party candidates, if not in 2008 then soon thereafter. When that candidate emerges, the 15 percent standard will continue to work well. It serves the public interest because it preserves the integrity of the debates while also providing a healthy chance for the upward movement of new parties and candidates. The standard is far preferable to the measures the Commission used between 1988 and 1996. Twice since 1980 a candidate has been included in the presidential debates because he had 15 percent or better public support. In 1980 the League of Women Voters refused to buckle under pressure from President Carter not to include independent John Anderson when his poll numbers qualified him to debate.[66] In doing so, the League set a precedent that the Commission followed in 1992 when it included Ross Perot. That decision was difficult, as Perot's late reentry into the race made his poll numbers difficult to evaluate fairly. The Commission included him because his earlier support had been so high—at 40 percent or better—and because by the additional measures of public support the Commission used Perot seemed clearly to qualify. That same calculus led to a different decision in 1996, confusing and in some cases angering the public and the press. As a result, the Commission revised its inclusion standards for 2000, jettisoning the possibility of any subjective judgments in favor of purely quantitative ones.

The 15 percent rule was adopted in that process, and it has since survived legal challenges. To lower the public support threshold now would lead to new and prolonged rounds of litigation on the grounds that any new threshold one might propose—12 percent, 10 percent, 5 percent—is even more arbitrary. The 15 percent rule is high enough to compel third-party candidates to speak to all Americans and to be more than protest candidates.[67] It is low enough to ensure that Americans will have an opportunity to see, hear, and judge a serious independent candidate in a forum with the major-party candidates, something overwhelming numbers of voters say they want.

Importantly, I believe that once a candidate meets the 15 percent standard, he or she should stay in to the end no matter what happens in the polls. The purpose of the debates is to promote a healthy interplay of ideas; therefore the Commission's standard for inclusion should honor that purpose. Any candidate who meets its 15 percent standard—in addition to being on enough state ballots to win the electoral vote—has already accomplished more than all but a small handful of presidential candidates have in the last century. The Commission should treat those candidates with the same seriousness the public has accorded them. Once in the debates, they should stay in.

5. *The Commission on Presidential Debates should be much more transparent in its operations, financing, and governance.* The Commission is often perceived, fairly or not, as a rubber stamp for the two major parties. I use this characterization purposefully because it is so widespread among critics — both those who are shrill and uninformed and even some who are thoughtful and scholarly. Despite the Commission's consistent court victories in cases challenging its nonpartisanship, the fact is there is some history to the "bipartisan" label its critics attach to it. Both the Harvard and the Georgetown studies that in the 1980s led to the creation of the Commission talked about "bipartisan" efforts to establish the debates' future. The Harvard study that I led explicitly approached the issue this way, as did some of the political science scholars who commented on our proposals. I have explained this history in previous chapters, and I do not believe there was ever anything sinister about it. To the contrary.

But the Commission must now put the bipartisan history firmly to rest. The Commission should be transparent about its internal operations, including the process of nominating board members. The Commission should also make public any negotiations with the candidates concerning formats, dates, locations, and other operational details of the debates. If the candidates negotiate a memorandum of understanding, the Commission should not sign it, following its own example from the 2004 election, when it rejected the campaigns' memorandum out of hand. Rather the Commission should post the document on its Web page where all can see it. There is of course no reason the Commission should not accommodate the reasonable concerns of the campaigns, but any accommodation it does make must be done in the best interests of the voters, not the candidates.

A second important step is for the Commission to plan for the succession of its leadership. The two cochairs, Frank Fahrenkopf and Paul Kirk, have served in those roles since 1988, taking their leadership positions when they were still active as chairs of their respective parties. They have done a fine job and deserve the thanks of the voters. I have never seen or heard one partisan word from either man in his role on the Commission (or from any other member of the Commission's board). But the Commission now needs to plan for new leadership if it is to endure as an institution. Such a change represents an opportunity to further establish its important role in the presidential debates.

What kind of leadership does the Commission need? Ideally, persons who are respected citizens without connection to either major party and who are widely regarded as impartial. I will reach the age of eighty-two before the 2008 presidential debates and plan to leave the Commission after those debates. Younger blood is needed. And as the country grows increasingly independent in its voting preferences and habits, the membership of the Commission board should reflect that change.

Finally, the Commission needs to be more transparent about its finances. A favorite charge of critics is that CPD is in the pocket of its corporate sponsors (the true foes, the argument goes, to including third parties in the debates). The Commission should identify with specificity the sources of its modest revenues and the amounts those sources provide.[68] The Commission's Web site does identify its sponsors, the majority of which are other not-for-profits, but it does not say how much any donor gives in any one year.[69] Neither is it clear if sponsors are donors or, if they are, what they donate—cash, expertise, equipment, technical assistance, and so on.[70] The Commission's most complete election-year tax form, from 2000, includes five pages of data on cash donations ranging from $200,000 to $1 million but does not identify the donors. That information is available to IRS-registered 527 organizations but not to the general public. It should be.

6. *The Commission on Presidential Debates should make every possible innovative use of the Internet to broaden the appeal and informative power of the debates.* Long-time Republican political consultant Doug Bailey told *Washingtonian* magazine in 2006, "Our society never asked the question, 'How can television best serve our democracy?' Let's not make the same mistake with the new technologies. Going online, podcasts—these present us with new opportunities for public involvement. . . . Our system needs a jolt. This must come from people who haven't yet participated, which means mostly younger people."[71]

The Commission has done some good online work already, but it will be able to do much more as greater public access to broadband makes video files easier to download and view and unmoderated exchanges between citizens—that is, a parallel citizen debate held in conjunction with the televised ones—easier to manage. Another obvious option is to hold an online debate between the candidates, which could be particularly attractive to younger citizens, those under forty, among whom the long-term decline in civic interest is most pronounced.[72]

In 1998 and 2000, the Markle Foundation tried to harness the Internet to a nonpartisan project called "Web, White, and Blue," which included a "rolling cyber debate" that in 2000 ran from October 1 through November 8 and included as its virtual participants George W. Bush, Al Gore, Pat Buchanan (Reform Party), Harry Browne (Libertarian Party), Howard Phillips (Constitution Party), and John Hagelin (Natural Law Party). (The site was also open to Ralph Nader, the only candidate who chose not to participate.) For the candidates, the cyber-debate featured both a "message of the day" and a "question of the day." The candidates could respond to questions in any way they chose and at any length, using video, audio, text, or links to other sites, including their own.

Unfortunately, the cyber-debate failed to generate any enthusiasm from the candidates, who left the job of "participating" to communications consultants who typed in talking points from press releases and policy papers available elsewhere. Still, Web, White, and Blue succeeded in a limited way to bring together citizens, media, and politicians on agreeable terms in a common online forum.[73] Web, White, and Blue's own postexperiment research suggested that an Internet debate between or among candidates could in time succeed with the proper sponsor and promotion. The Commission is ideally suited to do this—and I believe that if it fails to do so someone else surely will.[74]

Finally, the Commission should use the Internet to increase public participation in the televised debates. The Commission, to its credit, has made online efforts to broaden the debates' reach. In 2000 and 2004, for example, people could go to the Commission's site or the sites of various nonprofit partners and identify issues they wanted discussed in the debates. The Commission has also tried several other online projects—among them postdebate surveys, real-time "debate chats," and a weekly online poll. Probably the Commission's most successful program involving the debates, however, is a real world discussion, DebateWatch. Begun in 1996, the first DebateWatch brought together more than six hundred voters in seventeen U.S. cities to watch the debates, discuss them, and then share their suggestions for improvement with the Commission. Many voters found these face-to-face discussions the most useful and enjoyable part of the campaign. And most important, voters found they could disagree without becoming disagreeable.

* * *

One of the rich ironies of our presidential debates is that they were first proposed by a man who did not often watch or particularly like television.

When Governor Adlai Stevenson lived in the executive mansion in Springfield, Illinois, there was one television set there, but it almost never worked. In 1952, Adlai was traveling and I was working in my office in the mansion when Vice President Nixon gave his "Checkers" speech. I had to call my wife Jo, at home with our baby daughter Nell, so she could tell me what Nixon was saying. On the other line was the governor, to whom I relayed the news. When Adlai wanted to watch a football or baseball game, he would go to the home of Bill Flanagan, his press assistant. According to Porter McKeever, one of several Stevenson biographers, Adlai had never seen NBC's *Meet the Press* when he appeared on the program as a presidential candidate in 1952. That campaign was the highlight of a remarkable political career by a man who won only one election, serving for one term as Illinois governor. Adlai never had a chance against General Dwight Eisenhower, a popular war hero, and he knew it. But he ran anyway, and again in 1956, and in doing so he inspired millions of Americans. He believed in the idealism inherent to our political system, and he despised those who cynically appealed to our fears instead of our hopes.

As a politician, Adlai Stevenson would never have made it in a world of Madison Avenue advertisers, electronic mailing lists, political media consultants, television sound bites, and YouTube mash-ups. Even in his own day he was too thoughtful to fully understand the requirements of a modern presidential campaign. When in 1952 he learned the Eisenhower campaign would be airing television commercials, he responded, "What the hell do they think the White House is, a box of cornflakes?"[75] Adlai told me that campaigns should be educational for candidates as well as the voters. His idea of a responsible and informative campaign was to consult people like historian Bernard De Voto, Judge Carl McGowan, biographer John Bartlow Martin, lawyer and diplomat Wilson Wyatt, economist John Kenneth Galbraith, historian Arthur Schlesinger Jr., and Bill Blair, counselor, all of whom met regularly in a cramped room on the third floor of the decrepit old Elks Club on Sixth Street in Springfield. It is hard to imagine a presidential candidate doing such a thing today.

That building on Sixth Street is gone now, and of course so is Adlai. He died in 1965 of a heart attack. He had described Eleanor Roosevelt on her death as having "a glow that warmed the world," and anyone who ever knew Adlai Stevenson would say the same of him.

Today the glow that survives him is on television, every four years. I have been most fortunate in my own private life and in public service to be engaged for almost a half-century in trying to fulfill his vision for "great debates." I believe Americans have succeeded beyond what even Adlai thought possible, even if what we accomplished is not what he, nor I, nor my friend Frank Stanton first envisioned when that work began in CBS's Chicago studio in September 1960. The American presidential debates now have a record of continuity unmatched in the democratic world. The public demands them. That success has yielded another: our presidential candidates can no longer refuse to participate. We have established a great and enduring tradition. I am optimistic, as I know Adlai would be. We have an obligation to make the debates a still better public service, a gift to our country and to our children and grandchildren.

Memorandum of Understanding between the Bush and Kerry Campaigns, 2004

[Not signed or agreed to by the Commission on Presidential Debates]

MEMORANDUM OF UNDERSTANDING

This Memorandum of Understanding constitutes an agreement between Kerry-Edwards, '04, Inc. and Bush-Cheney, '04, Inc. (the "Campaigns") regarding the rules that will govern debates in which the campaigns participate in 2004. This agreement shall be binding upon the Bush-Cheney and Kerry-Edwards Campaign and, provided it agrees to sponsor the debates by executing this agreement on or before September 22, 2004, upon the Commission on Presidential Debates (the "Commission").

1. **Number, Dates, Time, Locations, Topics**
   (a) Presidential Debates

Date	Location
Thursday, September 30	University of Miami Coral Gables, Florida
Friday, October 8	Washington University in St. Louis St. Louis, Missouri
Wednesday, October 13	Arizona State University Tempe, Arizona

   (b) Vice Presidential Debate

Date	Location
Tuesday, October 5	Case Western Reserve University Cleveland, Ohio

   (c) Each debate shall being at 9 p.m., Eastern Daylight Time.
   (d) The parties agree that they will not (1) issue any challenges for additional debates, (2) appear at any other debate or adversarial forum with any other presidential or vice presidential candidate, or (3) accept any television or radio air time offers that involve a debate format or otherwise involve the simultaneous appearance of more than one candidate.

(e) The topic of the September 30 debate shall be foreign policy and homeland security. The topic of the October 13 debate shall be economic and domestic policy. The October 5 vice presidential debate and the October 8 presidential debate shall not be limited by topic and shall include an equal number of questions related to foreign policy and homeland security on the one hand and economic and domestic policy on the other.

2. **Sponsorship**

The two campaigns will participate in four debates sponsored by the Commission. However, if the Commission fails to execute this agreement on or before September 22, 2004, the two campaigns shall each have the option of terminating this agreement, or by agreement between them, seeking other sponsors for some or all of the proposed debates. The parties agree that the Commission's Nonpartisan Candidate Selection Criteria for 2004 General Election Debate Participation shall apply in determining the candidates to be invited to participate in these debates.

3. **Participants**

If one or more candidates from campaigns other than the two signatories is [sic] invited to participate pursuant to those Selection Criteria, those candidates shall be included in the debates, if those candidates accept the terms of this agreement. Any modifications to this agreement must be agreed upon by each of the signatories to this agreement as well as all other candidates selected to join the debates.

4. **Moderator**

(a) Each debate will have a single moderator.

(b) The parties have accepted the Commission's recommendations of the below listed moderators, provided that each proposed moderator executes a copy of this agreement at least seven (7) days prior to the debate that individual is to moderate in order to evidence his or her understanding and acceptance of, and agreement to, the provisions hereof pertaining to moderators. If any proposed moderator fails to execute a copy of this agreement at least seven (7) days prior to the proposed date of the debate he or she is to moderate, the two campaigns will agree upon and select a different individual to moderate that debate:

   i.   Jim Lehrer for the first presidential debate, September 30, 2004 at the University of Miami;

   ii. Charles Gibson for the second presidential debate, October 8, 2004 at Washington University in St. Louis;

   iii. Bob Schieffer for the third presidential debate, October 13, 2004 at Arizona State University, and;

   iv. Gwen Ifill for the vice presidential debate, October 5, 2004 at the Case Western Reserve University.

5. **Rules Applicable to All Debates**

The following rules shall apply to each of the four debates:

(a) Each debate shall last for ninety (90) minutes.

(b) For each debate there shall be no opening statements, but each candidate may make a two (2) minute closing statement.

(c) No props, notes, charts, diagrams, or other writings or other tangible things may be brought into the debate by any candidate. Neither candidate may reference or cite any specific individual sitting in a debate audience at any time during a debate. If a candidate references or cites any specific individual(s) in a debate audience, or if a candidate uses a prop, note, or other writing or other tangible thing during a debate, the moderator must interrupt and explain that reference or citation to the specific individual(s) or the use of the prop, note, or other writing or thing violates the debate rules agreed to by that candidate.

(d) Notwithstanding subparagraph 5(c), the candidates may take notes during the debate on the size, color, and type of paper each prefers and using the type of pen or pencil that each prefers. Each candidate must submit to the staff of the Commission prior to the debate all such paper and any pens or pencils with which a candidate may wish to take notes during the debate, and the staff of the Commission will place such, paper, pens, and pencils on the podium, table, or other structure to be used by the candidate in that debate.

(e) Neither film footage nor video footage nor any audio excepts from the debates may be used publicly by either candidate's campaign through any means, including but not limited to, radio, television, internet, or videotapes, whether broadcast or distributed in any other manner.

(f) The candidates may not ask each other direct questions, but may ask rhetorical questions.

(g) The order of questioning and closing statements shall be determined as follows:

    i. The Commission will conduct a coin toss at least seventy-two (72) hours before the first presidential debate. At that time, the winner of the coin toss shall have the option of choosing, for the September 30 debate, either (a) whether to take the first or second question, or (b) whether to give the first or second closing statement. At that time, the loser of the coin toss will have the choice of question order or closing statement order not exercised by the winner of the coin toss. For the October 8 debate, the loser of the coin toss shall have the option of choosing either (a) whether to take the first or second question, or (b) whether to give the first or second closing statement, with the winner of the coin toss having the choice of question order or closing statement not exercised by the winner of the coin toss. The Commission shall set a time at least seventy-two (72) hours before the October 8 debate at which the candidates shall make their choices for that debate.

    ii. For the October 13 debate, the order of questioning and closing statements shall be determined by a separate coin toss in the same manner as the September 30 debate, to take place at least seventy-two (72) hours before the debate.

   iii. The order of questioning and closing statements for the October 5 vice presidential debate shall be determined by a separate coin toss in the same manner as for the September 30 debate, to take place at least seventy-two (72) hours before the debate.

(h) Each candidate shall determine the manner by which he prefers to be addressed by the moderator and shall communicate this to the Commission, at least forty-eight (48) hours before the September 30 debate.

(i) Whether or not a debate runs beyond the planned ending time, each candidate shall be entitled to make a closing statement in accordance with subparagraph (b). The Commission shall use its best efforts to ensure that the TV networks carry the entire debate even if it runs past the specific ending time.

(j) No question shall be asked of a candidate by the moderator if less than six (6) minutes remain in the scheduled time of the debate.

(k) The candidates shall not address each other with proposed pledges.

(l) In each debate, the moderator shall:

   i. open and close the debate and enforce all time limits. In each instance where a candidate exceeds the permitted time for comment, the moderators shall interrupt and remind both the candidate and the audience of the expiration of the time limit and call upon such candidate to observe the strict time limits which have been agreed upon herein by stating, "I'm sorry . . . [Senator Kerry or President Bush as the case may be] . . . your time is up";

   ii. use his or her best efforts to ensure that the questions are reasonably well balanced in all debate and within the designated subject matter areas of the September 30 and October 13 debates in terms of addressing a wide range of issues of major public interest facing the United States and the world;

   iii. vary the topics on which he or she questions the candidates and ensure that the topics of the questions are fairly apportioned between the candidates;

   iv. use best efforts to ensure that the two candidates speak for approximately equal amounts of time during the course of each debate, and;

   v. use any reasonable method to ensure that the agreed-upon format is followed by the candidates and the audience.

6. **Additional Rules Applicable to September 30 and October 13 Debates**
For the September 30 and October 13 debates, the candidates will appear at podiums. The September 30 and October 13 debates shall be governed by the rules set forth in section 5 and the following additional rules:

(a) There shall be no audience participation in the September 30 and October 13 debates. After the start of each debate and in the event of and in each instance whereby an audience member(s) attempts to participate in the debate by any means thereafter, the moderator shall instruct the audience to refrain from any participation in the debates as described in section 9(a) (viii) below. The moderator shall direct the first question to the candidate determined by the procedure set forth in subparagraph 5(g). The candidate receiving the question shall be entitled to give an opening response not to exceed two (2) minutes, and thereafter the other candidate shall be permitted to comment on the question and/or the first candidate's answer for up to one and one-half (1½) minutes. Thereafter the moderator in his discretion may extend the discussion for a period of time not to exceed sixty (60) seconds, but the moderator shall begin each such discussion by calling upon the candidate who first received the question. To the extent that the moderator opens extended discussion, the moderator shall use beat efforts to ensure that each candidate has a maximum of approximately thirty (30) seconds to comment in the extended discussion period.

(b) The moderator shall then ask a question of the other candidate, and the answer, comments by the other candidate, and extension of discussion by the moderator shall be conducted as set out in paragraph 6(a) above for the first question. Thereafter the moderator shall follow the procedure in paragraph 6(a) above by asking a question of the candidate and shall continue with question of the candidates in rotation until the time for closing statements occurs.

(c) During the extended discussion of a question, no candidate may speak for more than thirty (30) seconds.

(d) The moderator shall manage the debate so that the candidates address at least sixteen (16) questions.

(e) At no time during these debates shall either candidate move from their designated area behind their respective podiums.

7. **Additional Rules Applicable to October 8 Debate**
The October 8 debate will be conducted in an audience participation ("town hall") format. This debate shall be governed by the rules set forth in section 5 and the following additional rules:

(a) There shall be no audience participation in the October 8 debate other than as described below. Other than an audience member asking a question as permitted by this section, at the start of the October 8 debate and in the event of and in each instance whereby an audience member(s) attempts to participate in the debate by any means thereafter, the moderator shall instruct the audience to refrain from any participation in the debate as described in section 9(a)(viii) below. The moderator shall facilitate audience members in asking questions to each of the candidates, beginning with the candidate determined by the procedure set forth in subparagraph 5(h). The candidate to whom the question is initially directed shall have up to two (2) minutes to respond, after which the other candidate shall have up to one and one-half (1½) minutes to respond to the question and/or to comment on the first candidate's answer. Thereafter, the moderator, in his or her discretion, may extend the discussion of that question for sixty (60) seconds, but the moderator shall begin each such discussion by calling up on the candidate who first received the question. The moderator shall balance additional discussion of the question with the interest in addressing a wide range of topics during the debate. To the extent that the moderator opens extended discussion, the moderator shall use best efforts to ensure that each candidate has a maximum of approximately thirty (30) seconds to comment in the extended discussion period.

(b) After completion of the discussion of the first question, the moderator shall call upon an audience member to direct a question to the candidate to whom the first question was not directed, and follow the procedures in this paragraph by calling upon another audience member to ask a question of the first candidate and shall continue facilitating the questions of the candidates in rotation until the time for closing statements occurs.

(c) During the extended discussion of a question, no candidate may speak for more than thirty (30) seconds.

(d) The audience members shall not ask follow-up questions or otherwise participate in the extended discussion, and the audience member's microphone shall be turned off after he or she completes asking the question.

(e) Prior to the start of the debate, audience members will be asked to submit their questions in writing to the moderator. No third party, including both the Commission and the campaigns, shall be permitted to see the questions. The moderator shall approve and select all the questions to be posed by the audience members to the candidates. The moderator shall ensure that the audience members pose to the candidates an equal number of questions on foreign policy and homeland security on the one hand and economic and domestic policy on the other. The moderator will further review the questions and eliminate any questions that the moderator deems inappropriate. At least seven (7) days before the October 8 debate the moderator shall develop, and describe to the campaigns, a method for selecting questions at random while assuring that questions are reasonably well balanced in terms of addressing a wide range of issues of major public interest facing the United States and the world. Each question selected will be asked by the audience member submitting that question. If any audience member poses a question or makes a statement that is in any material way different than the question that the audience member earlier submitted to the moderator for review, the moderator will cut-off the questioner and advise the audience that such non-reviewed questions are not permitted. Moreover, the Commission shall take appropriate step to cut-off the microphone of any such

audience member that attempts to pose any question or statement
different than that previously posed to the moderator for review.

(f) The debate will take place before a live audience of between 100 and
150 persons who shall be seated and who describe themselves as
likely voters who are "soft" Bush supporters or "soft" Kerry supporters as to their 2004 presidential vote. The number of "soft" Bush supporters shall equal the amount of "soft" Kerry supporters in the audience. The moderator shall ensure that an equal number of "soft"
Bush supporters and "soft" Kerry supporters pose questions to the
candidates. These participants will be selected by the Gallup Organization ("Gallup"). Gallup shall have responsibility for selecting the
nationally demographically representative group of voters. At least
fourteen (14) days prior to October 8, Gallup shall provide a comprehensive briefing on the selection methodology to the campaigns, and
both the Kerry-Edwards Campaign and Bush-Cheney Campaign shall
approve the methodology. Either campaign may raise objections on
the methodology to Gallup and to the Commission within twenty-
four (24) hours of the briefing.

(g) Participants selected shall not be contacted directly or indirectly by
the campaigns before the debate. The Commission shall not contact
the participants before the debate other than for logistical purposes.

8. **Additional Rules Applicable to October 5 Debate**
For the October 5 vice presidential debate, the candidates will be seated at
a table with the moderator. This debate shall be governed by the rules set
forth in sections 5 and 6. There shall be no audience participation in the
October 5 vice presidential debate. At the start of the October 5 debate
and in the even of and in each instance whereby an audience member(s)
attempts to participate in the debate by any means thereafter, the moderator shall instruct the audience to refrain from any participation in the
debate as described in section 9(a)(viii) below.

9. **Staging**
(a) The following rules apply to each of the four debates:
    i.   All staging arrangements for the debates not specifically ad-
dressed in this agreement shall be jointly addressed by representatives of the two campaigns.
    ii. The Commission will conduct a coin toss at least seventy-two (72)
hours before the September 30 debate. At that time, the winner
of the coin toss shall have the option of choosing stage position
for the September 30 debate; the loser of the coin toss will have
first choice of the stage position of the October 8 debate. The
loser of the coin toss or his representative shall communicate his
choice by written facsimile to the Commission and to the other
campaign at least seventy-two (72) hours before the October 8
debate. The stage position for the October 13 debate will be determined by a coin toss to take place at least seventy-two (72)
hours before the debate. The stage position for the October 5 vice

presidential debate will be determined by a separate coin toss to take place at least seventy-two (72) hours before the debate.

iii. For the September 30, October 8, and October 13 debates, the candidates shall enter the stage upon a verbal cue by the moderator after the program goes on the air, proceed to center stage, shake hands, and proceed directly to their positions behind their podiums or their stools in the case of the October 8 debate. For the October 5 vice presidential debate, the candidates shall be pre-positioned before the program goes on the air, and immediately after the program goes on the air the candidates shall shake hands.

iv. Except as provided in subparagraph (d)(viii) of this paragraph 9, TV cameras will be locked into place during all debate. They may, however, tilt or rotate as needed.

v. Except as provided in subparagraph (d)(viii), TV coverage during the question and answer period shall be limited to shots of the candidates or moderator and in no case shall any television shots be taken of any member of the audience (including candidates' family members) from the time the first question is asked until the conclusion of the closing statements. When a candidate is speaking, either in answering a question or making his closing statement, TV coverage will be limited to the candidate speaking. There will be no TV cut-aways to any candidate who is not responding to a question while another candidate is answering a question or to a candidate who is not giving a closing statement while another candidate is doing so.

vi. The camera locked at the rear of the stage shall be used only to take shots of the moderator.

vii. For each debate, each candidate shall have a camera-mounted, timing system described in section 9 (b)(vi) below, which shall be placed such that they are visible to the debate audiences and television viewers.

viii. All members of the debate audience will be instructed by the moderator before the debate goes on the air and by the moderator after the debate goes on the air not to applaud, speak, or otherwise participate in the debate by any means other than by silent observation, except as provided by the agreed upon rules of the October 8 town hall debate. In the even of and in each instance whereby an audience member(s) attempts to participate in a debate by any means, the moderator shall instruct the audience to refrain from any participation. The moderator shall use his or her best efforts to encore this provision.

ix. The Commission shall use best efforts to maintain an appropriate temperature according to industry standards for the entire debate.

x. Each candidate shall be permitted to have complete, private production and technical briefing and walk-through ("Briefing") at the location of the debate on the day of the debate. The order of the Briefing shall be determined by agreement, or, failing candidate agreement, a coin flip. Each candidate will have a maximum of one (1) hour for this Briefing. No media will be allowed into the auditorium where the debate will take place during a candidate's Briefing. All persons, including but not limited to the media, other candidates and their representatives, and the employees or other agents of the Commission, other than those necessary to conduct the Briefing, shall vacate the debate site while a candidate has his Briefing. The Commission will provide to each candidate's representatives a written statement and plan which describes the measures to be taken by the Commission to ensure the complete privacy of all Briefings.

xi. The color and style of the backdrop will be recommended by the Commission and mutually determined by representatives of the campaigns. The Commission shall make its recommendation known to the campaigns at least seventy-two (72) hours before each debate. The backdrops behind each candidate shall be identical.

xii. The set will be completed and lit no later than 3 p.m. at the debate site on the day before the debate will occur.

xiii. Each candidate may use his own makeup person, and adequate facilities shall be provided at the debate site for makeup.

xiv. In addition to Secret Service personnel, the President's military aide, and the President's physician and the Vice President's military aide and the Vice President's physician, each candidate will be permitted to have one (1) pre-designated staff member in the wings or in the immediate backstage area during the debate at a location to be mutually agreed upon by representatives of the campaigns at each site. All other staff must vacate the wings or immediate backstage areas no later than five (5) minutes before the debate commences. A PL phone line will be provided between each candidate's staff work area and the producer.

xv. Other than security personnel not more than two (2) aides will accompany each candidate on the stage before the program begins.

xvi. Each candidate shall be allowed to have one (1) professional still photographer present on the stage before the debate begins and in the wings during the debate as desired and on the stage immediately upon the conclusion of the debate. No photos shall be taken from the wings by these photographers during the debate. Photos taken by these photographers may be distributed to the press as determined by each candidate.

(b) In addition to the rules in subparagraph (a) the following rules apply
to the September 30 and October 13 debates:

i.   The Commission shall construct the podiums and each shall be
identical to view from the audience side. The podiums shall
measure fifty (50) inches from the stage floor to the outside top
of the podium facing the audience and shall measure forty-eight
(48) inches from the stage floor to the top of the inside podium
writing surface facing the candidates, and otherwise shall be
constructed in the style and specifications recommended by the
Commission, shown in attachment A. There shall be no writings or markings of any kind on the fronts of the podiums. No
candidate shall be permitted to use risers or any other devise to
create an impression of elevated height, and no candidate shall
be permitted to use chairs, stools, or other seating devices during the debate.

ii. Each podium shall have installed a fixed hardwired microphone, and an identical microphone to be used as backup per
industry standards.

iii. The podiums will be equally canted toward the center of the
stage at a degree to be determined by the Commission's producer. The podiums shall be ten (10) feet apart; such distance
shall be measured from the left-right center of a podium to the
left-right center of the other podium.

iv. The moderator will be seated at a table so as to be positioned in
front, between, and equidistant from the candidates, and between the cameras to which the candidates direct their answers.

v.   As soon as possible, the Commission shall submit for joint consultation with the campaigns a diagram for camera placement.

vi. At least seven (7) days before the September 30 debate, the
Commission shall recommend a system, to be used as a model
for each successive debate, of visible and audible time cues and
placement subject to approval by the campaigns. Such a system
shall be comprised of camera mounted timing lights placed in
the line of sight of each candidate and additional timing lights
that are clearly visible to both the debate audiences and television viewers. Time cues in the form of colored lights will be
given to the candidates and the moderator when there are thirty
(30) seconds remaining, fifteen (15) seconds remaining, and
five (5) seconds remaining, respectively for the two (2) minute,
one and one-half (1½) minute, and sixty (60) second response
times permitted under section 6(a). Pursuant to section 5(1)(i)
the moderators shall enforce the strict time limits described in
this agreement. The Commission shall provide for an audible
cue announcing the end of time for each candidate's responses,
rebuttals and rejoinder time periods to be used in the event the
moderators fail to take action to enforce the strict time limits

described in this Agreement. The audible cue shall be clearly audible to both candidates, and the debate audiences and television viewers. The Commission shall commence the use of the audible cue and continue its use through the conclusion of any debate where a moderator fails to take action described in section 5(1)(i) after two (2) instances in which either candidate has exceeded the time for responses, rebuttals, or rejoinders described in this Agreement.

(c) In addition to the rules in subparagraph (a), the following rules apply to the October 5 vice presidential debate:

   i.   The Commission shall construct the table according to the style and specifications proposed by the Commission in consultation with each campaign. The moderator shall be facing the candidates with his or her back to the audience.

   ii.   The chairs shall be swivel chairs that can be locked in place, and shall be of equal height.

   iii. Each candidate and the moderator shall have a wireless lapel microphone, and an identical microphone to be used as a backup per industry standards.

   iv.   At least seven (7) days before the October 5 debate the Commission shall recommend a system of time cues and placement subject to approval by both campaigns and consistent with the visual and audible time cues described in section 9(b)(vi).

   v.   As soon as possible, the Commission shall submit for joint consultation with each campaign a diagram for camera placement.

   vi.   The candidates shall remain seated throughout the debate.

(d) In addition to the rules in subparagraph (a), the following rules apply to the October 8 debate:

   i.   The candidates shall be seated on stools before the audience, which shall be seated in approximately a horseshoe arrangement as symmetrically as possible around the candidates. The precise staging arrangement will be determined by the Commission's producer subject to the approval of representatives of both campaigns.

   ii.   The stools shall be identical and have backs and a footrest and shall be approved by the candidates' representatives.

   iii. Each candidate shall have a place to put a glass of water and paper and pens or pencils for taking notes (in accordance with subparagraph 5(d)) of sufficient height to allow note taking while sitting on the stool, and which shall be designed by the Commission, subject to the approval of representatives of both campaigns.

   iv.   Each candidate may move about in a predesignated area, as proposed by the Commission in consultation with each campaign, and may not leave that area while the debate is underway. The pre-designated area of the candidates may not overlap.

v.   Each candidate shall have a choice of either wireless hand held microphone or wireless lapel microphone to allow him to move about as provided for in subparagraph (iv) above and to face different directions while responding to questions from the audience.

vi.   As soon as possible, the Commission shall submit for joint consideration by the campaigns a diagram for camera placement.

vii. At least seven (7) days before the October 8 debate the Commission shall recommend a system of time cues subject to approval by both campaigns, and consistent with the visual and audible cues described in sections 9(b)(vi).

viii. Notwithstanding sections 9(a)(iv) and 9(a)(v) a roving camera may be used for shots of an audience member only during the time that audience member is asking a question.

ix.   Prior to the start of the debate neither the moderator nor any other person shall engage in a "warm up" session with the audience by engaging in a question or answer session or by delivering preliminary remarks.

10. **Ticket Distribution and Seating Arrangements**

(a)   The Commission shall be responsible for printing and ensuring security of all tickets to all debates. Each campaign shall be entitled to receive directly from the Commission one-third of the available tickets (excluding those allocated to the participating audience in the October 8 debate), with the remaining one-third going to the Commission.

(b)   In the audience participation debate, the participating audience shall be separated from any nonparticipating audience, and steps shall be taken to ensure that the participating audience is admitted to the debate site without contact with the campaigns, the media, or the nonparticipating audience.

(c)   The Commission shall allocate ticket to the two (2) campaigns in such a manner to ensure that supporters of each candidate are interspersed with supporters of the other candidate. For the September 30, October 5, and October 13 debates, the family members of each candidate shall be seated in the front row, diagonally across from the candidate directly in his line of sight while seated or standing at the podium. For the October 8 debate, the family members of each candidate shall be seated as mutually agreed by representatives of the campaigns.

(d)   Any media seated in the auditorium shall be accommodated only in the last two (2) rows of the auditorium farthest from the stage. Two (2) still photo stands may be positioned near either side of the television camera stands located in the audience. (A media center with all necessary feeds will be otherwise available.)

(e)   Tickets will be delivered by the Commission to the chairman of each candidate's campaign or his designated representative by 12:00 noon on the day preceding each debate. The Commission will invite from its allotment (two (2) tickets each) an agreed upon list of officeholders such as the U.S. Senate and House Majority and Minority Leaders, the Governor and Lieutenant Governor of the State holding the debate, an appropriate list of other public officials and the President of the University sponsoring the debate. The Commission shall not favor one candidate over the other in the distribution of its allotment of tickets.

11. **Dressing Rooms/Holding Rooms**

(a) Each candidate shall have a dressing room available of adequate size so as to provide private seclusion for that candidate and adequate space for the staff the candidate desires to have in this area. The two (2) dressing rooms shall be comparable in size and in quality and in proximity and access to the debate stage.

(b) An equal number of other backstage rooms will be available for other staff members of each candidate. Each candidate shall have a minimum of eight (8) such rooms, five (5) of which shall be in the debate facility itself, and three (3) of which shall be located next to the press center. The rooms located next to the media center shall be located so that each campaign has equal proximity and ease of access to the media center. Each of the eight (8) rooms shall be a minimum of 10 feet by 10 feet. All of these rooms shall be furnished as deemed necessary by the candidates' representatives. Each candidate's rooms shall be reasonably segregated from those designated for the other candidate. If sufficient space to accommodate the above needs is not available at a particular debate facility, the Commission shall provide trailers or alternative space mutually agreeable to the candidates' representatives. Space that is comparable in terms of size, location, and quality shall be provided to the two campaigns. These rooms shall be made available at least seventy-two (72) hours in advance of the beginning of each debate. Each campaign may, at its own cost, rent one or more additional trailers so long as the Commission and authorities responsible for traffic and security do not object.

(c) The number of individuals allowed in these rooms or trailers shall be determined by each candidate. The Commission shall issue backstage passes (if needed) to the candidates' representatives as requested.

(d) The Commission shall provide each candidate with a direct television feed from the production truck to two (2) monitors placed in the candidate's dressing room and staff holding rooms as requested by the candidates' representatives. In addition, the Commission shall provide at least one (1) additional functioning TV set for each of the eight (8) rooms.

12. **Media**

(a) Each candidate will receive not fewer than thirty (30) press passes for the Media Center during the debate and more if mutually agreed upon by the campaigns.

(b) Each candidate will be allowed to have an unlimited number of people in the Media Center upon the conclusion of the debate.

(c) The Commission will be responsible for all media credentialing.

13. **Survey Research**

The sponsor of the debate agrees that it shall not, prior to two days after the Presidential Inauguration 2005, release publicly or to the media or otherwise make publicly available any survey research (including polls or focus group results or date) concerning the performance of the candidates in the debate or the preferences of the individuals surveyed for either candidate.

14. **Complete Agreement**

This memorandum of understanding constitutes the entire agreement between the parties concerning the debates in which the campaigns will participate in 2004.

15. **Amendments**

This Agreement will not be changed or amended except in writing signed by those persons who signed this Agreement or their designees.

16. **Ratification and Acknowledgement**

The undersigned moderators selected by the Commission agree to the terms contained herein and agree to fulfill their responsibilities as described in the Agreement.

Record of First Negotiations between the Ford and Carter Campaigns, 1976

NEGOTIATION MEETING NO. 1

August 26, 1976

ACTIONS	LEAGUE'S ORIGINAL PROPOSAL
	Number:
Not determined	Four or five
Tentative Agreement on 3	3 or 4 for Presidential Candidates
No agreement	1 for Vice Presidential Candidates
	Dates:
Thursday, Sept. 23	Tuesday, Sept. 28
	Week of Oct. 11
	Week of Oct. 18
No agreement	Week of Oct. 25
	If 5th Debate, week of Sept. 20
	Length:
	No less than one hour
No agreement	No more than 90 minutes
	Correspondents:
Agreement	Three, preferably
	—one from Print
	—one from Broadcast
	—one from Periodical or Wire Services

	Moderators:
Agreement, professional moderators . .	Alternate between 3 Chairs and Chairman of the Education Fund

ACTIONS

	Themes:
No agreement on: 1) any of these 2) if themes, which ones	Debate 1—America's Challenge at Home (If a 5th debate, have second on The Economy) Debate 2—America's Goal in The World Debate 3—(The Vice Presidency, Subject to be determined) Debate 4—Making Government Work: The Role of the Presidency

	First Half-Hour or 40 Minutes:
Agreement	No opening statements Questions from panel of journalists
Agreement: for entire length of each debate plus follow-up within each sequence	Alternate questioning from one candidate to another, each being able to respond to the answers of the other 2-1/2 minute limit on answers 1-1/2 minute limit on comments

	Second Half-Hour or 20 Minutes:
Agreed to drop	Direct questioning between candidates 3 minute closing, candidate A
Agreement	3 minute closing, candidate B

OTHER AGREEMENTS

1. Re: panelists selection	Each side submit a list of names (three times as many as needed), debate by debate. Project selects and informs candidates. Don't exclude reporters covering the candidates.
2. Re: moderators	Rotate moderator. Candidates will submit to Project possible choices.
3. Re: candidates	No notes to be used.

Section 312 of the Communications Act: "Reasonable Access" for Candidates for Federal Office

Section 312 of the Communications Act has existed since 1934, but in 1972 Congress added a critical subsection that created a right of "reasonable access" to the broadcast media for candidates running for federal office.[1] Congress added the provision as part of the 1971 Federal Election Campaign Act; before then, candidates' right of access had been limited by Section 315, whose equal time provisions applied only if a broadcaster, at its own discretion, provided time to a competing candidate for the same office. Discretion was the key: if a broadcaster declined to provide time to any candidate, no candidate had an independent, affirmative right of access to airtime.

The idea behind change in the law was "to give candidates for public office greater access to the media so that they may better explain their stand on the issues, and thereby more fully and completely inform the voters."[2] Theoretically, at least, law's affirmative access right also greatly enhances the ability of minor-party candidates for federal office to reach a mass audience, since they can now make a bid for time without having to rely on the equal opportunities rule. To further these goals, the law also seeks to reduce the costs of that access through an amendment to Section 315 requiring broadcasters to sell time to candidates at preferential rates.[3]

The legislative history of Section 312(a)(7) is thin, but what there is of it focuses overwhelmingly on Congress's desire to limit what it saw as the rocketing costs of political campaigns. The Senate Commerce Committee record, for example, talks about the "inherent" obligation that broadcasters have under the public interest standard to allow candidates "use" of the airwaves that goes beyond broadcaster discretion.[4] For whatever reason, Congress decided in Section 312 that this obligation applied only to candidates for federal office, while the equal opportunity rule in Section 315 applied to candidates for state and local office.[5] The result is that under Section 312 broadcasters have to give preferential treatment to federal campaigns at the expense of state and local candidates, even when state and local races may be more important, or more hotly contested, than a contest for federal office.[6]

The statute itself declares that broadcasters who flatly refuse to sell time to candidates can have their licenses revoked, but the legislative history is vague on just what constitutes a "reasonable" candidate request for time. In 1972, the Federal

Communications Commission devised guidelines to try to resolve that question, among other things deciding that the law's access obligations went into effect forty-five days before a primary election and sixty days before a general or special election.[7] The meaning of "reasonable," according to the Commission, lay first with the broadcaster, which could balance its own programming interests and those of its viewers with a candidate's request for time. The FCC would get involved only if the refusal to sell time was clearly unreasonable or if a broadcaster acted in bad faith in rejecting an initial request for time. Bad faith, presumably, would involve actual broadcaster hostility to a candidate, but it is easy to imagine instances in which a broadcaster's refusal to sell time, or its counter-offer to a candidate, is based entirely on its own interests. The FCC, therefore, has made it clear that the law applies to purchases candidates wish to make in primetime and to any time that a broadcaster ordinarily offers to commercial advertisers; broadcasters, in other words, cannot discriminate against federal candidates in favor of better-paying commercial advertisers.[8]

Readers may wonder how broadcasters can charge top dollar for time that by law is supposed to be sold at the "lowest unit rate." The short answer is that broadcasters can easily game the system. Charging higher rates is clearly inconsistent with the law, but in practice a broadcaster's advertising rate card means almost nothing. The purchase of time is always a negotiation, no matter who the advertiser may be, and candidates rarely know anything about that process. Even if he or she does, if the campaign is not for a federal office the station does not have to sell time under 312(a)(7), though under Section 315 it must offer equal time. And if the race is for a federal office, in the last week or so of the campaign the candidate is desperate to get on the air and does not want to lose time or money by complaining to the Federal Communications Commission.

The FCC has also ruled that candidates may buy spot time instead of longer, program-length periods.[9] In practice, of course, few candidates can afford to buy large chunks of time, and few believe that doing so would be an effective campaign strategy. Still, the agency's decision in 1976 to allow federal candidates to purchase spot ads was significant at the time. Today campaigns are dominated by thirty-second advertisements (and some even shorter). But when the agency made its spot ad decision it expressly overruled another decision it had made five years earlier under the equal time provisions of Section 315, which upheld in the circumstances (the station's offer of free time and lengthy segments) the judgment of a station not to sell spot time because no candidate could adequately explain his or her views in fewer than five minutes.[10]

One of the quirks of the Section 312 amendment is that the access requirement could be interpreted to mean free time to candidates rather than paid time. The FCC, however, has never read the statutory language that way. In the Commission's view, if a station is willing to sell time to a candidate it has no obligation to provide free time.[11] Further, the FCC has long argued that absent some clearer showing of Congress's intent, it has no authority to require broadcasters to provide free time, even if Section 312(a)(7) could be read to grant that authority.[12] In some cases, stations, in negotiating with candidates, have offered lesser amounts of uncharged time rather than the time the candidates originally sought to purchase, and the FCC has ruled these deals to be "reasonable" under the statute.[13]

Challenges to the Commission on Presidential Debates under Federal Election and Tax Law

Minor-party candidates who have argued that the Commission on Presidential Debates engages in illegal campaign activity have based such arguments on the 1971 Federal Election Campaign Act (FECA). That law is a complex collection of rules on campaign contributions, disclosure, requirements and prohibited activity, all of it regulated and enforced by the Federal Election Commission (FEC).[1] The law's campaign finance regulations have two broad goals.[2] The first is to ensure that the electoral process is insulated from corruption or the appearance of corruption from hidden campaign contributions.[3] The second is to make sure that money can flow into the campaigns, so that candidates can explain their ideas and their policy positions to the public through whatever channels they choose. To those ends, the law requires that whatever monies are raised and spent to elect or defeat a candidate for federal office are publicly reported. The presumption, writes legal scholar Anthony Corrado, is that "communications to the general public about federal candidates cost money; that those costs can be quantified, limited or prohibited; and that the costs must be reported and publicly disclosed."[4]

To whom or what do FECA's many requirements actually apply? FECA governs the activities of "political committees," which it defines as "any group of persons—whether established by a candidate, political party, corporation, labor union, or other organization or group of citizens—that receives contributions or makes expenditures of more than $1,000 in any calendar year for the purpose of influencing any election for federal offices."[5] The law also defines "contributions" and "expenditures" very broadly, to include not just money but "anything of value"[6] made for the purpose of influencing a federal election—including "any payment, gift, loan, or advance of money, goods, or services."[7] Finally, FECA prohibits corporations and labor unions from contributing to federal candidates or federal political committees.[8] If the Commission on Presidential Debates were a bipartisan organization, virtually all the corporate contributions would be illegal campaign contributions. But as a nonpartisan debate organizer it is exempt from these rules. According to the FEC, "nonpartisan debates are designed to educate and inform voters rather than to influence the nomination or election of a particular candidate," and therefore "funds expended . . . to defray costs incurred in staging nonpartisan debates" are legally acceptable.[9]

The critical thing, as evidenced by the FEC's language, is the emphasis on the nonpartisanship of the debate sponsor. Obviously, decisions about whom to include or exclude in a televised debate can make or break a candidate, and so they cannot be made arbitrarily. Under rules the agency established in 1995, neither the Commission on Presidential Debates nor any other would-be sponsor can use nomination by the two major parties as the sole test for debate inclusion. Moreover, the FEC said, any selection criteria used for the debates must be "pre-established" and "objective" so as to avoid "the real or apparent potential for a quid pro quo, and to ensure the integrity and fairness of the process."[10]

But the FEC also recognized that any debate organizer would want to, and probably have to, limit the number of participants in a debate if it was to serve its public purpose. So long as the selection criteria were not rigged to result in a predetermined outcome, the agency said, "the objective criteria may be set to control the number of candidates participating in the debate if the staging organization [the Commission or any other qualified organization] believes there are too many candidates to conduct a meaningful debate."[11]

*   *   *

The other federal agency to have been hauled into controversy over the presidential debates is the Internal Revenue Service, in response to challenges to the tax-exempt status of the debate sponsors. In 1988, for example, though the newly formed Commission on Presidential Debates sponsored the general presidential debates, the League of Women Voters continued to sponsor the primary debates—that year one for the Republicans and two for the Democrats. Candidate Lenora Fulani of the New Alliance Party challenged the League's tax-exempt status as a nonprofit organization after it denied her request to debate.[12] In order to qualify for federal 501(c)(3) tax-exempt status, an organization may not "participate in, or intervene in (including the publishing or distributing of statements), any political campaign on behalf of (or in opposition to) any candidate for public office." Fulani's theory was that by excluding candidates from parties other than the Democrats and Republicans, the League did precisely what Section 501 prohibits; that is, it had intervened on behalf of particular candidates to the detriment of others.[13] After agreeing that Fulani had standing to sue, the U.S. Court of Appeals for the Second Circuit dismissed Fulani's suit as baseless.[14] The court reasoned that primary debates (and primary elections as well) are exclusive by definition: "Fulani's attack on the League's primary voter education program essentially blurs the distinctions between the primary phase and the general election phase of the contest for the presidency, insofar as Fulani sought to compel the League to convert its 'primary season' voter education program into a 'general election' program for educating voters about inter-party differences."[15]

Thus advised, Fulani then filed a second suit, this time with the U.S. Court of Appeals for the District of Columbia, arguing that a nonpartisan, tax-exempt organization like the CPD could not exclude minor-party candidates from general election debates.[16] But this time Fulani sued the IRS, not the CPD, and this time the court gave her even shorter shrift, finding she had no legal standing to sue. "While the IRS's decision to provide the CPD with tax-exempt status is a cause of Fulani's claimed injury," the court said, "it is merely one in a chain of independent causal factors necessary to achieve this injury." Fulani's suit, wrote the court, was not "fairly traceable" to the IRS decision to exempt the CPD, nor would her injury have been "redressible" by revoking the CPD's tax-exempt status. Finally, the court noted its reluctance to "change the defendant's [the Internal Revenue Service's] behavior only as a means to alter the conduct of a third party [the CPD], not before the court, who is the direct source of the plaintiff's injury."[17] Commenting on the D.C. Circuit Court's holding nearly a decade later, the U.S. District Court for the District of Columbia wrote, "In Fulani v. Brady, the fact that the plaintiffs did not sue under FECA, but rather under the Internal Revenue Code, proved dispositive. . . . The FECA, unlike the Internal Revenue Code, confers a broad grant of standing."[18]

Chief Judge Abner Mikva dissented from the court's dismissal in Fulani v. Brady, arguing that Fulani's injury was in fact directly traceable to the Internal Revenue Service's exemption, because according to the law the CPD could only sponsor debates if it was a not-for-profit, tax-exempt entity. Therefore, Mikva argued, there existed a direct causal connection between the CPD's tax-exempt status and Fulani's injury. And even though the election at issue had already occurred, Mikva believed the court should hear Fulani's case because it presented issues "capable of repetition, yet evading review."[19]

Not to be dissuaded, in her next lawsuit against the IRS Fulani cited the CPD's practices in the 1992 election. For that year's presidential debates, the CPD had agreed to sponsor four meetings between President Bush and Governor Clinton, but it had invited Ross Perot only to the first of them. The CPD announced that "it was unable to determine at that time whether Perot met its Selection Criteria for the subsequent debates." President Bush and Governor Clinton both rejected this condition, telling the CPD that they would debate only if Perot were invited to all four debates. The following day, the CPD agreed to invite Perot to all four debates, a decision Fulani cited as evidence that the CPD did not "adhere to its Selection Criteria," and therefore she argued that the its tax-exempt status should be revoked. Again the court found that Fulani did not have standing to sue.[20]

Broadcast Debates and the First Amendment

Many decisions about televised debates involve matters of content and editorial discretion, and so they raise fundamental First Amendment issues for broadcasters. But as a regulated industry, broadcasting occupies a unique place in the American system of free expression.

From the earliest days of broadcasting, those who have received licenses to use the publicly owned electromagnetic spectrum have been required to provide something of public benefit in return. The most explicit of those benefits has been providing qualified candidates for public office with access to the airwaves. The historical and technological bases for that policy may now be obsolete, as many thoughtful critics argue, but the policy is still law and, whatever its faults, the democratic values that animate it are found throughout the world. Broadcasting is the world's most ubiquitous medium, available to those who are out of reach of newspapers and magazines, telephones and the Internet, and it is especially valuable to those who are poor, rural, or illiterate. In all of the nations that have become democracies in the last two decades, one of the first orders of business has been transforming what was once authoritarian or state broadcasting into a true public-service medium. And a major part of that transition has been providing citizens with information about parties and candidates so that they can meaningfully exercise their right to vote.

For this reason, Adlai Stevenson argued in his 1960 testimony before Senator John Pastore's Senate Communications Subcommittee, rules requiring the broadcast of campaign programming would not warrant the intense First Amendment scrutiny given to other kinds of regulations affecting political speech. Remember that Stevenson was not proposing debates but rather that candidates for the presidency—including qualified third-party candidates—be allotted thirty minutes of airtime on a weekly basis for the eight weeks prior to the election so they could present their views to the American public. This is not to say that broadcasters are without important First Amendment rights, particularly where political speech is concerned. As the Supreme Court stated in 1973: "For better or worse, editing is what editors are for; and editing is selection and choice of material. That editors—news-papers or broadcast—can and do abuse this power is beyond doubt, but that is no reason to deny the discretion Congress provided. Calculated risks of abuse are taken in order to preserve higher values."[1]

Candidates have also raised First Amendment objections to presidential debates. The first case to challenge Section 315 of the Communications Act on First Amend-ment grounds was brought by Senator Edward Kennedy in 1980. The issue, as Ken-nedy raised it, was whether the equal opportunity doctrine, as amended and inter-preted by the FCC and the courts, "transgress[ed] the First Amendment interest of a candidate demanding an opportunity to respond to another candidate's state-ments on an excepted occasion."[2] In other words, Kennedy argued, his First Amend-ment rights included a right of access to the airwaves irrespective of other consid-erations. To this proposal the Circuit Court of Appeals for the District of Columbia answered with a resounding *no*. As the court wrote, "No individual member of the public [has a right] to broadcast his own particular views on any matter."[3] Rather, it is the province of broadcasters, "as public trustees . . . to use their discretion in en-suring the public's access to conflicting ideas."[4]

Seven years later, feminist-activist Sonia Johnson ran for president as the nomi-nee of the Citizens Party. In *Johnson v. FCC*, she and her running mate, Richard Walton, demanded that the League of Women Voters give them access to the 1984 presidential debates on the theory that "by 1984 the televised presidential and vice-presidential debates had become so institutionalized as to be a prerequisite for elec-tion"; as a result, their exclusion from the debates deprived Johnson and Walton of their "access to the ballot," which, they claimed, "impinge[d] upon associational choices protected by the First Amendment." The FCC rejected Johnson's com-plaint, so she appealed to the DC Circuit Court of Appeals. The court acknowledged Johnson's argument that the broadcast media have "tremendous power to inform and shape public opinion, and the immutable scarcity of broadcast frequencies have created both tremendous opportunities and serious hazard for free expres-sion," but it was no more persuaded by Johnson's argument—which it said "boils down to a demand for broadcast access"—than it had been by Kennedy's four years earlier. Citing both a previous case involving CBS and the Kennedy case, the court wrote that Johnson and Walton "present a far weaker constitutional thesis than the ones those cases rejected. They seek not general access, as in the former, nor an opportunity to respond to a particular broadcast, as in the latter, but rather the specific right to appear on a specific program—a program not organized by the broadcasters, but by a third party. Thus, viewed in light of the First Amendment balance . . . petitioners have stated no legally cognizable claim to participate in the broadcast debates."[5]

More seriously, the court said, a ruling for access in the Johnson case would it-self violate the First Amendment through "the risk of an enlargement of Govern-ment control over the content of broadcast discussion of public issues."[6] It contin-ued, "We recognize the importance of preserving a large measure of journalistic discretion for broadcasters as a serious First Amendment issue."[7] As for Johnson's and Walton's claim that they were effectively denied ballot access by being denied a debate invitation and that voters were therefore denied the right to vote for them, the court gave the claim "realistic" scrutiny and decided any such injury was entirely conjectural. In the end, summarizing the spirit of its holding, the court wrote that "the Supreme Court has held that the Constitution does not demand that all candidates be subsidized to the point that all are equal in terms of financial strength and publicity."[8]

The Johnson case effectively ended the possibility that candidates could challenge on First Amendment grounds the decision by a *private* broadcaster to exclude them from a debate. Left unresolved was what a *public* broadcaster could do in a similar situation. Many public broadcast stations are independent not-for-profit institutions, and many rely almost exclusively on private donations for their funding. But many other public broadcasting organizations are owned and operated by state or city governments and depend largely on local, state, and federal dollars for their budgets. Many critics of public broadcasting make no distinction between private and state-run facilities. Public broadcasting of all kinds has long been subject to criticism from across the political spectrum about perceived "bias" in its public affairs programs. And because public broadcasters are more likely than commercial broadcasters to organize political debates as part of their public-service mission, it was inevitable that they would be drawn into the debate over debates.

Three years after Johnson, two separate suits—one in the Eighth Circuit and one in the Eleventh—would be brought by candidates objecting to their exclusion from debates on public broadcast stations. The Eighth Circuit cases involved a legally qualified third-party candidate for the U.S. Senate, Garry DeYoung, who sued Iowa Public Television (IPT) when it denied his request to join the two major-party candidates in a debate prior to that state's 1984 election. A federal district court dismissed the case, holding that DeYoung had no First Amendment right to airtime and that the decision by Iowa Public Television to exclude him did not amount to "state action" sufficient to trigger any other First Amendment claim. When DeYoung appealed to the Eighth Circuit, that court found that indeed IPT's decision did amount to state action—after all, public employees acting in their official capacity had made the decision to exclude him—but that it did not matter.[9] A political candidate, the court emphasized, "does not have a 'constitutional right of broadcast access to air for his or her views.'"[10] The court also rejected DeYoung's theory that IPT was a public forum to which he, or anyone else, was entitled access.[11]

In the Eleventh Circuit case, *Chandler v. Georgia Public Telecommunications Commission,* the Libertarian candidate for lieutenant governor, Walker Chandler, went to court to compel a public broadcast station to include him in a debate with the Democratic and Republican candidates. Chandler alleged that as a legally qualified candidate he had a right to participate in what amounted to a publicly funded debate. The district court agreed, enjoining the debate from taking place without him.[12] The Eleventh Circuit reversed. In a *per curiam* (but not unanimous) decision, the court held that the Georgia Public Telecommunications Commission's (GPTC) station was not "a medium open to all who have a message," and that therefore the station was not a true "marketplace of ideas." It followed, then, that the station's executives and producers rightfully exercised discretion by inviting only those candidates whom they believed "would be of the most interest and benefit to the citizens." As the judges concluded:

> We are not willing to establish a precedent that would require public television stations to forgo the broadcast of controversial views touching upon important public issues—environment, ecology, animal rights, ozone depletion—lest the airing of such programs require the inclusion of a cacophony of differing views on each subject. The values sought to be fostered by the First Amendment would be frustrated, not furthered, by the fitting of such harnesses on public television.[13]

The dissenting judge on the panel agreed with his colleagues that public television is not a public forum, but he questioned whether the station's criteria for inclusion were really made in good faith and, in constitutional terms, whether they were viewpoint neutral. By preventing anyone but the Democratic and Republican candidates from debating, he said, the station *necessarily* precluded certain parties—and in turn, certain viewpoints—from being aired. Further, "by discriminating against the viewpoints expressed by the Libertarians, GPTC has violated even the minimal First Amendment standards applicable to nonpublic forums."[14]

Four years later, in 1994, the Eighth Circuit departed from the Eleventh Circuit's precedent, finding First Amendment grounds for including third-party candidates in public television debates. The case involved an independent candidate for Congress in Arkansas's third congressional district, Ralph Forbes, a white supremacist who obtained enough petition signatures to appear on the ballot. The Arkansas Educational Television Commission (AETC) refused to invite Forbes to its debate.[15] The record strongly suggested that the AETC decision was based on Forbes's political views rather than its stated claim that he was not newsworthy; in another congressional district, for example, AETC invited a major-party candidate to debate who raised less money than Forbes and who enjoyed less public support.[16] Additionally, AETC was a state-supported organization whose board reported to and was appointed by the Arkansas governor. Forbes sued AETC, seeking an injunction requiring his inclusion in the debate. He alleged that, at least in AETC's case, public television was a *public* forum, not merely a forum for the two major parties.[17]

After dismissing Forbes's equal opportunity claim—by failing to file a timely FCC complaint, Forbes had not exhausted his administrative remedies—the court found that AETC was indeed a state entity and therefore that Forbes and all other legal candidates had a "qualified right to access." Decisions made by public stations, the court noted, "are fairly attributable to the State and subject to the Fourteenth Amendment, unlike the actions of privately owned broadcast licensees." The court also distinguished the issue in *Forbes* from that in *Kennedy*: "There is no First Amendment right to appear on television upon demand. However, the stations involved in *Kennedy* were private stations." In order to legally exclude Forbes from the debate, the station needed to satisfy the court that its decision was based on a compelling state interest and was not merely arbitrary. The court also examined the facts of the case through the lens of the public forum doctrine and arrived at the same holding. Whether the AETC was a limited public forum or even a nonpublic forum, in this case the state's exclusion of Forbes amounted to an unconstitutional discrimination based on Forbes's viewpoint.[18]

The *Forbes* decision suggested for the first time that third-party candidates might win themselves spots in debates on legal grounds other than the equal opportunities provision, federal election law, or federal tax law—all the approaches that had thus far failed. The Eighth Circuit had with a stroke changed the playing field. To leave debate-inclusion decisions exclusively in the hands of executive administrative bodies shielded from First Amendment scrutiny, the court said, would "allow a state-owned station to exclude all Republicans, or all Methodists, or all candidates with a certain point of view, except to the extent, if any, that the excluded candidates could obtain relief under the Communications Act. We believe the error of such a proposition is self-evident."[19]

Forbes's case then returned to the district court, which was charged with determining whether AETC had a compelling reason for not inviting Forbes to debate.[20] At trial, AETC claimed that it excluded Forbes because, as a perennial losing candidate for various Arkansas offices, he "lacked any campaign organization, had not generated appreciable voter support, and was not regarded as a serious candidate by the press covering the election." The jury found for AETC, but the Eighth Circuit again reversed, finding as a matter of law that the debate was a public forum and that AETC's reason for excluding Forbes—his viability—was not a legally compelling state interest. The Eighth Circuit was emphatic:

> It must be emphasized that we are dealing here with political speech by legally qualified candidates, a subject matter at the very core of the First Amendment, and the exclusion of one such speaker has the effect of a prior restraint—it keeps his views from the public on the occasion in question. . . . The question of political viability is, indeed, so subjective, so arguable, so susceptible of variation in individual opinion, as to provide no secure basis for the exercise of the First Amendment. . . . Political viability is a tricky concept. We should leave it to the voters at the polls, and to the professional judgment of nongovernmental journalists. A journalist employed by the government is still a government employee. . . . The First Amendment exists to protect individuals, not government.[21]

This time the Supreme Court got involved, and Justice Anthony Kennedy, writing for a 6–3 majority, reversed the Eighth Circuit's decision.[22] The Court held that public television was a nonpublic forum because the government had no intention of making the airwaves "generally available" to any particular class of speakers.[23] As Kennedy reasoned, "In the case of television broadcasting, . . . broad rights of access for outside speakers would be antithetical, as a general rule, to the discretion that stations and their editorial staff must exercise to fulfill their journalistic purpose and statutory obligations." But if AETC was not a public forum, Kennedy said, that did not mean the station could exclude speakers only because of their viewpoint; rather any such exclusions had to be "reasonable." Kennedy went on to conclude that because of Forbes's "objective lack of public support," the station's decision to exclude all but the Democratic and Republican candidates was "a reasonable, viewpoint-neutral exercise of journalistic discretion."[24]

It is hard to read the Court's decision in *Forbes* and not conclude that it is deeply rooted in the same policy considerations found in other kinds of challenges to debates.[25] But here the Court also found itself stuck between two competing and irreconcilable First Amendment claims—Forbes's desire to be included in a state-sponsored forum, AETC's desire for editorial independence—and chose the latter. The Court noted that "candidate debates are of exceptional significance in the electoral process," but it was clearly reluctant to scrutinize broadcast stations too severely if they wished to sponsor them. "The nature of editorial discretion," Justice Kennedy wrote, "counsels against subjecting broadcasters to claims of viewpoint discrimination." Partly for that reason, the Court took AETC at its word—that the station excluded Forbes because he had no chance of winning—and it found that reason good enough to warrant exclusion. But the Court also worried that applying a public forum analysis to public broadcasters had the undesirable public policy effect of producing "less speech, not more." As Kennedy wrote, "On logistical grounds alone, a public television editor might, with reason, decide that the inclusion of all ballot-qualified candidates would 'actually undermine the educational value and quality of debates'" and "might choose not to air candidates' views at all."[26]

In a vigorous dissent, Justice John Paul Stevens (along with Justices Ruth Bader Ginsburg and David Souter) condemned the "standardless character of the decision to exclude Forbes from the debate." It is odd, Stevens wrote, that "if a comparable decision were made today by a privately owned network, it would be subject to scrutiny under the Federal Election Campaign Act unless the network used 'pre-established objective criteria to determine which candidates may participate in [the] debate.'"[27] Justice Stevens argued that it made little sense for public stations to have "limitless discretion" to exclude candidates, while private stations were subject to exacting government regulation. After all, "because AETC is owned by the State, deference to its interest in making ad hoc decisions about the political content of its programs necessarily increases the risk of government censorship and propaganda in a way that protection of privately owned broadcasters does not."[28]

From the point of view of public broadcasters, certainly, the Supreme Court's ruling in Forbes was a relief—specifically, from litigation costs that they could ill afford. "Public, non-commercial stations do not have unlimited funds to dedicate to legal counsel," one commentator on the case wrote. "Such costs could . . . have a chilling effect on programming if excessive legal costs reduce funds available for programming or equipment."[29] Had the Court affirmed the Eighth Circuit's reading of the case, it would have had an immediate impact on a majority of the nation's 356 public television stations and 699 public radio stations, which in many places are the *only* broadcasters likely to sponsor candidate debates.[30] Commercial broadcasters, after all, face no requirement to sponsor debates, and they have substantial financial incentives not to do so. Both the actual costs and the opportunity costs of sponsoring debates are high, and it is far more lucrative, under Section 312 of the Communications Act, for broadcasters to, in effect, force candidates to purchase airtime to get their views before prospective voters. Public broadcasters operate under different financial constraints and incentives and so view candidate debates much more favorably. This was the essence of the policy compromise made in Forbes, in which the Court foresaw the risk of "less speech, not more" in the Eighth Circuit's analysis. Justice Kennedy, in fact, noted in his Forbes opinion that in the aftermath of the Court of Appeals ruling, Nebraska Educational Television, the public broadcasting authority for that state, had canceled an already-scheduled debate between the Democratic and Republican nominees for U.S. Senate.[31]

The flip side of this compromise, however, is exactly as Stevens described it, a policy environment in which public broadcasters that sponsor debates are subject to less regulation than commercial broadcasters. While Kennedy's opinion in *Forbes* made it clear that public broadcaster discretion in debates was not boundless, that it had "to be consistent with the First Amendment,"[32] it otherwise offered no guidance on the matter. The Court did suggest Congress could develop "neutral rules for access to public broadcasting,"[33] but Congress has not done so. By contrast, commercial broadcasters that wish to sponsor debates must comply with the debate regulations established by the Federal Election Campaign Act. Those regulations require commercial broadcasters to use "pre-established, objective criteria" for candidate selection, and they expressly forbid "nomination by a particular party as the sole objective criterion to determine whether to include a candidate in a debate."[34] However principled or wise this policy is, it introduces yet another disincentive to commercial broadcasters and could arguably have the effect of relegating candidate debates—or at least candidate debates for public offices other than president of the United States—to the less-watched precincts of public television. Of course if they were interested, commercial broadcasters could sponsor debates and develop their own eligibility criteria for them; they could, for instance, stipulate that to participate a candidate for office has at least 15 percent public support in the latest polls. Assuming such interest—which assumes a lot—there remains the problem that the candidate ahead in the polls can only lose by participating and so is not likely to do so.

Despite these limitations, we have come a long way from *Lar Daly* and from the debates of 1960, described in chapter 2. There is now no serious statutory inhibition on fully and fairly contributing to an informed electorate, so essential to the proper functioning of our democracy. The effort has been remarkably free from any reports of abuse. Indeed, the Federal Communications Commission has speculated that in a prominent race like that for president, the likelihood for broadcaster abuse is remote.[35] In the historically litigious United States, the journey has involved the courts at crucial junctions. Perhaps, in light of the need to balance conflicting policies, the effort could and should have been carried out far better by the legislative branch. But in the end, sound policy has prevailed, and the First Amendment bedrock principle of promoting robust, wide-open debate has been maintained and advanced. Americans have only to make the most of the opportunity.

The Televised Presidential Debates, 1960–2004

Source: Commission on Presidential Debates (www.debates.org).

1960

GENERAL ELECTION PRESIDENTIAL DEBATE

John F. Kennedy (D), U.S. Senator (MA), and Richard M. Nixon (R), U.S. Vice President

Date	September 26, 1960
Location	WBBM-TV, CBS affiliate
City	Chicago
Time	9:30–10:30 p.m. Eastern
Sponsor	Networks: ABC, CBS, NBC
Moderator	Howard K. Smith, CBS News
Panelists	Sander Vanocur, NBC News; Charles Warren, Mutual News; Stuart Novins, CBS
News	Bob Fleming, ABC News
Viewership	66.4 million
Format	Eight-minute opening statements; two-and-a-half-minute responses to questions; optional rebuttal; three-minute closing statements
Topic	Domestic issues

GENERAL ELECTION PRESIDENTIAL DEBATE

John F. Kennedy (D), U.S. Senator (MA), and Richard M. Nixon (R), U.S. Vice President

Date	October 7, 1960
Location	WRC-TV, NBC affiliate
City	Washington, DC
Time	7:30–8:30 p.m. Eastern
Sponsor	Networks: ABC, CBS, NBC
Moderator	Frank McGee, NBC

Panelists	Paul Niven, CBS; Edward P. Morgan, ABC; Alvin Spivak, UPI; Harold R. Levy, Newsday
News	Bob Fleming, ABC News
Viewership	61.9 million
Format	No opening or closing statements; each questioned in turn with optional rebuttal

GENERAL ELECTION PRESIDENTIAL DEBATE

John F. Kennedy (D), U.S. Senator (MA), and Richard M. Nixon (R), U.S. Vice President

Date	October 13, 1960
Location	Split-screen telecast with Nixon and panelists in ABC studio in Los Angeles and Kennedy in ABC studio in New York
Time	7:30–8:30 p.m. Eastern
Sponsor	Networks: ABC, CBS, NBC
Moderator	Bill Shadel, ABC
Panelists	Frank McGee, NBC; Charles Van Fremd, CBS; Douglass Cater, *Reporter* magazine; Roscoe Drummond, *New York Herald Tribune*
News	Bob Fleming, ABC News
Viewership	63.7 million
Format	No opening or closing statements; each questioned in turn with two and a half minutes to answer; one-and-a-half-minute rebuttals optional

GENERAL ELECTION PRESIDENTIAL DEBATE

John F. Kennedy (D), U.S. Senator (MA), and Richard M. Nixon (R), U.S. Vice President

Date	October 21, 1960
Location	ABC studios
City	New York City
Time	10:00–11:00 p.m. Eastern
Sponsor	Networks: ABC, CBS, NBC
Moderator	Quincy Howe, ABC News
Panelists	Frank Singiser, Mutual News; John Edwards, ABC News; Walter Cronkite, CBS News; John Chancellor, NBC News
News	Bob Fleming, ABC News
Viewership	60.4 million
Format	Eight-minute opening statements; each questioned in turn with two and a half minutes to answer; one-and-a-half-minute rebuttal; three-minute closing statements
Topic	Foreign affairs

1976

GENERAL ELECTION PRESIDENTIAL DEBATE

Jimmy Carter (D), Former Georgia Governor, and Gerald Ford (R), U.S. President

Date	September 23, 1976
Location	Walnut Street Theater
City	Philadelphia
Time	9:30–11:00 p.m. Eastern
Sponsor	League of Women Voters
Moderator	Edwin Newman, *Baltimore Sun*
Panelists	Frank Reynolds, ABC; James Gannon, *Wall Street Journal*; Elizabeth Drew, *New Yorker* magazine
Viewership	69.7 million (data provided by Nielsen Media Research)
Format	No opening statements; each questioned in turn with three minutes to answer; one optional follow-up question with two minutes to reply; two-minute rebuttal; three-minute closing statements
Topic	Domestic policy

GENERAL ELECTION PRESIDENTIAL DEBATE

Jimmy Carter (D), Former Georgia Governor, and Gerald Ford (R), U.S. President

Date	October 6, 1976
Location	Palace of Fine Arts
City	San Francisco
Time	9:30–11:00 p.m. Eastern
Sponsor	League of Women Voters
Moderator	Pauline Frederick, NPR
Panelists	Max Frankel, *New York Times*; Henry L. Trewitt, *Baltimore Sun*; Richard Valeriani, NBC News
Viewership	63.9 million (data provided by Nielsen Media Research)
Format	No opening statements; each questioned in turn with three minutes to answer; one optional follow-up question with two minutes to reply; two-minute rebuttal; three-minute closing statements
Topic	Foreign and defense issues

GENERAL ELECTION PRESIDENTIAL DEBATE

Jimmy Carter (D), Former Georgia Governor, and Gerald Ford (R), U.S. President

Date	October 22, 1976
Location	Phi Beta Kappa Hall, College of William and Mary
City	Williamsburg, VA
Time	9:30–11:00 p.m. Eastern
Sponsor	League of Women Voters
Moderator	Barbara Walters, ABC News

Panelists	Joseph Kraft, syndicated columnist; Robert Maynard, *Washington Post;* Jack Nelson, *Los Angeles Times*
Viewership	62.7 million (data provided by Nielsen Media Research)
Format	Candidates questioned in turn with two and a half minutes to answer; two-minute rebuttal; optional follow-up questions with two minutes to answer; three-minute closing statements

VICE-PRESIDENTIAL DEBATE

Bob Dole (R), U.S. Senator (KS), and Walter Mondale (D), U.S. Senator (MN)

Date	October 15, 1976
Location	Alley Theatre
City	Houston
Time	9:30–10:45 p.m. Eastern
Sponsor	League of Women Voters
Moderator	James Hoge, *Chicago Sun Times*
Panelists	Hal Bruno, *Newsweek;* Marilyn Berger, NBC News; Walter Mears, Associated Press
Viewership	43.2 million (data provided by Nielsen Media Research)
Format	Two-minute opening statements; each questioned in turn with two and a half minutes to answer; two-and-a-half-minute rebuttals; one-minute reply to rebuttal; three-minute closing statements
Topic	Domestic and economic policies; foreign and defense issues
Miscellaneous	First formal debate ever held between vice-presidential candidates

---

1980

GENERAL ELECTION PRESIDENTIAL DEBATE

John Anderson (I), Former U.S. Congressman (IL), and Ronald Reagan (R), Former California Governor

Date	September 21, 1980
Location	Convention Center
City	Baltimore
Time	10:00–11:00 p.m. Eastern
Sponsor	League of Women Voters
Moderator	Bill Moyers, PBS
Panelists	Carol Loomis, *Fortune* magazine; Daniel Greenberg, syndicated columnist; Charles Corddry, *Baltimore Sun;* Lee May, *Los Angeles Times;* Jane Bryant Quinn, *Newsweek;* Soma Golden, *New York Times*
Format	Candidates questioned in turn with two and a half minutes to answer; one-minute-fifteen-second rebuttal; three-minute closing statements

GENERAL ELECTION PRESIDENTIAL DEBATE

Jimmy Carter (D), U.S. President, and Ronald Reagan (R), Former California Governor

Date	October 28, 1980
Location	Public Music Hall
City	Cleveland, OH
Time	9:30–11:00 p.m. Eastern
Sponsor	League of Women Voters
Moderator	Howard K. Smith, ABC News
Panelists	Marvin Stone, *U.S. News & World Report;* Harry Ellis, *Christian Science Monitor;* William Hilliard, *Portland Oregonian;* Barbara Walters, ABC News
Viewership	80.6 million (data provided by Nielsen Media Research)
Format	First half: same questions posed to both candidates, who had two minutes to reply; follow-up by panelist permitted; each candidate allowed one-minute rebuttal. Second half: same questions posed to both candidates; no follow-up; each candidate given two opportunities per question for rebuttal
Topic	Domestic, economic, foreign policy, and national security issues

1984

GENERAL ELECTION PRESIDENTIAL DEBATE

Walter Mondale (D), Former U.S. Vice President, and Ronald Reagan (R), U.S. President

Date	October 7, 1984
Location	Center for the Performing Arts
City	Louisville, KY
Time	9:00–10:30 p.m. Eastern
Sponsor	League of Women Voters
Moderator	Barbara Walters, ABC News
Panelists	James Wieghart, *New York Daily News;* Diane Sawyer, ABC News; Fred Barnes, *New Republic*
Viewership	65.1 million (data provided by Nielsen Media Research)
Format	Same questions posed to each candidate, who had two and a half minutes to respond; follow-up by panelists permitted; one-minute rebuttal; four-minute closing statements
Topics	Economic and domestic issues

GENERAL ELECTION PRESIDENTIAL DEBATE

Walter Mondale (D), Former U.S. Vice President, and Ronald Reagan (R), U.S. President

Date	October 21, 1984
Location	Music Hall, Municipal Auditorium
City	Kansas City, KS
Time	8:00–9:30 p.m. Eastern

Sponsor	League of Women Voters
Moderator	Edwin Newman, *Baltimore Sun*
Panelists	Georgie Anne Geyer, Universal Press Syndicate; Marvin Kalb, NBC News; Morton Kondracke, *New Republic*
Viewership	67.3 million (data provided by Nielsen Media Research)
Format	Same questions posed to each candidate, who had two and one half minutes to respond; one-minute follow-up; one-minute rebuttal; four-minute closing statements
Topics	Defense and foreign policy issues

VICE-PRESIDENTIAL DEBATE

George Bush (R), U.S. Vice President, and Geraldine Ferraro (D), U.S. Congresswoman (NY)

Date	October 11, 1984
Location	Pennsylvania Hall Civic Center
City	Philadelphia
Time	9:00–10:30 p.m. Eastern
Sponsor	League of Women Voters
Moderator	Sander Vanocur, ABC News
Panelists	John Mashek, *U.S. News & World Report;* Jack White, *Time;* Norma Quarles, NBC News; Robert Boyd, Knight-Ridder Newspapers
Viewership	56.7 million (data provided by Nielsen Media Research)
Format	Same questions posed to each candidate, who had two and a half minutes to respond; follow-up permitted by panelists; one-minute rebuttal; four-minute closing statements
Topics	First half: domestic affairs. Second half: foreign affairs

---

1988

GENERAL ELECTION PRESIDENTIAL DEBATE

George Bush (R), U.S. Vice President, and Michael Dukakis (D), Massachusetts Governor

Date	September 25, 1988
Location	Wait Chapel, Wake Forest University
City	Winston-Salem, NC
Time	8:00–9:30 p.m. Eastern
Sponsor	Commission on Presidential Debates
Moderator	Jim Lehrer, PBS
Panelists	John Mashek, *Atlanta Constitution;* Peter Jennings, ABC; Ann Groer, *Orlando Sentinel*
Viewership	65.1 million (Data provided by Nielsen Media Research)
Format	No opening statements; each candidate questioned in turn with two minutes to respond; one-minute rebuttal; follow-up questions permitted by panelists; two-minute closing statements
Topic	Questions divided between foreign and domestic policy

GENERAL ELECTION PRESIDENTIAL DEBATE

George Bush (R), U.S. Vice President, and Michael Dukakis (D), Massachusetts Governor

Date	October 13, 1988
Location	Pauley Pavillion, University of California at Los Angeles
City	Los Angeles
Time	9:00–10:30 p.m. Eastern
Sponsor	Commission on Presidential Debates
Moderator	Bernard Shaw, CNN
Panelists	Andrea Mitchell, NBC; Ann Compton, ABC; Margaret Warner, *Newsweek*
Viewership	67.3 million (data provided by Nielsen Media Research)
Format	No opening statements; each candidate questioned in turn with two minutes to respond; one-minute rebuttal; follow-up by panelists permitted; two-minute closing statements
Topics	Defense and foreign policy issues

VICE-PRESIDENTIAL DEBATE

Lloyd Bentsen (D), U.S. Senator (TX), and Dan Quayle (R), U.S. Senator (IN)

Date	October 5, 1988
Location	Omaha Civic Auditorium
City	Omaha, NE
Time	9:00–10:30 p.m. Eastern
Sponsor	Commission on Presidential Debates
Moderator	Judy Woodruff, PBS
Panelists	Tom Brokaw, NBC; Jon Margolis, *Chicago Tribune*; Brit Hume, ABC
Viewership	46.9 million (data provided by Nielsen Media Research)
Format	No opening statements; each candidate questioned in turn with two minutes to respond; one-minute rebuttal; two-minute closing statements

---

1992

GENERAL ELECTION PRESIDENTIAL DEBATE

George Bush (R), U.S. President, Bill Clinton (D), Arkansas Governor, and Ross Perot (I), Businessman

Date	October 11, 1992
Location	Field House, Washington University
City	St. Louis
Time	8:00–9:30 p.m. Eastern
Sponsor	Commission on Presidential Debates
Moderator	Jim Lehrer, PBS
Panelists	Sander Vanocur, independent journalist; Ann Compton, ABC; John Mashek, *Boston Globe*

Viewership   62.4 million (data provided by Nielsen Media Research)

Format   No opening statements; each candidate questioned in turn with two minutes to respond; one-minute rebuttal by other candidates; two-minute closing statements

Topic   Questions divided between foreign and domestic policy

GENERAL ELECTION PRESIDENTIAL DEBATE

George Bush (R), U.S. President, Bill Clinton (D), Arkansas Governor, and Ross Perot (I), Businessman

Date	October 15, 1992
Location	Robbins Field House, University of Richmond
City	Richmond, VA
Time	9:00–10:30 p.m. Eastern
Sponsor	Commission on Presidential Debates
Moderator	Carole Simpson, ABC
Questioners	209 uncommitted voters
Viewership	69.9 million (data provided by Nielsen Media Research)
Format	Town hall meeting; two-minute closing statements

GENERAL ELECTION PRESIDENTIAL DEBATE

George Bush (R), U.S. President, Bill Clinton (D), Arkansas Governor, and Ross Perot (I), Businessman

Date	October 19, 1992
Location	Wharton Center, Michigan State University
City	East Lansing
Time	9:00–10:30 p.m. Eastern
Sponsor	Commission on Presidential Debates
Moderator	Jim Lehrer, PBS
Panelists	Gene Gibbons, Reuters; Helen Thomas, UPI; Susan Rook, CNN
Viewership	66.9 million (data provided by Nielsen Media Research)
Format	First half: single moderator with option of follow-ups; roughly two minutes to answer, one-minute rebuttal. Second half: panelists posed questions in turn with no follow-ups; two-minute closing statements

VICE-PRESIDENTIAL DEBATE

Al Gore (D), U.S. Senator (TN), Dan Quayle (R), U.S. Vice President, and James Stockdale (I), Retired Admiral

Date	October 13, 1992
Location	Theater for the Arts, Georgia Tech
City	Atlanta
Time	7:00–8:30 p.m. Eastern
Sponsor	Commission on Presidential Debates
Moderator	Hal Bruno, ABC

Viewership	51.2 million (data provided by Nielsen Media Research)
Format	Two-minute opening statements; issue presented to candidates with one minute, fifteen seconds to respond, then five-minute discussion period about same topic; two-minute closing statements

---

1996

GENERAL ELECTION PRESIDENTIAL DEBATE

Bill Clinton (D), U.S. President, and Bob Dole (R), U.S. Senator (KS)

Date	October 6, 1996
Location	The Bushnell
City	Hartford, CT
Time	9:00–10:30 p.m. Eastern
Sponsor	Commission on Presidential Debates
Moderator	Jim Lehrer, PBS
Viewership	46.1 million (data provided by Nielsen Media Research)
Format	Single moderator; two-minute opening statements; candidates questioned in turn with ninety seconds to answer; sixty-second rebuttal; thirty-second response; two-minute closing statements

GENERAL ELECTION PRESIDENTIAL DEBATE

Bill Clinton (D), U.S. President, and Bob Dole (R), U.S. Senator (KS)

Date	October 16, 1996
Location	Shiley Theater, University of San Diego
City	San Diego
Time	9:00–10:30 p.m. Eastern
Sponsor	Commission on Presidential Debates
Moderator	Jim Lehrer, PBS
Questioners	113 uncommitted voters
Viewership	36.3 million (data provided by Nielsen Media Research)
Format	Town hall meeting; two-minute opening statements; candidates questioned in turn with ninety seconds to answer; sixty-second rebuttal; thirty-second response; two-minute closing statements

VICE-PRESIDENTIAL DEBATE

Al Gore (D), U.S. Vice President, and Jack Kemp (R), Former Secretary of Housing and Urban Development

Date	October 9, 1996
Location	The Bayfront Center's Mahaffey Theater
City	St. Petersburg, FL
Time	9:00–10:30 p.m. Eastern
Sponsor	Commission on Presidential Debates
Moderator	Jim Lehrer, PBS

Viewership	26.6 million (data provided by Nielsen Media Research)
Format	No opening statements; candidates questioned in turn with ninety seconds to answer; sixty-second rebuttal; thirty-second response; three-minute closing statements

---

2000

GENERAL ELECTION PRESIDENTIAL DEBATE

George W. Bush (R), Texas Governor, and Al Gore (D), U.S. Vice President

Date	October 3, 2000
Location	University of Massachusetts
City	Boston
Time	9:00–10:30 p.m. Eastern
Sponsor	Commission on Presidential Debates
Moderator	Jim Lehrer, PBS
Viewership	46.6 million
Format	Single moderator; candidates questioned in turn with two minutes to answer; sixty-second rebuttal; two-minute closing statements

GENERAL ELECTION PRESIDENTIAL DEBATE

George W. Bush (R), Texas Governor, and Al Gore (D), U.S. Vice President

Date	October 11, 2000
Location	Wake Forest University
City	Winston-Salem, NC
Time	9:00–10:30 p.m. Eastern
Sponsor	Commission on Presidential Debates
Moderator	Jim Lehrer, PBS
Viewership	37.5 million
Format	Single moderator; candidates questioned in turn with two minutes to answer; sixty-second rebuttal; two-minute closing statements

GENERAL ELECTION PRESIDENTIAL DEBATE

George W. Bush (R), Texas Governor, and Al Gore (D), U.S. Vice President

Date	October 17, 2000
Location	Washington University
City	St. Louis
Time	9:00–10:30 p.m. Eastern
Sponsor	Commission on Presidential Debates
Moderator	Jim Lehrer, PBS
Viewership	37.7 million
Format	Town hall style debate; single moderator; candidates questioned in turn with two minutes to answer; sixty-second rebuttal; two-minute closing statements

VICE-PRESIDENTIAL DEBATE

Dick Cheney (R), Former Defense Secretary, and Joseph Lieberman (D), U.S. Senator (CT)

Date	October 5, 2000
Location	Centre College
City	Danville, KY
Time	9:00–10:30 p.m. Eastern
Sponsor	Commission on Presidential Debates
Moderator	Bernard Shaw
Viewership	28.5 million
Format	Single moderator; candidates questioned in turn with two minutes to answer; two-minute rebuttal

---

2004

GENERAL ELECTION PRESIDENTIAL DEBATE

George W. Bush (R), U.S. President, and John F. Kerry (D), U.S. Senator (MA)

Date	September 30, 2004
Location	University of Miami
City	Coral Gables, FL
Time	9:00 10:30 p.m. Eastern
Sponsor	Commission on Presidential Debates
Moderator	Jim Lehrer, PBS
Viewership	62.4 million (data provided by Nielsen Media Research)
Format	Ninety-minute debate with candidates standing at podiums. Candidates questioned in turn with two-minute responses, ninety-second rebuttals and, at moderator's discretion, discussion extensions of one minute
Topic	Foreign policy

VICE-PRESIDENTIAL DEBATE

Dick Cheney (R), U.S. Vice President, and John Edwards (D), U.S. Senator (NC)

Date	October 5, 2004
Location	Case Western Reserve University
City	Cleveland, OH
Time	9:00–10:30 p.m. Eastern
Sponsor	Commission on Presidential Debates
Moderator	Gwen Ifill, PBS
Viewership	43.5 million (data provided by Nielsen Media Research)
Format	Ninety-minute debate with candidates seated at a table with the moderator. Candidates questioned in turn with two-minute responses, ninety-second rebuttals and, at moderator's discretion, discussion extensions of one minute
Topic	Domestic and foreign policy

GENERAL ELECTION PRESIDENTIAL DEBATE

George W. Bush (R), U.S. President, and John F. Kerry (D), U.S. Senator (MA)

Date	October 8, 2004
Location	Washington University in St. Louis
City	St. Louis
Time	9:00–10:30 p.m. Eastern
Sponsor	Commission on Presidential Debates
Moderator	Charles Gibson, ABC
Viewership	46.7 million (data provided by Nielsen Media Research)
Format	Ninety-minute town hall meeting debate. Candidates questioned by uncommitted voters identified by the Gallup Organization. Two-minute responses, ninety-second rebuttals, and, at moderator's discretion, discussion extensions of one minute
Topic	Domestic and foreign policy

GENERAL ELECTION PRESIDENTIAL DEBATE

George W. Bush (R), U.S. President, and John F. Kerry (D), U.S. Senator (MA)

Date	October 13, 2004
Location	Arizona State University
City	Tempe
Time	9:00–10:30 p.m. Eastern
Sponsor	Commission on Presidential Debates
Moderator	Bob Schieffer, CBS
Viewership	51.1 million (data provided by Nielsen Media Research)
Format	Ninety-minute debate with candidates standing at podiums. Candidates questioned in turn with two-minute responses, ninety-second rebuttals, and, at moderator's discretion, discussion extensions of one minute
Topic	Domestic policy

Notes

INTRODUCTION

1. A note to the reader: Though this book has two authors, it is written as a policy memoir told in the voice of its senior author, Newton N. Minow, whose half-century of personal experience with the presidential debates is essential to the narrative.

2. Don Hewitt, who produced the debate for CBS, later said that "the only thing anybody remembers about that night is Nixon's makeup. I frequently have scholars say to me, 'Well, what about Quemoy and Matsu?' To which I usually answer, 'Okay, where are Quemoy and Matsu and who said what and who cares?' We talked for years about who won that debate. They say if you listened to it on radio, Nixon won, and if you watched it on television, Kennedy won."

3. Richard Nixon, speaking in the third 1960 presidential debate in response to a question by Douglass Cater, October 13, 1960. The debate was a split-screen telecast, with the vice president speaking from an ABC studio in Los Angeles. Senator Kennedy spoke from an ABC studio in New York.

4. See Leo Bogart, *The Age of Television* (New York: Frederick Ungar, 1956).

5. Don Hewitt, speaking in "Debating the Debates: Defining Moments in Presidential Campaigns," a panel discussion sponsored by the Ronald Reagan Center for Public Affairs, October 15, 1996 (transcript, 27–28).

6. Former Ronald Reagan aide and press secretary Lynn Nofziger said in a 1996 forum on the presidential debates that President Kennedy had promised Goldwater the opportunity to debate in 1964. Nofziger made the claim in "Debating the Debates: Defining Moments in Presidential Campaigns," a panel discussion sponsored by the Ronald Reagan Center for Public Affairs, October 15, 1996 (transcript, 29).

7. President Kennedy had said unequivocally that he would debate his Republican opponent in 1964. At the time of his death, Kennedy had already asked Congress for another temporary suspension of the law, and two bills had been introduced that would have permanently suspended the law's application to presidential and vice presidential campaigns. See Stanley Kelley Jr., "Campaign Debates: Some

Facts and Issues," *Public Opinion Quarterly* 26, no. 3 (Autumn 1963): 351–66, at 351; see also S204, 87th Cong, 1st session, and S2035, 87th Cong, 1st session. The latter bill would have exempted from the law campaigns for U.S. senator, U.S. representative, and governor in addition to races for president and vice president.

8. Aaron Henry, speaking in *On Television: Public Trust or Private Property?* a documentary by Films Incorporated, New Brunswick, NJ, 1989.

9. Ibid.

10. Medgar Evers was the Mississippi state field secretary for the National Association of Colored People (NAACP). He was killed in his own driveway by an assassin on June 12, 1963, and was buried in Arlington National Cemetery. The accused killer, a white supremacist and Ku Klux Klansman named Byron De La Beckwith, was tried twice in 1964 but not convicted. In a third trial in 1994, a Mississippi jury convicted Beckwith of the murder and sentenced him to life in prison. He died in prison in 2001.

11. *Office of Communications of the United Church of Christ v. Federal Communications Commission,* 359 F2d 994 (D.C. Circuit), March 25, 1966. The opinion in the case was written for a three-judge panel by Judge Warren Burger and issued on the day Burger was sworn in as the new chief justice of the United States Supreme Court.

12. The League of Women Voters of the United States was founded in 1920, the same year that the 19th Amendment to the Constitution was ratified by thirty-six of the then forty-eight states (Tennessee was the 36th state to ratify, in August of that year), giving women the right to vote. The League has been organizing local, state and national political debates ever since.

13. "First Presidential Debate Seen by 63 Mil," *Mediaweek* 14, no. 35 (October 4, 2004): 3.

14. "Debates draw 47 million viewers," *Mediaweek,* October 18, 2004, Vol. 14, Issue 37, 42.

15. John Harwood and Jeanne Cummings, "Debates Take Center Stage," *Wall Street Journal,* October 15, 2005, A4.

16. "Veep Debate Draws 43 Million Viewers," *Mediaweek* 14, no. 36 (October 11, 2004): 34.

17. See Newton N. Minow, *Voters' Time* (New York: Twentieth Century Fund, 1969).

18. In 1948, *America's Town Meeting of the Air* became an NBC television program.

19. Quoted in J. Jeffrey Auer, "The Counterfeit Debates," in *The Great Debates: Background, Perspective, Effects,* ed. Sidney Kraus (Bloomington: Indiana University Press, 1962), 142–50, 145.

20. Though nineteenth- and early-twentieth-century America may have been a period of memorable political rhetoric, it was also a time when it was considered unseemly for a presidential candidate to debate; surrogates did the job instead. See Kathleen Hall Jamieson and David S. Birdsell, *Presidential Debates: The Challenge of Creating an Informed Electorate* (New York: Oxford University Press, 1988), 6.

21. See, for example, Anthony Marro, "The Quadrennial Sham: The Case for Truly Open Debates," *Columbia Journalism Review,* May/June 2004, 55; see also "Gingrich Harkens Back to Bygone Age of Lengthy Debate," *Congress Daily/A.M.,* May 28, 1999;

and Jeff Cohen, "Allow Nader, Buchanan into Debates," *Baltimore Sun*, September 28, 2000, available at www.fair.org/articles/allow-debates.html. (Cohen is founder of Fairness and Accuracy in Reporting [FAIR].)

22. See, for example, George Farah, *No Debate: How the Republican and Democratic Parties Secretly Control the Presidential Debates* (New York: Seven Stories, 2004); see also Julie Hilden, "Controlling the Presidential Debates: The First Amendment Issues Raised by Limiting the 'Town Hall' to Uncommitted Voters," *FindLaw*, October 12, 2004, available at http://write.findlaw.com/hilden/20041012.html (accessed November 8, 2005).

23. "Lincoln-Douglas vs. Nixon-Kennedy," *Wall Street Journal*, September 26, 1960, 12.

24. Alan L. Otten, "Issues or Entertainment? TV Debates May Feature Packaging More Than Ideas," *New York Times*, September 14, 1960, 14.

25. Ibid.

26. Jack Gould, "Details of Nixon-Kennedy Encounters Seen as Victory of Matter over Mind," *New York Times*, September 7, 1960, 83.

27. Lloyd B Dennis, "Lincoln Debates Easily Arranged," *New York Times*, September 26, 1960, 25.

28. The journalists on the first debate panel were Sander Vanocur of NBC (my college roommate at Northwestern University), Robert Fleming of ABC, Stuart Novins of CBS, and Charles Warren of the Mutual Broadcasting System, a radio network. See "TV Panel Chosen to Quiz Nominees," *New York Times*, September 23, 1960, 19; see also "Press Panel Complaint Fails to Scuttle Tonight's Kennedy-Nixon TV Spectacular," *Broadcasting*, September 26, 1960, 80.

29. "DC Politician Files Sec. 315 Suit," *Broadcasting*, September 12, 1960, 58.

30. Ibid.

31. "Lid's Off for Air Campaigning," *Broadcasting*, August 29, 1960, 33.

32. "Free Time for Campaigns Certain," *Broadcasting*, May 23, 1960, 72.

33. "Debates Set; Time-Buying Begins," *Broadcasting*, September 5, 1960, 44.

34. Roger B. May, "Nervous Pollsters Polish Techniques as Election Nears," *Wall Street Journal*, September 23, 1960, 11.

35. Ibid.

36. "TV Debate Switched Few Votes, Nation-Wide Survey Shows," *New York Times*, September 28, 1960, 26.

37. Claude Sitton, "Kennedy Gets Full Backing of 10 Southern Governors: Senator's 'Control' of TV Debate Cited," *New York Times*, September 28, 1960, 1.

38. See Richard S. Salant, "The Television Debates: A Revolution That Deserves a Future," *Public Opinion Quarterly* 26, no. 3 (Autumn 1962): 341.

39. Quoted in "Editorial Comments on N-K Debate," *Broadcasting*, October 3, 1960, 90.

40. "The TV Debate," *Wall Street Journal*, September 28, 1960, 14.

41. Quoted in "Excerpts from Editorials on TV Debate," *New York Times*, September 28, 1960, 24.

42. Ibid.

43. Ibid.

44. Ibid.

45. Henry Steele Commager, "Washington Would Have Lost a TV Debate," *New York Times Magazine,* October 30, 1960, 13.

46. Norman Cousins, "Presidents Don't Have to be Quiz Champions," *Saturday Review,* November 5, 1960, 34.

47. Quoted in "British Find Debate 'Brilliant Lesson,'" *New York Times,* September 29, 1960, 27.

48. Ibid.

49. "'Great Debate' Rightly Named: Nixon, Kennedy Set a Precedent That Will Be Hard to Abandon," *Broadcasting,* October 3, 1960, 88; see also, "73,500,000 Viewers Estimated to Have Seen Television Debate," *New York Times,* September 28, 1960, 77.

50. All quotes in this paragraph from "Most TV Viewers Give Kennedy Edge in Debate With Nixon," *Wall Street Journal,* September 28, 1960, 18.

51. *Broadcasting,* November 7, 1960, 27–28.

52. Salant, "Television Debates," 338.

53. William Schneider, "The 1960 Debates' Long Shadow," *Atlantic Monthly,* October 11, 2000.

CHAPTER ONE

1. See Samuel Becker and Elmer Lower, "Broadcasting in Presidential Campaigns," in *The Great Debates: Background, Perspective, Effects,* ed. Sidney Kraus (Bloomington: Indiana University Press, 1962), 44–47.

2. The Federal Communications Commission in those days had seven members; today it has five. All are appointed by the president and confirmed by the Senate. The FCC's chairman is ordinarily a member of the same political party as the president. The other seats on the Commission are divided equally between the Democrats and Republicans, with commissioners replaced by presidential appointment on the occasion of their leaving the agency or completing their terms of office. The FCC was established in 1934, a successor to the Federal Radio Commission.

3. *Columbia Broadcasting System,* 14 R.R. 720 (1956). The FCC's decision noted that the agency had no standards for determining what constituted a candidate's "use" of the airwaves, and it declined to develop any.

4. Adlai E. Stevenson, "Adlai Stevenson's Plan for a Great Debate," *This Week,* March 6, 1960.

5. Ibid.

6. Ibid.

7. See CNN.com, "Debates History," at www.cnn.com/ELECTION/2000/debates/history.story/intro3.html (accessed June 18, 2006).

8. Quoted in Becker and Lower, "Broadcasting in Presidential Debates," 39.

9. Alec Kirby, "A Major Contender: Harold Stassen and the Politics of American Presidential Nominations," *Minnesota History* 65, no. 4 (Winter 1996–97): 150.

10. See Commission on Presidential Debates, "1948 Debate," at www.debates.org/pages/his_1948_p.html (accessed February 11, 2006).

11. Kirby, "Major Contender," 162.

12. Stevenson, "Adlai Stevenson's Plans for a Great Debate."

13. Ibid.

14. The Presidential Campaign Broadcasting Act was cosponsored by Senators Ralph Yarborough of Texas and Mike Monroney of Oklahoma. A companion bill in the House, sponsored by Arizona representative Morris Udall, mirrored the Senate version almost exactly. The Senate bill was S-3171; the companion bill in the House was HR-11260.

15. S. 3171, 86th Congress, 2nd Session: "A bill to provide for the use of television broadcasting stations by candidates for the Office of President of the United States."

16. Ibid., section 2(e).

17. Ibid., section 2(a).

18. S. 3171, Presidential Campaign Broadcasting Act, *Hearings before the Communications Subcommittee of the Committee on Interstate and Foreign Commerce, United States Senate, Sixty-eighth Congress, May 16, 17, 18, 1960* (Washington: United States Government Printing Office, 1960); hereafter *Subcommittee Hearings, 1960.*

In the 1956 election, Eisenhower had won 57 percent of the popular vote, Stevenson 31 percent. Of the other parties with candidates, the Liberal Party did best with 0.5 percent of the popular vote; the Socialist Party did the worst, with 0.001 of the popular votes. Dozens of "other" candidates combined to win 0.4 percent of the vote.

19. Ibid., 5.

20. Testimony of Adlai E. Stevenson in ibid., 8–9.

21. Ibid, 18.

22. Ibid., Statement of the Honorable Herbert Hoover, 182.

23. Ibid., Statement of the Socialist Party-Social Democrat Federation, 312. CBS President Frank Stanton also raised this issue in his testimony, saying that the bill did not encourage or protect "other significant candidates for the presidency." See Statement of Dr. Frank Stanton, President, Columbia Broadcasting System, Inc., May 17, 1960.

24. Ibid., Statement of the American Civil Liberties Union, 314.

25. Statement of the Honorable Richard Nixon, Vice President of the United States, 179–80, and Statement of the Honorable Thomas Dewey, 180–81, in ibid.

26. "Free Time for Candidates Certain: But Will It Be Voluntary or Imposed by Federal Legislation?" *Broadcasting,* May 23, 1960, 72. Of course, real First Amendment issues could have arisen depending on how the legislation proceeded.

27. *Subcommittee Hearings, 1960,* 73 (Adams), 76 (Seymour).

28. Ibid., 72.

29. Frank Stanton, "The History-Making Kennedy-Nixon Debates in 1960 Were Eight Years in The Making: I Know; I Was There," *Newsweek,* September 25, 2000, 11.

30. Testimony of Dr. Frank Stanton, President, Columbia Broadcasting System, *Subcommittee Hearings, 1960,* 18284.

31. Ibid., 190, 196–98.

32. Ibid., 191.

33. Ibid., 188.

34. Ibid., Statement of Frank Stanton, 227, 201, 211.

35. Joint Resolution of Aug. 24, 1960, Pub. L. no. 86-677, 74 Stat. 554 (1960) (also

known as Joint Resolution 207): "Resolved by the Senate and House of Representatives of the United States of America in Congress assembled, That that part of section 315(a) of the Communications Act of 1934, as amended, which requires any licensee of a broadcast station who permits any person who is a legally qualified candidate for any public office to use a broadcasting station to afford equal opportunities to all other such candidates for that office in the use of such broadcasting station, is suspended for the period of the 1960 presidential and vice presidential campaigns with respect to nominees for the offices of President and Vice President of the United States. Nothing in the foregoing shall be construed as relieving broadcasters from the obligation imposed upon them under this Act to operate in the public interest."

During debate on the Senate bill, the FCC, at the subcommittee's urging, sent a questionnaire to the nation's television stations asking each to explain its general policy "with respect to political broadcasts and to the forthcoming election campaign." The questionnaire asked broadcasters whether they provided time without charge to politicians at the local, state, or national level, and if they did, how much time during what hours of the day. If broadcasters had needed further convincing of Congress's intent to act and of the need to offer substantial concessions of airtime, the questionnaire did the job. The legislation was set aside in favor of the networks' promises to act voluntarily, over the vigorous objections of Senator Yarborough, who immediately set up a "watchdog group" within the subcommittee to monitor the broadcasters' performance on their promises.

36. NBC president Robert Sarnoff wrote afterward that it was a mistake for the networks to forgo advertising as a way to finance the debates. "It is an antiquated notion that a so-called public service program is not a public service if it is sponsored. By this odd reasoning, a broadcaster cannot serve the public unless he loses money. . . . That is why we at NBC saw no more objection to appropriate sponsorship already found acceptable for the presidential inauguration or, indeed, the current sponsorship of various network programs in which the candidates themselves are appearing. However, after one network (CBS) publicly opposed any sponsorship of 'The Great Debate,' the question was foreclosed." See Robert W. Sarnoff, "An NBC View," in *The Great Debates: Background, Perspective, Effects,* ed. Sidney Kraus (Bloomington: Indiana University Press, 1962), 61.

37. The complete transcripts and video excerpts of all the televised presidential debates from 1960 forward are available online through the Museum of Broadcast Communications; see www.museum.tv/debateweb/html/history/index.htm. The Commission on Presidential Debates Web site also publishes full transcripts of all presidential and vice-presidential debates from 1960 forward; see www.debates.org/pages/trans60c.html.

38. Stanton, "History-Making Kennedy-Nixon Debates," 11.

39. Ibid.

40. See Sidney Kraus, *Televised Debates and Public Policy,* 2nd ed. (Mahwah, NJ: Lawrence Erlbaum, 2000), 208–10.

41. Theodore H. White, *The Making of the President, 1960* (New York: Atheneum, 1962), 279.

42. Quoted in Stanley Kelley Jr., *Political Campaigning* (Washington, DC: Brookings Institution, 1960), 14.

CHAPTER TWO

1. Because broadcasting is a regulated industry, the First Amendment does not apply to broadcasters in the same way it does to print media. The reasons for this treatment are historical and technological. Thoughtful people from across the political spectrum believe the law's treatment of broadcasting is ineffective or even unconstitutional, but the law is nonetheless clear: Congress may treat mass media differently under the First Amendment, and broadcasters have obligations that print media do not. See, for example, *Red Lion Broadcasting v. FCC*, 395 U.S. 367 (1969); see also *Turner Broadcasting System, Inc. v. FCC*, 114 S.Ct. 2445, 2456–57 (1994).

2. We have tried to be complete and precise in recounting this legal history while not tying up the reader with technical legal details, which interested readers can find in endnotes and the appendices.

3. All of these issues arise because of a fundamental property of broadcasting that has long been the foundation of government regulation of the technology: spectrum scarcity. Because only a limited number of operators can use the electromagnetic spectrum without creating interference that would render all broadcasts impossible to receive, those who do receive a license to broadcast are statutorily assumed to have service obligations to the many who do not receive licenses, i.e., the public at large. If soapboxes rather than spectrum were at issue, there would be no basis for regulation and no need for it.

4. Still today the equal opportunities provision pops up in curious, sometimes comical circumstances. Most famous was the decision by the 1960s television serial *Death Valley Days* to take on a different host when its regular host, Ronald Reagan, was running for governor of California. More recently, the 2003 gubernatorial recall in election in California created a situation in which stations could not air any of Arnold Schwarzenegger's movies without risking a claim for equal time from any of the dozens of other candidates running for governor. Neither could stations air reruns of *Diff'rent Strokes*, which featured candidate Gary Coleman. By contrast, candidate appearances on programs like *Entertainment Tonight, Access Hollywood,* and even the *Tonight Show* have been judged news broadcasts. Governor Schwarzenegger, for example, announced his candidacy on the *Tonight Show* and appeared again on the program during the campaign.

The equal time rule has also applied to local races in which, for example, a candidate is a local broadcast personality. See *Branch v. FCC*, 824 F.2d 37, 43 (D.C. Cir. 1987), cert. denied, 485 U.S. 959 (1988). In 2007, for instance, an Indianapolis sportscaster running for a city council seat withdrew from the race after opponents asked his station for equal time.

5. See 47 USC Sections 307(a), 315(a) (Supp. II 1996 and 1994). Broadcast licenses are awarded "if public interest, convenience and necessity will be served thereby," and radio and television licensees are required to "operate in the public interest."

6. *Office of Communication of the United Church of Christ v. FCC*, 359 F.2d 994, 1003 (D.C. Cir., 1966).

7. See *Farmers Education and Cooperative Union v. WDAY*, 360 U.S. 525 (1959), at 534–5.

8. See 47 USC Section 315(a)(b).

9. See 47 USC Section 312(a)(7). Regulations concerning the sale of political advertising were first introduced in Section 315 in 1952. That year, on a proposal by Washington congressman Walter Horan, Congress amended 315 so that "the charges made for the use of any broadcast station for any of the purposes set forth in this section shall not exceed the charges made for the comparable use of the station for other purposes" (47 USC Section 315(b)(1)). The change in the law came after many years of candidate complaints about radio stations' charging exorbitant fees for political broadcasts, often twice or more their normal commercial rate for same time periods.

10. Nicholas Zapple, "Historical Evolution of Section 315," in *The Past and Future of Presidential Debates*, ed. Austin Ranney (Washington, DC: American Enterprise Institute, 1979).

11. See "Equal Time Rule," Chicago Museum of Broadcast Communications, at www.museum.tv/archives/etv/E/htmlE/equaltimeru/equaltimeru.htm.

12. *Congressional Record*, 1926, remarks of Senator Earl B. Mayfield, 12,502.

13. Ibid., remarks of Senator Clarence Dill.

14. Ibid., remarks of Rep. Frank D. Scott, 2,567; Hoover's words are on 2,571.

15. Because of this legislative history, some federal district courts would later decide that they had no jurisdiction over disputes about Section 315 of the 1934 act. In 1926 the House rejected one proposal to give district courts the power to prosecute violations and another that would have allowed stations to appeal license revocations to district courts. The House did decide to allow stations to appeal revocations and refusals to the DC Court of Appeals. But the Senate decided to allow appeals either to district courts or to the DC appeals court. The final version reported to the Senate allowed license holders to appeal to the DC appeals court in the case of a rejected application for a license and to either the DC appeals court or a federal district court in the case of a license revocation.

16. *Congressional Record*, 1926, 12,356.

17. 47 USC Section 315(a).

18. See Leo Bogart, *The Age of Television* (New York: Frederick Unger, 1956).

19. *Felix v. Westinghouse Radio Stations*, 186 F2d 1 (3d Cir. 1950).

20. 47 CFR, Section 73.1940(a).

21. Ibid., Section 73.1940(a)(1–5).

22. *Columbia Broadcasting System, United Fund*, 14 R.R. 524, FCC 1956.

23. *Columbia Broadcasting System, Suez Crisis*, 14 R.R. 720, FCC 1956.

24. *Voters' Time: Report of the Twentieth Century Fund Commission on Campaign Costs in the Electronic Era* (New York: Twentieth Century Fund 1969), 41.

25. *In Re Telegram to CBS, Inc.*, 18 Rad. Reg. (P & F) 238, recon. denied, 26 F.C.C. 715 (1959)—hereafter *Lar Daly*.

26. *In Re Petitions of the Aspen Institute Program*, 55 F.C.C.2d 697, 698 (1975)—hereafter *Aspen*.

27. Beyond news programs, the equal time rule applies to entertainment pro-

gramming. When Lar Daly ran as a third-party candidate for president in 1960, for example, he demanded equal time after NBC's *Tonight Show* host Jack Parr invited Senator John Kennedy to be a guest on the program in June of that year. The FCC granted the request. When Daly appeared on the *Tonight Show*, Parr was visibly irritated at having him there, and the audience booed the candidate. Parr later publicly criticized the FCC ruling, calling it "an abuse of equal time."

28. See Howard K. Smith, "Behind the News," CBS News broadcast, July 26, 1959; see also Samuel Becker and Elmer Lower, "Broadcasting in Political Campaigns," in *The Great Debates: Background, Perspective, Effects*, ed. Sidney Kraus (Bloomington: Indiana University Press, 1962), 49.

29. Senate Report 86-562, at 9 (1959), reprinted in 1959 US CCAN 2564, at 2572, 2571.

30. See Susan L. Brinson, "Epilogue to the Quiz Show Scandal: A Case Study of the FCC and Corporate Favoritism," *Journal of Broadcasting and Electronic Media* 47, no. 2 (2003): 276–88.

31. 47 U.S.C. § 315(a)(1)–(4) (1959). The FCC's criteria for determining whether a candidate's appearance fell under any of these exemptions were the following: (1) Is the program regularly scheduled? (2) What are the format, nature, and content of the program? (3) Has the format or nature of the program changed since its inception, and, if so, in what respects? (4) Who initiates the program? (5) Who produces and controls the program? (6) When was the program initiated? See John Dean, "Political Broadcasting: The Communication Act of 1934 Reviewed," *Federal Communications Bar Journal* 20 (1966): 27.

32. Remarks of Senator John O. Pastore, *Congressional Record*, 1959, 14,446.

33. Remarks of Representative Walter Rogers, ibid., 16,235; Remarks of Representative John E. Moss, ibid., 16,244.

34. Remarks of Senator Spessard L. Holland, ibid., 14,443.

35. Remarks of Senator Jacob K. Javits, ibid., 14,452.

36. Ibid., 14,443.

37. Ibid., 16,230.

38. Remarks of Representative Emanuel, ibid., 16,226.

39. Remarks of Representative Samuel S. Stratton, ibid., 16,242.

40. Dean, "Political Broadcasting," at 42.

41. Remarks of Senator Warren G. Magnuson, *Congressional Record*, 1959, 14,447.

42. Senate Report 86-562, at 10.

43. Remarks of Senator Pastore, *Congressional Record*, 1959, 14,454.

44. See the D.C. Circuit Court's explanation of this balancing act in *Kennedy for President Comm. v. FCC*, 636 F.2d 417, 423–24 (D.C. Cir. 1980).

45. Remarks of Pastore, 14,455.

46. Ibid., 17,780.

47. Ibid., 16,228. In the aftermath of the *Lar Daly* decisions, broadcasters argued vigorously that application of the equal opportunities rule, with or without the 1959 amendments, was arbitrary and inconsistent. For instance, the FCC decided that NBC's *Today* program was exempt from 315 requirements while the network's *Tonight Show* was not. The Commission based its decision on the fact that the *Tonight Show* was listed as a variety program in newspaper listings while the *Today* program was not listed

at all. In a later case, the FCC decided that *Today* was exempt after all because it was produced by NBC's News, but that ABC's *Good Morning America* was not because it was produced by the network's entertainment division. See Richard Singer, "The FCC and Equal Time: Never-Neverland Revisited," *Maryland Law Review* 27 (1967): 233.

48. *Fairness Report*, Federal Communications Commission, 48 FCC2d, 46n16. Just as significant as the increase in coverage of the two major party candidates made possible by the 315 exemption in 1960 was the equally substantial *decrease* in coverage of the minor-party candidates, who saw their time drop by 90 percent from the levels of the 1956 campaign. See Lee Mitchell, *With the Nation Watching: Report of the Twentieth Century Fund Task Force on Televised Presidential Debates* (New York: Twentieth Century Fund, 1979), 84.

49. "Debates Set; Timebuying Begins," *Broadcasting*, September 5, 1960, 46.

50. Val Adams, "Parties Weighing Surplus TV Time: Plethora of Free Invitations Raises Doubt as to Need for All Paid Telecasts," *New York Times*, September 20, 1960, 79.

51. Richard S. Salant, "The Television Debates: A Revolution That Deserves a Future," *Public Opinion Quarterly* 26, no. 3 (Autumn 1962): 345.

52. The industry's hope for repeal of Section 315 after the success of the 1960 debates is well documented. See, for example, Robert W. Sarnoff, "An NBC View," and Frank Stanton, "A CBS View," in *The Great Debates: Background, Perspective, Effects,* ed. Sidney Kraus (Bloomington: Indiana University Press, 1962), 56–64, 65–72.

53. "A Chance to Clean Up the Image," *Broadcasting*, May 23, 1960, 77.

54. "315 Emancipation," *Broadcasting*, June 6, 1960, 114.

55. The networks were not alone in this effort. Many critics upset by the Republicans' use of television spot advertising in 1952 and 1956, among them the Speech Communication Association and the American Forensic Association, had urged Congress to promote more meaningful presidential debates by suspending Section 315 of the Communications Act for the 1960 election.

56. I was thirty-four years old when President Kennedy appointed me FCC chair. Shortly before he did, my local public library had declined to nominate me to its board of directors, citing my youth and inexperience.

57. *In Re Inquiry concerning Section 315 of the Communications Act of 1934 as Amended*, 40 F.C.C. 362 (1962)—hereafter *Goodwill Stations, Inc.*

58. *Aspen*, 55 F.C.C.2d at 699 (citing *Goodwill Station, Inc.*, 40 F.C.C., at 363).

59. Ibid.

60. *Goodwill Station, Inc.*, 40 F.C.C. at 363 (emphasis added).

61. Petitions of the Aspen Institute Program on Communications and Society and CBS, Inc., *Memorandum Opinion and Order,* 55 F.C.C.2d at 700 (citing *In Re Complaint Under "Equal Time" Requirements of Section 315*, 40 F.C.C. 370 [1962], popularly known as *National Broadcasting Co.*).

CHAPTER THREE

1. The relevant section of the law is 315(a)(4).

2. *In Re Petitions of the Aspen Institute Program*, 55 F.C.C.2d 697 (1975), at 703, 697, 706, 710 (hereafter *Aspen*).

3. See *Aspen*, at 712. See also *Chisholm v. FCC*, 538 F2d 349, at 353 (D.C. Cir. 1976),

cert denied, 429 U.S. 890 (1976). In that decision, the Court wrote (at 366) that "the legislative history is inconclusive, but we find much support for the [FCC's] new interpretation. In these circumstances, we are obligated to defer to its interpretation, even if it is not the only interpretation possible."

4. *Aspen*, at 711. If a rhetorical flourish, the agency's reference to *New York Times v. Sullivan* was also consistent with the view, advanced by many First Amendment scholars, that *Sullivan* is the singular transforming case in modern free speech law. In the decades after *Sullivan*, the Supreme Court has come to protect a range of public speech and speech activities that, prior to 1964, had fallen well outside the First Amendment's protections.

5. At the time the FCC had seven commissioners, including the chair. Today the total number of commissioners is five.

6. *Aspen* (Hooks, Comm'r, dissenting).

7. Ibid., at 714 (Lee, Comm'r, dissenting).

8. Ibid., at 353–54.

9. Ibid., at 366 (citing 47 U.S.C. § 315(d): "The Commission shall prescribe appropriate rules and regulations to carry out the provision.") and at 366–69 (Wright, J., dissenting).

10. Importantly, the *Aspen* decision also changed the rules with respect to broadcaster coverage of press conferences under the Section 315 exemptions. The Commission had long held that press conferences were not excluded from the equal opportunity requirement and in 1964, in *Columbia Broadcasting System, Inc.*, had concluded "that broadcast of a press conference . . . would not constitute either a bona fide news interview or on-the-spot coverage of a bona fide news event within the meaning of Sections 315(a)(2) and (4), respectively." But there remained a conceptual problem: what made a press conference a press conference? Two weeks before the presidential election of 1964, President Johnson had asked the networks for time to give a speech about a sudden change of leadership in the Soviet Union and the explosion of a nuclear device in China. When the Republican National Committee sought time to respond, the Commission decided the circumstances were very much like those involving President Eisenhower's speech in response to the 1956 Suez Crisis and ruled that the president's talk was not a "use" under the law but was instead a bona fide news event covered by the exemptions to Section 315. The challenge went to the D.C. Circuit Court of Appeals, which affirmed the FCC's decision without opinion, and the Supreme Court declined to review the case. However, two justices, Arthur Goldberg and Hugo Black, dissented, arguing that the Commission's decisions in matters such as these were inconsistent enough to warrant review.

Four years later, Senator Eugene McCarthy sued the FCC when it refused his request for time to respond to what he perceived as President Johnson's criticisms of him during a televised interview with reporters. McCarthy had already announced his intention to seek the Democratic nomination, but Johnson had not. The Commission thus denied the senator's request on the grounds that Johnson was not a "legally qualified candidate" for anything. The D.C. Circuit upheld that decision, and shortly afterward Johnson announced that he would not seek reelection to the presidency.

In 1972, problems arose when several presidential aspirants complained about their exclusion from the networks' Sunday-morning interview programs. CBS, for example, faced challenges from Democratic presidential candidates Sam Yorty and Shirley Chisholm when it invited only Senators Hubert Humphrey and George McGovern to appear on *Face the Nation* the Sunday before the California primary. The network claimed the program was a bona fide news interview and thus exempt, and the FCC agreed. This time the D.C. Circuit reversed, finding the format for the program more akin to a debate conducted by the network itself than an interview. Thus corrected, the FCC grudgingly ordered the networks to grant Chisholm thirty minutes of prime time before the election.

On this matter of press conferences, as with debates, the U.S. Court of Appeals for the District of Columbia affirmed the FCC's new policy. In order "to achieve more complete broadcast coverage," the court declined to second-guess the networks' judgment when it came to press conferences. Based on this ruling, an opposing candidate no longer had recourse to equal opportunity scrutiny as long as a broadcast station could show that (1) it had broadcast the press conference live, (2) the station had chosen to cover the press conference based on good faith determinations, *prior* to the conference, that it was a bona fide news event (with the burden on the plaintiff to demonstrate bad faith) and (3) there was no "evidence of broadcaster favoritism."

11. Commissioner Benjamin L. Hooks wondered what relation those two qualifications had to being bona fide news events. "Inasmuch as ninety-nine percent of the usual news broadcast is of taped excerpts, the 'live' and 'entirety' limitations have no plausible relationship to the question of 'on-the-spot coverage of bona fide news events.' . . . If 'bona fide news events' are only those covered live and in totality, then there is no such thing as broadcast news currently available." *Aspen*, at 715 (Hooks, Comm'r, dissenting).

12. Almost immediately the sponsorship of the League came under legal attack. American Independent Party presidential candidate Lester Maddox and independent candidate Eugene McCarthy each challenged the validity of the 1976 debates on different grounds. Maddox argued, in effect, that the involvement of the League of Women Voters was a fig leaf, that President Ford and Governor Carter had exercised control over the format of the debates and the selection of moderator. He claimed that arrangements between the candidates violated *Aspen*'s requirement that, in order to fall under the Section 315(a)(4) exemption, debates "must be under the exclusive arrangement and control of an independent party not associated with either the opposing candidates or broadcasters." The FCC answered that, as a matter of law, "the *Aspen* ruling made no reference to candidate participation in the arrangement of a debate." And as a practical matter, the agency said:

> It is unreasonable to assume that any candidate would agree to a debate without any input into the arrangements for the debate, such as date, duration, method of questioning, participants and subject matter, nor would such input destroy the newsworthiness of political candidates appearing before the public face-to-face to present their positions on the issues. Therefore, the fact that Ford and Carter had some say in the arrangements does not remove the instant debates from the 315(a)(4) exemption.

The Commission addressed McCarthy's complaint in the same advisory letter it had sent to the American Independent Party, even though the senator had challenged his exclusion by claiming the networks had violated the FCC's "fairness doctrine" by broadcasting debates that excluded McCarthy, a self-described "serious" and "major" candidate. The Commission first defined the "fairness doctrine" as a rule instructing broadcasters to afford reasonable opportunity to those who wished to present contrasting viewpoints on "controversial issue[s] of public importance." Candidates, the Commission noted, are not issues. "In an election for public office each candidate cannot be considered a separate controversial issue of public importance merely by reason of his or her candidacy or partisan campaign." But the vote was not unanimous. As he had done in *Aspen*, Commissioner Benjamin Hooks dissented:

> We are all victims—the League, the candidates, the voters, the media—of the *Aspen* ruling which makes everyone pretend that these debates are a spontaneous occurrence (like a forest fire) or a routinely-scheduled newsworthy event (like the Super Bowl) which would have occurred anyway, with or without the conspired presence of the media. The world-at-large is not fooled into believing that these debates would have taken place without the direct involvement and commitment of the networks. However, like Shakespeare, the FCC by its action affirms that "The play's the thing."

13. "Great Debates?" *Cincinnati Post*, May 11, 1976, 8.

14. "League of Women Voters Plans Debates between Democratic, Republican Finalists," League of Women Voters Education Fund news release, May 5, 1976.

15. Quoted in Jim Karayn, "Presidential Debates: A Plan for the Future," manuscript, May 1977, 1.

16. Thousands of ticket requests from the general public came in to the League, but because of limited seating in the chosen venues none were honored. Both the campaigns and the League agreed that no elected officials should be included in the audience. I personally received several requests for tickets from people I had never met and, before that, solicitations from politicians across the country wanting to host the debates. The Secret Service received a complete list of invitees prior to each debate.

17. Douglass Cater, "The Potential for Great Political Debates," *Washington Post*, July 6, 1976, A17.

18. If the networks were upset with the League, the League was not altogether confident about journalists acting as questioners. "The network pros," Cater said, "abhor anything that smacks of amateurism. Television has become conditioned to the slick and the fast-paced" (ibid.).

19. Former NBC president Reuven Frank publicly blasted both the League and the candidates for trying "to limit and control the picture at the other end, the audience end." See Frank, "Programming the Presidential Debates," *New Leader*, October 11, 1976, 9.

20. Jim Karayn, undated memorandum on the debates, from the personal files of Newton N. Minow.

21. Dorothy H. Kuper, director of research and development, League of Women Voters Education Fund, personal correspondence to Newton N. Minow, October 29, 1976.

22. Journalist Edwin Newman, who had moderated the first debate between Ford and Carter, later said he thought Ford "had been answering a question that had not been asked, and he was giving an answer to a question on the same subject, but phrased differently, which was, 'Do we accept Soviet domination of Eastern Europe?' Then when he realized what he had done, he really had a dilemma." Newman explained his theory in "Debating the Debates: Defining Moments in Presidential Campaigns," transcript of a panel discussion sponsored by the Ronald Reagan Center for Public Affairs, October 15, 1996, 14.

23. In fact Reagan *had* paid for the microphone. Two days before his debate with George Bush, the Federal Election Commission ruled that the sponsorship of the *Nashua Telegraph* newspaper made the debate an illegal political contribution. Reagan offered to split the $3,500 cost for the event with Bush. Bush refused, so Reagan paid for the entire event. See "We Were Sandbagged," *Time*, March 10, 1980, available at www.time.com/time/magazine/article/0,9171,950323,00.html (accessed February 2, 2006).

24. CBS newsman Don Hewitt noted later that Reagan's "I paid for this microphone" objection was a line from a movie: *State of the Union*, a 1948 film starring Spencer Tracy. Hewitt's observation is in "Debating the Debates: Defining Moments in Presidential Campaigns," transcript of a discussion about the debates at the Ronald Reagan Center for Public Affairs, October 15, 1996, 41.

25. Chevy Chase, "Mr. Ford Gets the Last Laugh," *New York Times*, January 6, 2007.

26. In 2004, for example, vice-presidential candidate John Edwards became the subject of criticism from the Bush campaign and Fox News after he complimented Vice President Richard Cheney's devotion to his gay daughter. Edwards did so immediately after Cheney had answered a question about how he could reconcile his own family's experience with his party's opposition to gay unions.

27. Importantly, Lehrer does not view himself as a journalist when he participates in the debates but as a "moderator" bound by the rules the candidates themselves have agreed on. "I would never let these guys get away with not answering a question or with giving a canned speech on the *News Hour*," Lehrer told us in an interview. "When I do the debates I very consciously take off my journalism hat and serve in the role of moderator. I keep the time, I enforce the rules."

28. Bill Clinton, interviewed in "Debating Our Destiny," PBS, 2000. The entire documentary can be viewed online at www.pbs.org/newshour/debatingourdestiny/.

29. Michael Beschloss, "Debate Your Way to Defeat," *New York Times*, October 17, 2004, 11. The tendency of journalists to grandstand in debates is made worse when there are multiple candidates, because there is so little opportunity for any candidate to engage another in serious and uninterrupted discussion. In June 2007, for example, CNN hosted a debate among eight Democratic aspirants for their party's presidential nomination. Host Wolf Blitzer repeatedly asked the candidates to respond to highly charged statements (for example, "English should be the official language of the United States") by raising their hand if they agreed with them. At one point, Delaware senator Joseph Biden said the United States should use military force to end the genocide in Darfur, Sudan, and Blitzer asked the other candidates to raise their hand if they agreed. "We're not going to engage in these hypotheticals," responded New York senator Hillary Clinton. "One of the jobs of a president is

being very reasoned in approaching these issues. And I don't think it's useful to be talking in these kinds of abstract terms." Illinois senator Barack Obama agreed and added, "I don't want to raise my hand anymore." *Washington Post* columnist David Ignatius later described the Republican and Democratic debates as "mass questionings" that "looked like police-station lineups." See David Ignatius, "Debates to Dream About," *Washington Post*, June 17, 2007, B7.

30. The question was "If Kitty Dukakis were raped and murdered, would you favor an irrevocable death penalty for the killer?" Shaw's conclusion: "For presidential debates, candidates should be locked in a studio with only the moderator, no audience, no staff, no panels of questioners. Voters do not need a screening committee. They do that in the voting booth." See "Debating the Debates: Defining Moments in Presidential Campaigns," transcript of a panel discussion sponsored by the Ronald Reagan Center for Public Affairs, October 15, 1996, 7–8.

31. John Anderson, quoted in *Debating Our Destiny*, a 2000 PBS documentary hosted by Jim Lehrer. Transcripts are available at www.pbs.org/newshour/debatingourdestiny/interviews.html, 3.

32. The existing requirements had been constitutional eligibility to be president and a mathematical possibility of an electoral victory. League of Women Voters Education Fund, "The 1980 Presidential Debates: Behind the Scenes" (Washington, DC: LWVEF, 1981), 3–4.

33. Ibid., 4–5.

34. See Nicholas Zapple, "Historical Evolution of Section 315," in Austin Ranney, ed., *The Past and Future of Presidential Debates* (Washington, D.C.: American Enterprise Institute, 1979), 64.

35. Anderson at one point had more than 20 percent support among voters, and on that basis the League believed he should be invited to participate. Then in late in October 1980, just a week or so before the election, his standing in the polls went down below the threshold percentage of 15 percent public support that the League required for participation. The League's view, which I did not share, was that since Anderson had gone down in the polls he no longer belonged in the debates. I believed that the League was pulling the hook on a credible candidate.

36. The moderator of the Baltimore debate was Bill Moyers of PBS. The panelists were Charles Corddry of the *Baltimore Sun*, Soma Golden of the *New York Times*, syndicated columnist Daniel Greenberg, Carol Loomis of *Fortune*, Lee May of the *Los Angeles Times*, and Jane Bryant Quinn of *Newsweek*.

37. Disappointingly, there was no vice-presidential debate in 1980; Vice President Mondale's staff was upset with Bob Strauss for not insisting on a debate with George H. W. Bush.

38. In the November election, Anderson received 5.7 million votes (6.6 percent of the total), compared to more than 79 million for Carter and Reagan combined. Trailing Anderson was Libertarian Party candidate Ed Clark, with 921,000 votes or just over 1 percent of the total.

39. The participants in that "presidential forum" were Governor Ronald Reagan, Representative John Anderson, Senator Howard Baker, Ambassador George Bush, Governor John Connelly, Representative Phillip Crane, and Senator Robert Dole.

40. See William A. Henry III, "In Search of Questioners: The League Runs into Problems Putting Together a Panel," *Time,* October 22, 1984, 84.

41. According to Nielsen Media Research, the second largest audience for a presidential debate was the nearly 70 million Americans who watched the second 1992 debate among President George H. W. Bush, Bill Clinton, and Ross Perot.

CHAPTER FOUR

1. Author (C. LaMay) interview with Dorothy Ridings, Commission on Presidential Debates, Louisville, KY, October 25, 2005. Ridings was also president of the League of Women Voters of the United States from 1982 to 1986, and on its board of directors from 1976 to 1986.

2. See *Voter's Time: Report of the Twentieth Century Fund Commission on Campaign Costs in the Electronic Era* (New York: Twentieth Century Fund, 1969), 20–21. Over the sweep of U.S. history, once-powerful parties such as the Federalists and the Whigs lost the support of the electorate and disappeared, replaced by or absorbed into new parties. But for most of American history we have had a two-party system.

3. Today Clifford Sloan is the president of *Washington Post/Newsweek* Interactive.

4. The Georgetown study was published as R. E. Hunter, ed., *Electing the President: A Program for Reform* (Commission on National Elections, April 1986); the Harvard report was published as Newton Minow and Clifford Sloan, *For Great Debates: A New Plan for Future Presidential Debates* (New York: Priority, 1987).

5. Kathleen Hall Jamieson and David S. Birdsell, *Presidential Debates: The Challenge of Creating an Informed Electorate* (New York: Oxford University Press, 1988), 213.

6. The Commission's cochairs are Frank J. Fahrenkopf Jr. and Paul G. Kirk Jr. As of spring 2007, its board consists of Howard Buffett, John C. Danforth, Jennifer Dunn, Antonia Hernandez, Caroline Kennedy, Michael D. McCurry, Dorothy Ridings, Alan K. Simpson, H. Patrick Swygert, and me. According to its bylaws (1995), the Commission must have at least eight and no more than seventeen board members.

7. Among them have been Brazil, Ecuador, Jamaica, Japan, Mexico, Namibia, Nicaragua, Nigeria, Russia, South Africa, Taiwan, and Ukraine.

8. The Commission maintains an advisory Web page for any organization wishing to host a debate, available at www.debates.org/pages/education.html (accessed September 4, 2006).

9. An adequate debate facility, according to the Commission, is difficult to find. First there are the physical requirements. A debate hall must be at least 17,000 square feet, with a minimum ceiling height of 35 feet and an overall floor depth of at least 140 feet. The stage must be at least 65 feet long, 30 feet deep, 4 feet above the hall floor, and it must have a backdrop at least 30 feet high. The distance from the candidates' position on the stage to the television camera platforms must be no more than 90 feet. The debate hall must have sufficient air conditioning to maintain a temperature of 68 degrees Fahrenheit on the floor and 65 degrees on the stage, while being quiet enough not to interfere with the broadcast of the debates. In addition, the hall must have excellent acoustic qualities, fully padded seats for the audience, and fully carpeted floors.

The Commission requires 3,000 square feet of workspace for itself, 200 square feet of storage space, and a conference room large enough to accommodate 30 people. Candidate "holding rooms" must be at least 350 square feet and have bathrooms and telephone and cable television connections. Campaign staff workrooms must have the same facilities and be no less than 2,000 square feet. A holding room for reporters must be equipped with tables and chairs for 20 people, a closed-circuit television system, and telephone, electronic, and audiovisual transmission capacity.

Outside the debate hall there must be reasonable vehicular access and ample parking, including space for 30 television remote trucks up to 48 feet long. A separate press hall of at least 17,500 square feet, sufficient to hold 2,000 journalists, must be part of the debate facility or immediately adjacent to it. The press hall must have a closed-circuit television system with 40 TV monitors and cable access, as well as work stations for 750 reporters, each with a telephone line and two 110-volt AC plus, and of course space for food.

All of this must be located no more than ten to fifteen minutes away from a hotel or hotels that will accommodate 2,500 people.

10. Community support means above all that the host facility and host city understand that having the presidential debates in town means significant disruptions in the lives of its citizens and the operations of city services. The Commission requires the host city to guarantee complete city services—police, fire, bomb disposal, and rescue services—necessary to ensure the security of the debate. The Commission requires information on the size of the local police force, the location of the trauma center nearest the debate hall, and the availability of mobile medical services at the debate. All these city services personnel will be under the direction of agents of the U.S. Secret Service. The host city or facility must contribute $750,000 or more to the production costs of a single debate and in addition cover the transportation and hotel costs of Commission visits to inspect the site.

11. Minutes, annual meeting of the board of directors, Commission on Presidential Debates, November 21, 2006.

12. The University of Richmond, for instance, hosted the second 1992 presidential debate (and the first ever "town hall" debate) with President George H. W. Bush, Bill Clinton, and Ross Perot, and moderator Carole Simpson of ABC News. In 1995, the university's director of external relations and its provost told coauthor Craig LaMay that despite the enormous success of the event, the university would forgo the debates in the future for reasons of cost and inconvenience.

13. David S. Broder, "Open Up the Debates," *Washington Post*, September 30, 2004, A25.

14. Anthony Marro, "Quadrennial Sham: The Case for Truly Open Debates," *Columbia Journalism Review*, May/June 2004, 55–56, 56.

15. Norman Ornstein, "Moderation in Excess," *Wall Street Journal*, April 3, 2007, A14.

16. For the Citizens Debate Commission, see www.citizensdebate.org/. Quote is from "Efforts Building to Take Back the Presidential Debates," *Chicago Sun-Times*, July 5, 2004.

17. George H. W. Bush, speaking with Jim Lehrer in "Debating Our Destiny," PBS, 2000. The full transcript of President Bush's interview is available online at

http://www.pbs.org/newshour/debatingourdestiny/interviews.html (accessed December 9, 2006).

18. According to an internal Commission memorandum from December 2006, the cost in 2008 for one debate plus out-year preparation will be approximately $1.35 million, assuming there are no unexpected expenses from litigation or insurance coverage.

19. James A. Barnes, "Is Anybody Listening?" *National Journal,* January 2, 1988, 6–12, 12.

20. George Farah, *No Debate: How the Republican and Democratic Parties Secretly Control the Presidential Debates* (New York: Seven Stories, 2004), at 33.

21. James A. Barnes, "Debates, If Not Debaters, Win Praise," *National Journal,* October 24, 1992, 2444.

22. Jamieson and Birdsell, *Presidential Debates,* 64.

23. Article I, Section 3 of the Constitution as it was first ratified read: "The Senate of the United States shall be composed of two Senators from each state, chosen by the legislature thereof for six Years; and each Senator shall have one Vote." The Seventeenth Amendment, providing for the direct election of senators, was ratified in 1913.

24. Candidates for the U.S. House of Representatives, unlike those running for the Senate or the presidency, have engaged in public debates with one another since the earliest days of the republic. James Madison and James Monroe, for example, met in several face-to-face public encounters in 1788 while campaigning for a House seat from Virginia.

25. *Union* (Washington, DC), September 2, 1858.

26. *Cincinnati Commercial,* September 23, 1858.

27. Jamieson and Birdsell, *Presidential Debates,* 50–63.

28. Adam Howard Hoffman, "The Effects of Campaign Contributions on State Legislatures," PhD diss., University of Maryland, 2005, 32; see also George Thayer, *Who Shakes the Money Tree? American Campaign Financing Practices from 1789 to the Present* (New York: Simon and Schuster, 1973).

29. Hoffman, "Effects of Campaign Contributions." See also Richard Brookhiser, "What Would the Founders Do Today?" *American Heritage,* June/July 2006.

30. Jamieson and Birdsell, *Presidential Debates,* 94.

31. Ibid., 97.

32. Quoted in Richard S. Salant, "The Television Debates: A Revolution That Deserves a Future," *Public Opinion Quarterly* 26, no. 3 (Autumn 1962): 342.

33. Jamieson and Birdsell, *Presidential Debates,* 86.

34. Sidney Kraus, *Televised Presidential Debates and Public Policy,* 2nd ed. (Mahwah, NJ: Lawrence Erlbaum Associates, 2000), 34.

35. In 1960, for example, ABC refused to call the Nixon-Kennedy appearances "debates," instead calling them "joint appearances" and "face-to-face."

36. See David Zarefsky, "The Lincoln-Douglas Debates Revisited: The Evolution of Political Argument," *Quarterly Journal of Speech,* no. 72 (1986): 162–84 (quote is from 181).

37. Jim Lehrer, interview with the authors, Washington, DC, September 7, 2006.

38. Farah, *No Debate.*

39. The ten other participating groups were the Brennan Center for Justice; Center for Voting and Democracy; Common Cause; Democracy Matters; Democracy South; Judicial Watch; National Voting Rights Institute; Public Campaign; Rock the Vote; and the Voting Rights Project of the Institute for Southern Studies. The report is available online at www.opendebates.org/documents/REPORT2.pdf.

40. Ibid, 3–4.

41. Theodore H. White, *The Making of the President: 1960* (New York: Atheneum, 1960), 282.

42. Jack Gould, "TV: Rebuttal on 'Debate': Details of the Nixon-Kennedy Encounters Seen as Victory of Matter over Mind," *New York Times*, September 7, 1960, 39M.

43. U.S. Senate Committee on Commerce, *Final Report, Part 2: The Speeches, Remarks, Press Conferences, and Study Papers of Vice President Richard M. Nixon, August 1 through November 7, 1960*, Report 994, Part 2 (Washington, DC: U.S. Government Printing Office, 1961), 1143.

44. Herb Klein, speaking in "Debating the Debates: Defining Moments in Presidential Campaigns," transcript of a panel discussion sponsored by the Ronald Reagan Center for Public Affairs, October 15, 1996, 30–31.

45. H. A. Seltz and R. D. Yoakam, "Production Diary of the Debates," in *The Great Debates: Kennedy vs. Nixon, 1960*, ed. Sidney Kraus (Bloomington: Indiana University Press, 1977), 74–77.

46. Sig Mickelson, *The Electric Mirror: Politics in an Age of Television* (New York: Dodd, Mead, 1972), 200.

47. Ibid.

48. See Seltz and Yoakam, "Production Diary of the Debates"; see also R. Drummond, "Candidates' Aides and TV Bosses Clash over News Men on Panels for Debates," *New York Herald Tribune*, September 12, 1960.

49. Kevin Klose, "Echoes of the Great Debate: Remembering Nixon-Kennedy Twenty-five Years Later," *Washington Post*, September 25, 1985.

50. Don Hewitt, *Tell Me a Story: Fifty Years and 60 Minutes in Television* (New York: Public Affairs, 2001), 69.

51. John W. Self, "The First Debate over the Debates: How Kennedy and Nixon Negotiated the 1960 Presidential Debates," *Presidential Studies Quarterly* 35, issue 2 (2005): 361–76.

52. Ibid., 369.

53. P. Potter, "Kennedy Denies Violation," *Baltimore Sun*, October 14, 1960.

54. L. Fleming, "Nixon Charges Kennedy Used Notes in Debate," *Los Angeles Times*, October 14, 1960, 2.

55. Self, "First Debate over the Debates," 372–74.

56. Tom Wicker, "Accord Indicated on Fifth Debate: Candidates' Representatives Report Making 'Progress' on New TV Meeting," *New York Times*, October 27, 1960, C24.

57. Richard Lyons, "Kennedy Demands TV Debate Answer Today," *Washington Post*, October 29, 1960, A7.

58. Fred Scribner Jr., "Statement of Fred C. Scribner, Kennedy-Nixon Debate: September 22, 1960–October 28, 1960," manuscript, Robert F. Kennedy Papers, n.d.

59. Don Hewitt, in "Debating the Debates: Defining Moments in Presidential

Campaigns," transcript of a panel discussion sponsored by the Ronald Reagan Center for Public Affairs, October 15, 1996, 23.

CHAPTER FIVE

1. A frequent charge made by the Commission's critics is that it is beholden to its corporate sponsors. The Commission's Web page lists sponsors for each debate year (www.debates.org/pages/natspons.html), though it does not show how much each sponsor donated. Because it is a tax-exempt charity, the Commission's 990 tax forms are also online (see Guidestar.com), but those forms show only a total of gifts, grants, and donations for each tax year, not how much or what the Commission received from individual donors. At the time of this writing, the most recent election year for which donation data are available, 2000, shows total donations of a little more than $5 million.

Without question, the Commission should be much more transparent about its revenue sources, but even so its critics willfully miss an obvious point: *all* nonprofit organizations require operating revenue and are limited to only three sources: government subsidies, private donations (of money, labor, facilities, expertise, and so on), and sales of goods or services clearly related to their tax-exempt mission. Universities, hospitals, zoos, aquariums, libraries, botanical gardens, museums, and virtually all other nonprofit educational organizations depend for a majority of their revenue on donations. From an economist's point of view, it is obvious that any source of revenue a nonprofit may receive will affect the nature of the mission goods and services it produces. But there is no way out of that dilemma, and the Commission's critics never propose a realistic alternative strategy. Would they prefer, for example, that the Commission (or any other hypothetical debate sponsor) survive on government grants? Some might argue that this is desirable as candidates increasingly choose to forgo federal campaign contributions, but that choice would raise new issues. Would such grants increase or decrease the Commission's independence and thus its ability to organize nonpartisan debates?

2. In 2004, when the European Union consisted of fifteen member nations, all of its members except for Italy had held leader debates. France has held televised presidential debates since 1974. West Germany had televised debates beginning in 1969, a practice that was interrupted briefly after reunification when Chancellor Helmut Kohl refused to debate "reformed Communists." See Stephen Coleman, "The Televised Leaders' Debate in Britain: From Talking Heads to Headless Chickens," *Parliamentary Affairs* 51, no. 2 (April 1998): 16.

3. In May 1997, however, Major called for a national election and proposed that he debate Labour candidate Tony Blair. The Conservative and Labour parties then engaged in lengthy and occasionally acrimonious negotiations over the debate's format, with each of the nation's two largest broadcasters, the BBC and the Independent Television Network, submitting competing formats to both parties. The Conservatives objected to the more formal debate format proposed by the BBC, which also included special provisions for the major third-party candidate, Paddy Ashdown, a Liberal Democrat. The Labour Party insisted in every case on having a panel

of journalists ask questions, rather than a single moderator, and for the full inclusion of Ashdown. Negotiations eventually broke down with the broadcasters, at which point the *Times of London* challenged the two major-party candidates to a debate, again excluding Ashdown. There were no debates.

See Jill Sherman, "Major Negotiates Showdown Debate with BBC and ITV," *Times of London*, March 20, 1997, 1; Sherman, "Regulator Likely to Allow ITV Debate without Ashdown," *Times of London*, March 21, 1997, 1; and "The Times Challenge," *Times of London*, April 11, 1997, 1.

4. See Helen Clark, "The Worm That Turned: New Zealand's 1996 General Election and the Televised 'Worm' Debates," in *Televised Election Debates: International Perspectives* , ed. Steven Coleman, 122–30, (Basingstoke, Hampshire, UK: Palgrave Macmillan, 1999).

5. See Shoshana Blum-Kulka and Tamar Liebes, "Peres versus Netanyahu: Television Wins the Debate, Israel 1996," in *Televised Election Debates,* ed. Coleman, 66–92.

6. Larry Rohter, "Brazil Heads to Polls in Shadow of Yet Another Scandal," *New York Times*, October 1, 2006, 4.

7. ITAR-TASS, February 14, 2004. Putin ran as an independent against six other candidates and won the election with approximately 80 percent of the vote.

8. Note that these are English translations from the Italian. See "Quotable Quotes From Italy's Election Campaign," Agence France Presse, April 9, 2006. See also Peter Popham, "Berlusconi and Prodi Exchange Insults in Debate," *Independent* (London), April 4, 2006, 17.

9. In a separate debate, Neofascist candidate Allessandra Mussolini called transgender Communist Party candidate Vladimir Luxuria a "faggot."

10. *Question Time* first aired on BBC Radio 4 in 1979 and was intended to have only a short run. Today it is the BBC's most popular televised public affairs program. The broadcast typically includes politicians from each of the parties as well as other public figures who take questions from the studio audience.

11. Czech News Agency (CTK), "Meciar, Gasparovic Clash Again in Presidential Debate," April 13, 2004. For a slightly different interpretation of these remarks, see "Europe's Black Sheep Returns to the Fold," *Guardian Unlimited,* April 28, 2004, at www.guardian.co.uk/eu/story/0,,1202011,00.html (accessed March 12, 2007).

12. "Popular Puppetry," *Financial Times*, March 4, 2004, 12.

13. "Debate Scored for Two Voices," *America*, September 18, 1976, 135–36. According to internal documents from the League of Women Voters, there were 102 candidates for the presidency in 1976.

14. Lampl, "The Sponsor: The League of Women Voters Education Fund," in *The Great Debates: Carter vs. Ford, 1976,* ed. Sidney Kraus (Bloomington: Indiana University Press, 1979), 88.

15. "Debate Scored for Two Voices."

16. Ibid.

17. Often missing from all the criticism of the Commission is recognition of the fact that *any* organization can host a debate provided it meets the requirements for nonpartisanship of the Federal Election Campaign Act. A critical part of demon-

strating nonpartisanship is the selection criteria an organization uses to invite debate participants, and since 1995 the law has required the following:

> For all debates, staging organizations must use pre-established objective cri-
> teria to determine which candidates may participate in a debate. For general
> election debates, staging organization(s) shall not use nomination by a particu-
> lar party as the sole objective criterion to determine whether to include a candi-
> date in a debate.

This rule marked a significant change. Under rules the FEC had devised in 1979,
a staging organization like the League of Women Voters, if it had wished, could have
restricted debate invitations to the major-party candidates. That the League very
conscientiously did *not* do this is again a testament to the organization's commitment to its larger purpose—informing the public about serious candidates for the
presidency. With the FEC's reinterpretation of the law in 1995, nomination by a major party could be one consideration among many but not the only one. The purpose
of the requirement, according to the FEC, is to "avoid the real or apparent potential
for a quid pro quo, and to ensure the integrity and fairness of the process," but the
decision about which objective criteria to use is a matter for the staging organization to decide. So long as the criteria are not "designed to result in the selection of
certain pre-chosen participants," the FEC says, they can be chosen purposefully to
limit "the number of candidates participating in a debate if the staging organization
believes there are too many candidates to conduct a meaningful debate."

18. If, for example, there are three candidates, A, B, and C, and we have three citizens choosing among them, their individual voting preferences might be ABC,
CBA, BCA, CAB, ACB, or BAC. Under these conditions, whichever candidate is selected, the winner may not have a plurality of the vote and a majority will prefer
someone else. Put another way, there is no single election procedure that can always fairly decide the outcome of an election (or other public choice) that involves
more than two candidates or alternatives. We cannot rule out conflicting orderings,
nor can we say a voting system will go from individual to group preferences without
restraining or discounting the choices of some citizens. These conditions have especially worrisome implications for democracy, since they can lead to group decisions that are either nonsensical or manifestly undemocratic. As political scientists
Ken Shepsle and Mark Bonchek have written, "The group is either dominated by a
single distinguished member or has intransitive preferences" (Kenneth A. Shepsie
and Mark S. Bonchek, *Analyzing Politics: Rationality, Behavior, and Institutions* [New
York: W. W. Norton, 1997], 85). "Single distinguished member" is just a nice way of
saying "dictator," and so Arrow's theorem is also known as the dictator theorem.

19. In May 2007, for example, MSNBC and Fox News each sponsored a debate
among Republican presidential candidates. Both networks were sharply criticized
for their decision to exclude some candidates on grounds that the excluded candidates claimed were arbitrary and failed to adhere to the sponsors' published criteria for debate participation. One candidate, John Cox, threatened to sue when, in a
South Carolina debate, Fox required candidates to have "garnered at least 1% in recent state and national polls" but relied only on its own Fox News/Opinion Dynamics Poll of likely South Carolina voters, conducted a month before the May debate,

as the basis for inclusion. Two candidates, Jim Gilmore and Ron Paul, were included in the debate on this basis, while Cox was not because his name was not included in the poll.

20. In addition to me, the advisory panel's members were Charles Benton, Ambassador Holland Coors, Marian Wright Edelman, Mary Hatwood Futrell, Carla A. Hills, Barbara Jordan, Melvin Laird, Ambassador Carole Laise, William Leonard, Kate Rand Lloyd, Richard Neustadt, Paul H. O'Neill, Nelson W. Polsby, Jody Powell, Murray Rossant, Jill Ruckelshaus, Lawrence Spivak, Robert Strauss, Richard Thornburgh, Marietta Tree, Anne Wexler, and Mrs. Jim Wright.

21. Richard E. Neustadt, letter to Paul G. Kirk Jr. and Frank J. Fahrenkopf Jr., September 17, 1996.

22. Ibid.

23. "Fixing the Presidential Debates," *New York Times*, September 18, 1996, A20.

24. "Include Perot in Debates, Abolish Dysfunctional Debate Commission," *South Florida Sun-Sentinel*, September 20, 1996, A22.

25. Clarence Page, speaking on PBS's *NewsHour*, September 11, 1996; full transcript available at www.pbs.org/newshour/bb/election/september96/perot_9-11.html (accessed March 3, 2007).

26. General Counsel's Report, Federal Election Commission, February 6, 1998, 58.

27. Ibid.

28. Federal Election Commission, Matters under Review 4451 and 4473, 1998, 8–9.

29. At the beginning of the 1996 campaign, both Clinton and Dole opposed Perot's participation. The Democrats, according to Clinton aide George Stephanopoulos, tried to use Dole's opposition to Perot as a bargaining chip in negotiations with the Republicans ("Comments of Richard Neustadt," Commission on Presidential Debates Symposium, "Planning for the Year 2000: A Review of the 1996 Debates," October 20–21, 1997).

Later in the 1996 campaign, the Clinton campaign saw Perot's participation as a advantage and supported his inclusion in the debates. See Federal Election Commission, "Federal Election Commission Statement of Reasons re: Complaints 4451 and 4473," April 6, 1998, 7.

30. Federal Election Commission, First General Counsel's Report, 9–10.

31. In 1968, Governor Wallace had public support as high as 20 percent two months before the election.

32. Commission on Presidential Debates, "Nonpartisan Candidate Selection Criteria for 2000 General Election Debate Participation," January 5, 2000.

33. League of Women Voters Education Fund, "The 1980 Presidential Debates: Behind the Scenes," 4.

34. And just as the League of Women Voters had done with Anderson in 1980, the Commission requires that candidates meet its eligibility requirements for each of the debates.

35. John Anderson, quoted in *Debating Our Destiny*, a 2000 PBS documentary on the debates hosted by Jim Lehrer. Full transcripts of the program are available at www.pbs.org/newshour/debatingourdestiny/interviews.html.

36. Peter Hart, "The League Passes the Buck," *Washington Post*, August 22, 1980.

37. The five polling organizations the League used were Louis Harris Associates, the Los Angeles Times, the Roper Organization, NBC/Associated Press, and the Gallup Poll. The League also consulted with three polling experts: Mervin Field, Lester R. Frankel, and Herbert Abelson.

38. League of Women Voters Education Fund, "The 1980 Presidential Debates: Behind the Scenes," 4.

39. League of Women Voters, "Statement of Dr. Herbert Adelson, Mervin Field, and Lester Frankel," press release, Washington, D.C., September 19, 1980.

40. League of Women Voters Education Fund, "1980 Presidential Debates," 4.

41. "Stop Arguing and Start Debating," *New York Times,* August 22, 2000, A20.

42. "Extra Debates—with Other Faces," *Washington Post,* September 19, 2000, A22.

CHAPTER SIX

1. According to the International Telecommunications Union, Internet penetration in the United States was 69.4 percent in late 2006. Ninety percent of Americans had Internet access either at home or at work, or used public terminals. See also Henry Jenkins and David Thorburn, "The Digital Revolution, the Informed Citizen, and the Culture of Democracy," in *Democracy and New Media,* ed. Henry Jenkins and David Thorburn (Cambridge, MA: MIT Press, 2003), 1.

2. In the United States, the WELL (the Whole Earth 'Lectronic Link) was the first important example of community building on the Web, indeed the place where the term *virtual community* was coined. Now hosted by Salon.com, the San Francisco–based WELL is a group of like-minded individuals interacting in an electronic venue, exhibiting important social bonds, and observing normative expectations of behavior. Other early virtual communities with explicit political agendas included Cleveland FreeNet, PeaceNet, EcoNet, and GreenNet, all of which made it possible for like-minded activists around the world to communicate and organize. Some of these early online communities played key roles in bringing the world's attention to the 1989 student uprising in China that ended at Tienanman Square and to opposing, then monitoring, the 1991–92 Persian Gulf War.

This book's discussion of the Internet and politics is limited to the United States. We acknowledge and admire many of the important uses of the Internet and other digital communications to advance democracy in the developing world, including in particular those that provide political information in support of free and fair elections. Among the most notable examples are Malaysiakini.com, an online paper in Malaysia; Kantor Barita Radio 68H in Jakarta, an Internet-based radio network that serves the Indonesian archipelago; and B92 in Belgrade, a terrestrial and online radio broadcaster in Serbia.

3. "More Adults Tap Internet for Election News," Reuters, September 9, 2006. See also "Campaign and Political News Online: More Americans Turn to the Internet for News about Politics," Pew Internet and American Life Project, at www .pewinternet.org/PPF/r/187/report_display.asp. See also David Carr, "Online Player in the Game of Politics," *Wall Street Journal,* November 6, 2006, C1; Will Lester, "Candidates, Parties Target Web Audience," Associated Press, October 29, 2006.

4. For a theoretical discussion of this idea, see Thomas Emerson, "Toward a Gen-

eral Theory of the First Amendment," *Yale Law Journal* 72 (1963): 877; see also *Associated Press v. United States*, 326 US 1, 1945.

5. See Democracy Network at www.dnet.org.

6. In July 1952, for example, NBC president Pat Weaver told *Variety* magazine that television would

> create a new stature in our citizens. The miracles of attending every event of importance, meeting every personality of importance in your world, getting to observe members of every group, racial, national, sectional, cultural, religious; recognizing every city, every country, every river and mountain on sight; having full contact with the explanations of every mystery of physics, mechanics and the sciences; sitting at the feet of the most brilliant teachers, and be exposed to the whole range of diversity of mankind's past, present and the aspirations for mankind's future—these and many other miracles are not assessed yet. But I believe that we vastly underestimate what will happen.

Perhaps the most famous academic critique of the idea that new media promote democratization is Raymond Williams's 1974 essay "Television: Technology and Cultural Form." Williams's view was that technological deterministic arguments are not only wrong but, because they assume humans are essentially powerless to choose how new technologies are used, politically and morally dangerous.

7. See Mark Halperin and John F. Harris, *The Way to Win* (New York: Random House, 2006).

8. See Michael Cornfield, "The Internet and Politics: No Revolution Yet," Pew Internet and American Life Project, November 6, 2006.

9. See Adam Nagourney, "Politics Is Facing Sweeping Change via the Internet," *New York Times*, April 2, 2006.

10. M. Margolis and D. Resnick, *Politics as Usual: The Cyberspace Revolution* (Thousand Oaks, CA: Sage, 2000).

11. Jenkins and Thorburn, "Digital Revolution," 2.

12. In one of the more unusual features of the 2000 presidential campaign, for example, the campaign of Green Party candidate Ralph Nader urged voters in heavily Democratic states like Massachusetts and Rhode Island to "trade" their votes on the Web with those of Nader supporters in contested states like Florida and Oregon. The point of this trading was to increase Nader's percentage of the national vote and thus improve the Green Party's chances of qualifying for federal matching funds in 2004. Some fifteen thousand of these trades were logged on the Nader Web site. Some commentators deplored the activity as corrupt, while others praised it as a way to increase the viability of third parties in national elections.

13. Some communities on the Internet may of course take on some of the characteristics of thick communities. One of the best-known political Web sites, for example, Dailykos.com, is devoted to re-creating the Democratic Party as something other than a confederacy of single-issue constituencies and political insiders. In June 2006, several thousand "kossacs," as readers of the site call themselves, held their first convention in Las Vegas, meeting one another face to face.

Internet enthusiasts will argue, with some justification, that thick community has its own problems, in particular insulating elite decisions and popular prejudices from outside scrutiny and criticism. Thick community can also be majoritarian and thus may be dismissive of or hostile to minority viewpoints. The Internet's fluid and thin communities, the argument goes, mitigate or even undo these tendencies. Whether either is to be preferred is democracy's oldest question.

14. See, for example, Bruce Bimber, "The Internet and Political Transformation: Populism, Community, and Accelerated Pluralism," *Polity*, Fall 1998.

15. Bruce Bimber, quoted in "Use of Internet in Presidential Campaigns: Lessons of 2000 Race," press release, University of California at Santa Barbara, November 18, 2003. For Bimber's complete analysis of Internet use in campaigns, see Bruce Bimber and Richard Davis, *Campaigning Online: The Internet in U.S. Elections* (New York: Oxford University Press, 2003).

16. See Cornfield, "Internet and Politics."

17. See Racine Group, "White Paper on Televised Political Campaign Debates," *Argumentation and Advocacy: The Journal of the American Forensic Association,* Spring 2002, 199–218.

18. Numerous researchers have reached this conclusion, even those who are critical of the debates. See, for example, David J. Lanoue and Peter R. Schrott, *The Joint Press Conference: The History, Impact, and Prospects of American Presidential Debates* (Westport, CT: Greenwood, 1991).

19. Kathleen Hall Jamieson and David S. Birdsell, *Presidential Debates: The Challenge of Creating an Informed Electorate* (New York: Oxford University Press, 1988), 5.

20. Quote from "Moderating Presidential Debates: A Conversation with Jim Lehrer, April 6, 2001," *Miller Center Forum* (Miller Center of Public Affairs, University of Virginia), Spring 2001, 13.

21. See Ronald Faucheux, "What Voters Think about Political Debates: Key Findings from a Nationwide Poll," *Campaigns and Elections*, June 2002, 22. Faucheux found that 71 percent of voters thought the debates would be better if candidates had more time to explain their views on complex issues. This view was particularly prevalent among young voters, 82 percent of whom wanted candidates to explain themselves at greater length. About 38 percent of voters expressed some willingness to participate in an exclusively online political debate by asking questions through e-mail. A much larger percentage, 63 percent, were willing to submit questions by e-mail but have candidates answer them on live television. Again, the voters most willing to submit questions online were those under 25 (28 percent) and those 45 to 54 (also 28 percent).

22. See Jodi Wilogren, "Commission on Debates Rejects Prompt Signing of Campaigns' Accord on the Events," *New York Times*, September 22, 2004, A15; see also Mark Memmott, "Journalists Alarmed by Provision That Debate Moderators Must Sign Statement," *USA Today*, September 23, 2004, 6A; and "The Rules of Engagement," *Chicago Tribune*, September 30, 2004, C1.

23. The single debate between the finalists in French presidential elections works this way, for example. In May 2007, candidates Nicolas Sarkozy and Segolene Royal met for a single two-and-a-half-hour debate in which they asked the questions, confronted each other, pointed fingers at each other, and repeatedly interrupted each other. The *International Herald Tribune* reported that the debate was "reminiscent of a couple bickering at the breakfast table," though the *Washington Post* praised the for-

mat for "allowing far more drama and confrontation than the staid American presidential debates." Approximately 23 million French voters watched the debate. See Molly Moore and John Ward Anderson, "Debate Turns Bitter as France's Presidential Rivals Trade Jabs," *Washington Post,* May 3, 2007, A20; Elaine Sciolino, "Candidates Spar Vigorously as French Presidential Vote Nears," *International Herald Tribune,* May 3, 2007, at www.iht.com/articles/2007/05/03/europe/03france.php (accessed June 13, 2007).

24. Jamieson and Birdsell, *Presidential Debates,* 201.

25. See Theodore H. White, *The Making of the President 1960* (New York: Atheneum, 1961).

26. Newton N. Minow and Nell Minow, "Let's Improve Presidential Debates," *Christian Science Monitor,* August 20, 1987.

27. *Voter's Time: Report of the Twentieth Century Fund Commission on Campaign Costs in the Electronic Era* (New York: Twentieth Century Fund, 1969), 1. The commission members who served with me were Dean Burch, who served as Barry Goldwater's campaign manager in 1964 and later served as FCC chair; Thomas G. Corcoran, a Washington attorney who served as an adviser to Franklin D. Roosevelt; Alexander Heard, a political scientist, chair of President Kennedy's Commission on Campaign Costs, and chancellor of Vanderbilt University; and Robert Price, a New York attorney and investment banker who managed several Republican campaigns.

28. See "Presidential Campaign TV Ad Spending, 2004," at Journalism.org, www .stateofthenewsmedia.org/2005/chartland.asp?id=451 (accessed November 4, 2006). The Bush campaign spent $188 million, the Kerry campaign $165 million, and 527 groups $207 million.

29. See "Local Stations Are Big Winners in Campaign 2004," *Alliance for Better Campaigns,* December 2004, 1. See also "Political Ad Spending on Television Sets New Record: $1.6 Billion," November 24, 2004, at http://bettercampaigns.org/press/ release.php?ReleaseID=65. In 2004, the top ten states for spending on political advertising were, in order, Florida, California, Ohio, Pennsylvania, Missouri, New Jersey, Delaware, Michigan, Wisconsin, and North Carolina. The top ten markets for ad spending were, in order, Los Angeles, Cleveland, Miami, Philadelphia, Tampa, St. Louis, San Francisco, Orlando, Las Vegas, and Denver.

Trade magazine *Broadcasting and Cable* also put the total for television spending in 2004 at $1.6 billion, with the two presidential campaigns spending $386 million, 527 groups $207 million, PACs $188 million, House races $234 million, and Senate races $213 million. About 10 percent of that total ($173 million), according to the magazine, was for "soft money" attack advertising.

30. See Jonathan Weisman and Chris Cillizza, "Campaigns Set for TV Finale," *Washington Post,* November 3, 2006, A1. Total political ad spending for all media for the 2006 elections, according to PQ Media, was $3.14 billion; see also Katy Bachman, "Midterm Elections Spending More Than Doubles to $2.1 Billion for Broadcast TV," MediaWeek.com, November 14, 2006; see also John M. Higgins, "Stations Log Record Windfall," November 6, 2006, at www.broadcastingcable.com.

31. Christopher Stern, "Foley, Iraq War Fuel Record Political Ad Sales," Bloomberg.com, October 26, 2006, available at www.bloomberg.com/apps/news ?pid=20670001&refer=politics&sid=a0atgwoU0jNg. (accessed October 28, 2006).

32. I agree with Supreme Court justice John Paul Stevens, who wrote in 2006 that "the Framers would have been appalled by the impact of modern fundraising practices on the ability of elected officials to perform their public responsibilities." See *Randall et al. v. Sorrell et al.*, no. 04-1528, decided June 26, 2006.

33. In a 2002 study of 4,850 half-hour local news broadcasts from 122 randomly selected stations in the country's fifty top markets, researchers from the Annenberg School of Communication at the University of Southern California and the University of Wisconsin found that just over one in three stations carried any campaign coverage at all. At the same time, three out of four aired at least one paid political advertisement, and just over half (52 percent) carried at least two paid political advertisements.

The 2004 study examined 44 stations in 11 markets, and a total of 435 hours of regularly scheduled news programming between October 4 and October 10, 2004. In the sample as a whole, the time the stations gave to coverage of the one presidential debate and the vice-presidential debate that fell within the time frame of the research was four times the total amount of election coverage that aired during the stations' regularly scheduled news programs. The presidential campaign, in other words, got far more news coverage than any other race, about 70 percent of the total. Independent of their regularly scheduled new programs, the 44 stations in the sample gave a total of 27 hours of time to the broadcast of town-hall meetings and other campaign-related programming.

A University of Wisconsin study of 2006 midterm election coverage by local stations in six Midwestern states found that political campaigns received an average of 36 seconds per 30-minute broadcast.

34. Quoted in Robert M. Entman, ed., *American Media and the Quality of Voter Information* (Washington, DC: Aspen Institute, 2004), 6.

35. One might object that negative campaigning is as old as the republic. In the bitter presidential election of 1800, for example, Jefferson supporters accused President Adams of using his vice president to procure prostitutes from the Russian czar, while Adams supporters accused Jefferson of being a compulsive philanderer who favored legalized prostitution. The differences between then and now are many, not least that the world is more interconnected through globalization and the issues that face the country and the world are more complex and potentially lethal.

36. Michael Kinsley, "Election Day," *New York Times Book Review*, November 5, 2006, 1.

37. Many commentators and certainly most broadcasters prefer to call air time used by candidates without compensation "free time." But this characterization is incorrect. By law the broadcasters do not own the time; the public does. The time therefore is not broadcasters' to donate or give away, but for use in the public interest. It is therefore properly called public-service time.

38. See *King Broadcasting v. Federal Communications Commission*, 860 F2d 465 (D.C. Cir., 1988). In *King*, the FCC decided that the broadcast of back-to-back statements by political candidates on a Seattle television station in the days right before an election was a bona fide news program and therefore not subject to the equal time rule.

39. In 1969, as chair of the Twentieth Century Fund's Voter's Time Commission,

I recommended with my colleagues that time be allotted to (1) candidates of parties that had placed first or second in the popular vote in two of the three preceding presidential elections; (2) candidates of all parties that had received at least one-eighth of the popular vote in the preceding presidential election; and (3) candidates of all parties that show evidence of a fair degree of potential voter support but not necessarily past electoral significance. Candidates from each of these categories would in addition have to appear on the ballot in at least three-quarters of the states, and in enough states to represent a majority in the Electoral College. See *Voter's Time*, 20–25.

40. The problem of how to allocate broadcast time for political uses is much the same as deciding whom to include in debates: stability of the system has to be balanced against principled accessibility to the political arena.

The British system allocates time through a panel known as the Committee on Party Political Broadcasts, which consists of representatives from the political parties, the BBC, and the Independent Broadcasting Authority. The panel calculates the amount of free television and radio time for each party by considering several factors, including the number of votes the party attracted in the previous election and the relative strength of the parties at the time the elections are announced. There is no sale or purchase of broadcast time; no money is involved. The campaign is mercifully short, and the voters are well informed.

Another common way of allocating broadcast time, particularly in parliamentary systems (as in France and Canada), is to relate it to the number of seats a party holds in the legislature. Still another method, used by Mexico and Brazil, is to stipulate that a fixed percentage of time—in Mexico's case, 30 percent—be distributed equally between the parties, with the balance distributed according to electoral strength.

41. Once we add in the many further programming hours available to broadcasters made possible through multiple streams of digital transmission, that six hours becomes an even smaller time commitment.

42. See Ellen Mickiewicz, Charles Firestone and Laura Roselle, *Television and Elections*, 2nd ed. (Durham, NC: DeWitt Wallace Center, Duke University, 1999), 13–18.

43. First Rupert Murdoch announced that Fox would provide free time to presidential candidates, and then CBS, CNN, NBC, PBS, UPN, and NPR announced that they, too, would give time to Bill Clinton and Bob Dole. CNN also gave time to Reform Party candidate Ross Perot, Libertarian candidate Harry Browne, Natural Law Party candidate John Hagelin, and Howard Phillips of the U.S. Taxpayers Party. Each broadcast organization offered time in different lengths, times, and formats, with no uniformity or coordination among them with respect to what they did or when they did it. Fox Television, for example, aired ten one-minute segments on Tuesdays, Saturdays, and Sundays in September and October between 7:30 and 9:30 p.m. Eastern Time. Candidates responded to questions posed by the network, which then aired their responses back to back. NBC also asked questions of the candidates, then aired five of their ninety-second responses in paired segments during regular broadcasts of *Dateline*. CNN, UPN, PBS, and NPR all aired the same two-and-a-half-minute candidate statements, with the topics determined by the candidates themselves.

These national programmers were joined in these efforts by the A. H. Belo company, which at the time owned seven stations in seven states and in each of those markets offered free five-minute blocks of time to candidates for governor and U.S. Senate and House seats.

44. Howard Kurtz, "Campaign for Free Air Time Falls Short of Organizers' Goals," *Washington Post,* October 31, 1996, A17.

45. *National Broadcasting Co., Inc. v. United States,* 319 U.S. 190 (1943); *Red Lion Broadcasting Co., Inc., et al. v. Federal Communications Commission,* 395 U.S. 367 (1969); *Turner Broadcasting System, Inc. v. Federal Communications Commission,* 512 U.S. 622 (1994); *Turner Broadcasting System, Inc. v. Federal Communications Commission,* 520 U.S. 180 (1997).

46. Under the law, broadcasters were eligible to receive new digital television channels, which all have now received. Congress directed that, unlike other telecommunications service providers, broadcasters would not have to pay for their new channels. They got them for free, and no one else was allowed even to bid for them. Digital transmission of broadcast television, which the FCC now says will be complete by 2009, will allow broadcasters to offer multiple channels instead of one and, if they wish, to use those extra channels for services such as data transmission, paging services, or pay-per-view movies.

47. One popular explanation for Ross Perot's relatively poor showing in the 1996 election, when he won 9 percent of the popular vote, far less than the 19 percent he won in 1992, was that he had been excluded from the 1996 debates. Two years later, Jesse Ventura went from obscurity to the governorship of Minnesota after he was included in statewide televised gubernatorial debates.

48. The Presidential Election Campaign Fund Act stipulates that to be eligible for campaign funding in the general election a third-party candidate must be on the ballot in at least ten states, must have obtained at least 5 percent of the national popular vote in the previous presidential election, and of course must comply with all the Federal Election Commission's disclosure and filing requirements for campaign contributions. According to the Presidential Primary Matching Payment Account Act, to be eligible for matching funds in the primaries a candidate must raise $100,000 in contributions from individuals, with at least $5,000 of that coming in contributions of $250 or less from residents in no fewer than twenty different states.

49. See "What Does He Want?" *Newsweek,* September 28, 1992, 16.

50. Of these, only Wallace, Anderson, and Perot would have been included based on scientifically valid preelection polls. The others would have been included on the presumption that the percentage of the popular vote they received in the election is an approximate measure of their preelection public support.

51. Robert A. Dahl, "The American Oppositions: Affirmations and Denial," in *Political Oppositions in Western Democracies,* edited by Robert A. Dahl (New Haven, CT: Yale University Press, 1966), 62.

52. See Daniel A. Mazmanian, *Third Parties in Presidential Elections* (Washington, DC: Brookings Institution, 1974), 81.

53. John Hicks, "The Third Party Tradition in American Politics," *Mississippi Valley Historical Review* 20 (1933): 26–27.

54. Most third-party presidential candidates have run in only one election. Be-

tween 1840 and 1980, only forty-five third-party or independent candidates received popular votes in more than one state; of those, 58 percent ran just once. See Stephen J. Rosenstone, Roy L. Behr, and Edward H. Lazarus, *Third Parties in America: Citizen Response to Major Party Failure* (Princeton, NJ: Princeton University Press, 1996).

55. See Eleanor Clift and Ginny Carroll, "Perot: Pulling the Race out of the Mud," *Newsweek*, October 26, 1992, 34; see also Robin Toner, "Perot Re-enters the Campaign, Saying Bush and Clinton Fail to Address Government 'Mess,'" *New York Times*, October 2, 1992, A1.

56. The federal government does not collect data on registered independents, and only half the states and some counties do, so counting heads turns up numbers that, if not consistent, are clear on one point: a lot of Americans think of themselves as independent no matter what their party registration actually is, and by that they mean they are not enthusiastic about strictly partisan politics. Not just Americans think this way either. In each of the few democratic countries that have reliable longitudinal data—the United States, Great Britain, and Canada—party identification has been declining for more than forty years.

Researcher Curtis Gans notes that the number of voters who register as independents or as supporters of third parties has risen from 1.4 percent of eligible voters in 1962 to 16.7 percent in 2006, with each new election cycle bringing another increase. The oldest continuous measurement of party identification in the United States is the American National Election Study (ANES), which has tracked party identification in every presidential and congressional election since 1948. According to the ANES, voters who identify themselves as independent have since the early 1990s consistently constituted about 35 percent of the electorate—more than identify with either of the major parties. The National Annenberg Election Survey at the University of Pennsylvania found that 26 percent of registered voters thought of themselves as independents in 2000, 25 percent in 2004.

57. In 1960, for example, almost 63 percent of eligible voters cast ballots. By 1988 only 50 percent did, and nearly a million of those cast their ballots for third-party candidates. Not until Perot's candidacy in 1992 was there a notable reversal in that downward trend, with 55 percent of eligible voters casting ballots. See Robert Pear, "55% Voting Rate Reverses 3-Year Decline," *New York Times*, November 5, 1992, B4. Much of that reversal was attributed directly to Perot, who "pulled many who might not have voted otherwise." See Richard Benedetto, "Presidential Election: Voter Turnout," *USA Today*, November 5, 1992, 13A.

58. See Todd Donovan, Janine A. Parry, and Shaun Bowler, "O Other, Where Art Thou? Support for Multiparty Politics in the United States," *Social Science Quarterly* 86, no. 1 (March 2005): 146–59. The ANES was conducted in 2000, with a sample of 2,000 and responses from 1,487 individuals. See also Jeffrey Koch, "Political Cynicism and Third Party Support in American Presidential Elections," *American Politics Research* 31, no. 1 (2003): 48–65.

59. Faucheux, "What Voters Think about Political Debates," 26. Only one out of twenty voters thought third-party candidates should never be included. Another 39 percent said third-party candidates should be included only if they have a "reasonable chance" to win the election.

60. Aside from the problems of fairness and relevance with a measure based on previous election performance, there is also a problem of reliability. Ballot counts are state matters, and states record votes in widely different and often noncomparable ways. Many states, for example, list any third-party candidate as an "independent," irrespective of party label. Votes cast for a Green Party candidate, for example, would not be officially counted in the Green Party's vote total. There is the possibility, then, that a 5 percent popular vote for an independent candidate is either an undercount or an overcount. Given the well-known problems with state voting systems, perhaps that should not matter, since an independent presidential candidate who wins even 2 or 3 percent of the national popular vote is remarkable. Independent presidential candidates in the past century have rarely won as much as one-tenth of one percent of the popular vote. Public opinion polls may not be a perfect device for determining a candidate's qualifications for debate inclusion, but they are not as opaque as state voting records, and they are more easily reviewed by competent critics using accepted social science methods.

61. One thoughtful proposal for debate participation comes from the Debate Advisory Standards Project (DASP), a program funded by the Pew Charitable Trusts and sponsored by the University of Maryland. The DASP proposes that debates be divided between those that occur in an "out-period" and an "in-period," the latter limited to the thirty days before Election Day and the first to the weeks and months before. During the out-period, DASP recommends that debates include all candidates who demonstrate "seriousness of purpose." Seriousness, in DASP's formulation, is at one level highly subjective, excluding "joke" candidates or those "who do not campaign in any meaningful way" and those "who admit that their candidacies have only symbolic or trivial intentions." After these qualitative measures, DASP offers several possible quantitative ones, among them a showing of 5 percent or more of the vote in a "professionally conducted public opinion survey" or the nomination of a party that received at least 3 percent of the vote in the prior election. During the in-period, DASP urges that "serious" candidates show 10 percent public support or be the nominee of a party that received at least 10 percent of the vote in the previous election.

Leaving aside the problems of legality in DASP's more subjective recommendations, at least one of its measures is biased toward what voters say they want *today*, not four or more years ago. Still, I question the wisdom of including or excluding any candidate in a debate on the basis of previous election performance.

62. The utility of the Internet for political organizing has become steadily more apparent since the World Wide Web made the Internet widely accessible to the public. In one of the best known examples, two people angry at the impeachment of President Bill Clinton in 1998 created a Web site they called "Censure and Move On" on which they posted a petition protesting the impeachment and asking for signatures. The creators did no marketing or promotion for their site, but by the end of the first week 100,000 people had signed. By Election Day 1998, 300,000 people had signed. By Election Day 2000, the site—by then known as MoveOn.org—had collected more than $13 million in donations and commitments from volunteers to work more than 750,000 hours in the congressional elections.

More recently, a 2003 Internet campaign resulted in the recall of California governor Gray Davis, and another online effort launched the presidential campaign of retired army general Wesley Clark in 2004. But it was the 2004 presidential campaign of former Vermont governor Howard Dean that proved the Internet's organizing and fund-raising power. Dean's campaign used the Web site MeetUp.com to help organize supporters. According to Michael Cornfield, "the Dean Meetup population eventually constituted a virtual midsize city, with several hundred thousand activists situated across the nation and beyond." In late June 2003, Dean won a virtual Democratic primary staged by MoveOn.org, and a week later he reported the largest fundraising totals to the Federal Election Commission among candidates for the second quarter of 2003. He eventually raised a total of almost $50 million through online donations, most of them small gifts of $100 or less.

Online fundraising also transformed campaigns for Senate and House offices in 2004. The Democratic Web site Dailykos, for example, raised $500,000 of the total $850,000 campaign budget of Paul Hackett, an Iraq War veteran challenging an incumbent in a traditionally Republican Ohio congressional district. On Election Day, when Hackett suddenly needed $60,000 to help get out the vote, Dailykos put out the word and raised the money through online donations in six hours.

63. See http://unity08.com/.

64. Ibid.

65. See Jonathan Alter, "A New Open-Source Politics," *Newsweek*, June 5, 2006; see also Jim VandeHei, "From the Internet to the White House," *Washington Post*, May 31, 2006, A1.

66. The League used the 15 percent standard on the advice of legal counsel because it was objective, and the League then admirably stuck by its decision in the face of Carter's refusal to participate in any debates that included independent Anderson. After that, wrote League president Nancy N. Neuman, the League abandoned the 15 percent standard as "unworkable." Not until 2000 would the Commission on Presidential Debates revive it. See Nancy N. Neuman, "Setting the Record Straight: Discussion on Presidential Debates," *Miller Center Journal* (University of Virginia), Spring 1994, 152.

67. In most presidential election years there are two hundred or more candidates seeking the office, and very few of those are on enough state ballots to have even a theoretical chance of winning the Electoral College. The National Archives lumps into this vast group of "other" candidates all those who get less than one two-thousandth of the popular vote.

68. Commission revenue from donations was reported as $5 million for fiscal year 2000 and $4.13 million in fiscal year 2004.

69. See www.debates.org/pages/natspons.html. Among the Commission's sponsors in 2004, for example, were the Ford Foundation, Century Foundation, the John S. and James L. Knight Foundation, the Marjorie Kovler Fund, the Howard G. Buffett Fund, and the AARP (formerly the American Association of Retired Persons). Corporate sponsors in 2004 were Anheuser-Busch and the Ford Motor Company, US Airways and 3Com. Past election-year corporate sponsors have included the Philip Morris Companies, Lucent Technologies, Sprint, Sara Lee Corporation, Prudential, Hallmark, IBM, AT&T, J. P. Morgan, Atlantic Richfield, and Dun and Bradstreet.

70. The Commission's publicly available 990 tax forms do not provide this information either. Guidestar.com has 990 tax forms for the Commission on Presidential Debates going back only to 1997.

71. Ken Adelman, "Meeting in the Middle," *Washingtonian,* October 2006, 41.

72. See David Mindich, *Tuned Out: Why Americans under Forty Don't Follow the News* (New York: Oxford University Press, 2004). One of the more innovative proposals for engaging young people in the debates comes from political scientist Michael Cornfield, who has suggested an *American Idol* format in which each party has citizen-contestants compete for the opportunity to ask a question of the opposing party's nominee in a town meeting debate. Another competition Cornfield suggests is "Ninety with the Next," in which competition winners would get ninety seconds to interact with one of the candidates who might be the next president, with the exchange placed on the Web. Cornfield notes that in 2004, seventy thousand Americans auditioned for the chance to become the next "American idol." If even 1 percent of that total were to compete in his contests, Cornfield writes, it would give the "politically disaffected . . . an incentive to pay closer attention to the presidential campaign."

73. *Slate* magazine was critical of Web, White, and Blue but nonetheless concluded that "the site holds much promise. Yes, questions got answered with memos. But these are more thorough and accurate answers than the ones in town hall debates, where responses are essentially rote. True, the campaigns' daily messages are crafted by staff. But no more so than out on the stump. And the third-party candidates (save for Nader, who hasn't participated) are finally getting a voice. In fact, they're going to town—rebutting everything in sight. Pat Buchanan, at least, even seems to write his own entries." See Seth Stevenson, "The Cyber-Debate That Wasn't," *Slate,* October 11, 2000.

74. In April 2007, the political blog Huffington Post, together with Yahoo and the online magazine *Slate,* announced two online presidential debates for the following September, one between Democratic candidates and a second between Republican candidates, both to be hosted by PBS's Charlie Rose. Yahoo would sponsor the debates and produce them. Candidates would participate from remote locations, and voters would be invited to submit questions and share their views on the candidates in real time. Real-time video of the events would appear on both the Huffington Post and *Slate.* In June 2007, the online video-sharing site YouTube announced that in July it would cohost with CNN a presidential debate to be moderated by journalist Anderson Cooper. See Beth Fouhy, "Online Presidential Debates Planned," *Time,* April 23, 2007, available at www.time.com/time/business/article/0,8599,1613497,00.html (accessed April 23, 2007); see also Katherine Q. Seelye, "YouTube Passes Debates to a New Generation," *New York Times,* June 14, 2007, A1.

75. Adlai Stevenson, quoted in Porter McKeever, "Setting the Record Straight," *Miller Center Journal* (University of Virginia), Spring 1994, 150.

APPENDIX C

1. 47 USC 312(a)(7). The amendment says that the Federal Communications Commission may revoke a broadcaster's license for "willful and repeated failure to allow reasonable access to or to permit purchase of reasonable amounts of time for

the use of a broadcasting station by a legally qualified candidate for federal elective office on behalf of his candidacy."

2. Statement of Senator John Pastore, Senate Report no. 96, 92nd Congress, 1st Session 20 (1971), reprinted in *U.S. Code Congressional and Administrative News*, 1,774.

3. Section 315(b)(1) of the Communications Act was amended in 1952 to ensure that candidates could purchase time at "the lowest unit charge" for the time they sought. This reduced charge led to the adoption of Section 312(a)(7) to ensure against broadcasters' declining to sell to federal candidates (members of Congress).

4. Senate Report no. 96, at 34: "The presentation of legally qualified candidates for public office is an essential part of any broadcast licensee's obligation to serve the public interest, and the FCC should continue to consider the extent to which each licensee has satisfied his obligation in this regard in connection with the renewal of his broadcast license."

5. A plausible explanation for 312(a)(7)'s focus on federal candidates is that when Congress passed the Federal Election Campaign Act in 1971, it cited its constitutional authority to regulate the time, place, and manner of federal elections. See *Congressional Record* 117 (1971): 28,794.

6. Another feature of Section 312(a)(7) was that it did not allow noncommercial educational broadcasters (public broadcasters) to charge more than the cost of production for campaign advertisements, in effect creating something very near a free time obligation for public broadcasters. In 2000, Congress amended subsection (a)(7) to exempt such stations from the obligation to carry political advertisements.

7. Federal Communications Commission, *Use of Broadcast and Cablecast Facilities, Federal Register* 37 (1972): 5,796.

8. See *Baltazar Corrada del Rio*, 67 FCC2d 12, 1976; Federal Communications Commission, *Enforcing Section 312(a)(7) of the Communications Act, Federal Register* 43 (1978): 33,772.

9. See *Campaign '76 Media Communications v. Stations WGN and WGN-TV*, 58 FCC2d 1142, 1976.

10. See *Rosenbush Advertising Agency*, 31 FCC2d 782, 1971.

11. See *Dennis I. Morrisseau*, 48 FCC2d 436, 1974; and *Morrisseau v. Mt. Mansfield Television Inc.*, 380 F.Supp. 512 (D.Vt., 1974).

12. The statute says that broadcasters must provide "reasonable access to or to permit purchase of reasonable amounts of time." If the word *or* were read conjunctively, the statute would seem to require both free and paid time for federal candidates.

13. See, for example, *WALB-TV*, 59 FCC2d 1246, (1976), at 1247–48.

APPENDIX D

1. The FEC was created by a 1974 amendment to the law, written after the Watergate investigation uncovered unsavory campaign practices in the Nixon administration.

2. The FEC's statutory duties are "to disclose campaign finance information, to enforce the provisions of the law such as the limits and prohibitions on contributions, and to oversee the public funding of Presidential elections."

3. In that role, the FEC publishes electronic and fully searchable reports filed by Senate, House, and presidential candidates that specify how much each campaign has raised and spent. Campaigns must identify the source of any donation more than $200.

4. Anthony Corrado, *Campaigns in Cyberspace: Toward a New Regulatory Approach* (Washington, DC: Aspen Institute Communications and Society Program and American Bar Association Standing Committee on Election Law, 2000), 10.

5. Ibid.

6. See 2 U.S.C. 431(8)(A)(I) and 431(9)(A)(I).

7. Corrado, *Campaigns in Cyberspace,* 10.

8. 2 U.S.C. 441b(a). The law does provide, however, that corporations and labor unions can spend money for communication on any subject, including candidates for federal office, with their own employees or members of some other "restricted class," such as a corporation's stockholders. If those communications cost more than $2,000, they must be reported to the Federal Election Commission.

9. *Federal Register* 44 (1979): 76, 734.

10. 11 C.F.R. 110.13; 60 Fed. Reg. 64, 262 (1995).

11. Ibid.

12. *Fulani v. League of Women Voters Educ. Fund,* 882 F.2d 621 (2d Cir. 1989). Under IRS regulations the League is a 501(c)(3) nonprofit, tax-exempt organization.

13. Ibid., 624.

14. Ibid., 630.

15. Ibid.

16. *Fulani v. Brady,* 935 F.2d 1324 (D.C. Cir. 1991), *cert. denied,* 502 U.S. 1048 (1992).

17. Ibid., 1325, 1329, 1330 (in this last, quoting *Common Cause v. Dep't of Energy,* 702 F.2d 245, 251 [1983]).

18. *Buchanan,* 112 F. Supp. 2d at 64.

19. *Fulani,* 935 F.2d at 1334 (Mikva, C. J., dissenting); citations omitted. See 11 C.F.R. § 110.13.

20. *Fulani v. Bentsen,* 862 F. Supp. 1,140, 1,146–47 (S.D.N.Y. 1994).

APPENDIX E

1. *CBS, Inc. v. Democratic National Committee,* 412 U.S. 94, 125–25 (1973).

2. *Kennedy for President Committee v. Federal Communications Commission,* 636 F.2d 432 (D.C. Cir. 1980).

3. Ibid. at 432, quoting *Columbia Broadcasting Sys. v. Democratic Nat'l Comm.,* 412 U.S. 94, 112–13 (1973).

4. Ibid., quoting *Red Lion Broadcasting Co. v. FCC,* 395 U.S. 367, 390 (1969). See also *Turner Broadcasting System v. FCC,* 114 S.Ct. 2445 (1994), at 2456–57, where the Court unanimously states that while much criticized, Red Lion remains the Court's broadcast jurisprudence. On the issue of technological obsolescence and the public-interest standard, *Red Lion* was a case involving radio when there were seven thousand radio stations in the United States; now there are eleven thousand, but it is hard to see why that change should matter to the law. *Red Lion* was based on the fact that more people want to broadcast than there are available frequencies, which is

still true today. The crucial sentence in *Red Lion* is that Congress could have divided the broadcast day, week, month, or year among many different users; instead it chose a system whereby a single user has to serve the entire community.

5. *Johnson v. FCC*, 829 F.2d 157–62 (1987).

6. Ibid. at 162.

7. Ibid. at 164, citing *Columbia Broadcasting Sys.*, 412 U.S., at 126.

8. Ibid. at 164–65.

9. *DeYoung v. Patten*, 898 F2d 628 (8ᵗʰ Cir., 1990), at 631–32.

10. Ibid., quoting *Kennedy v. FCC*, 636 F2d 417, 430–31 (D.C. Cir. 1990).

11. Ibid. at 633.

12. *Chandler v. Georgia Public Telecommunications Commission*, 917 F.2d 486, 487–88 (11th Cir. 1990).

13. Ibid. at 488–90.

14. Ibid. at 491 (Clark, J., dissenting).

15. *Forbes v. Arkansas Educational Television Commission*, 22 F.3d 1423, 1426 (8th Cir. 1994).

16. Micah L. Sifry, "Minor-Party Blackout; US Supreme Court Rules Public Broadcaster Can Block Appearance of Minor Political Candidates," *The Nation*, June 15, 1998.

17. *Forbes*, 22 F.3d at 1426, 1429.

18. Ibid. at 1427–29.

19. Ibid. at 1428–29 (internal citations omitted).

20. Ibid. at 1430.

21. *Ark. Educ. TV Comm'n v. Forbes*, 523 US. 666, 669 72, 504–5 (1998).

22. Ibid. at 679.

23. Ibid., citing *Widmar v. Vincent*, 454 U.S. 263, 264 (1981).

24. Ibid. at 673, 682, 669.

25. It seems hard to dispute that, by excluding unpopular candidates, a broadcast station discriminates, at least de facto, against particular viewpoints. This is especially true of single-issue parties.

26. *Forbes*, 523 US. at 675, 763, 681.

27. Ibid. at 684–85 (Stevens, J., dissenting), citing 11 CFR § 110.13(c) (1997).

28. Ibid. at 685, 689 (Stevens, J., dissenting).

29. See Thomas Berg, "Excluding a Candidate from a Debate on State-Owned Television Station: Editorial Judgment or Suppression of Free Speech?" *Preview U.S. Supreme Court Case*, September 18, 1997, 44.

30. See "Public Affairs Programming by Public Broadcasters at Risk in Court Case," *Communications Daily*, April 18, 1997, 4.

31. *Forbes*, 523 U.S., at 681. See also David C. Kotok, "ETV Cancels Debate between Nelson, Hagel," *Omaha World Herald*, August 23, 1996, 1.

32. *Forbes*, 523 U.S., at 682.

33. Ibid. at 675.

34. See 11 C.F.R Section 110.13(c) (1998).

35. See *King*, at 5000; *Aspen*, at 707.

Index